The Miracle Lady

LIBRARY OF RELIGIOUS BIOGRAPHY

Mark A. Noll and Heath W. Carter, series editors

Long overlooked by historians, religion has emerged in recent years as a key factor in understanding the past. From politics to popular culture, from social struggles to the rhythms of family life, religion shapes every story. Religious biographies open a window to the sometimes surprising influence of religion on the lives of influential people and the worlds they inhabited.

The Library of Religious Biography is a series that brings to life important figures in United States history and beyond. Grounded in careful research, these volumes link the lives of their subjects to the broader cultural contexts and religious issues that surrounded them. The authors are respected historians and recognized authorities in the historical period in which their subject lived and worked.

Marked by careful scholarship yet free of academic jargon, the books in this series are well-written narratives meant to be read and *enjoyed* as well as studied

Titles include:

*Her Heart Can See: The Life and Hymns of **Fanny J. Crosby***
by Edith L. Blumhofer

***Emily Dickinson** and the Art of Belief*
by Roger Lundin

***Aimee Semple McPherson**: Everybody's Sister*
by Edith L. Blumhofer

***Francis Schaeffer** and the Shaping of Evangelical America*
by Barry Hankins

***Harriet Beecher Stowe**: A Spiritual Life*
by Nancy Koester

*Prophetess of Health: A Study of **Ellen G. White***
by Ronald L. Numbers

***George Whitefield**: Evangelist for God and Empire*
by Peter L. Choi

For a complete list of published volumes, see the back of this volume.

THE MIRACLE LADY

Kathryn Kuhlman
and the Transformation of
Charismatic Christianity

Amy Collier Artman

WILLIAM B. EERDMANS PUBLISHING COMPANY
GRAND RAPIDS, MICHIGAN

Wm. B. Eerdmans Publishing Co.
4035 Park East Court SE, Grand Rapids, Michigan 49546
www.eerdmans.com

Published 2019
Printed in the United States of America

28 27 26 25 24 23 22 21 20 19   1 2 3 4 5 6 7 8 9 10

ISBN 978-0-8028-7670-6

Library of Congress Cataloging-in-Publication Data

Names: Artman, Amy Collier, 1970- author.
Title: The miracle lady : Kathryn Kuhlman and the transformation of
    charismatic Christianity / Amy Collier Artman.
Description: Grand Rapids : Eerdmans Publishing Co., 2019. | Series: Library
    of religious biography | Includes bibliographical references and index.
Identifiers: LCCN 2018041858 | ISBN 9780802876706 (pbk. : alk. paper)
Subjects: LCSH: Kuhlman, Kathryn. | Evangelists—United States—Biography. |
    Healers—United States—Biography. | Pentecostalism—United States. |
    United States—Church history—20th century.
Classification: LCC BV3785.K84 A78 2019 | DDC 269/.2092 [B] —dc23
    LC record available at https://lccn.loc.gov/2018041858

Contents

Foreword

In an age of female Christian superstars—leaders like Joyce Meyer, Beth Moore, or Jen Hatmaker—it is easy to forget that women were not always allowed under the spotlight and behind the pulpit. Today's religious celebrities owe much of their success to a handful of pioneers who battled convention and prejudice to convince American Christians that a woman's voice could win the crowds.

One of those trailblazers was Kathryn Kuhlman, once named "the best-known woman preacher in the world" and "the Miracle Lady." She emerged from obscurity, overcame a scandalous divorce and a muckraking investigation, and fashioned for herself a ministerial career that moved from backwoods crusades to the heights of popular awareness on television. Though largely forgotten now, Kuhlman was responsible for helping usher Pentecostalism into middle-class respectability and win conservative American religion over to the possibility of female stardom.

Amy Collier Artman ably traces Kuhlman's remarkable rise to fame, which began shortly after World War I when Kathryn first felt the call to preach. She was an unlikely candidate with scant theological training and a failing grade in her homiletics class in a small Canadian Bible college. But it was also a time of a short-lived fashion for "girl evangelists"—the ill-fated Uldine Utley, for example, preached to thousands at Madison Square Garden at age fourteen—and Kuhlman began to find modest audiences in churches and auditoriums. She would eventually establish her own church, the Denver Revival Tabernacle, but her career was nearly doomed when, possibly distraught at the recent death of her father, she agreed to marry evangelist Burroughs Waltrip, who left his wife and two children for Kuhlman. Their marriage was a disaster, as was their mutual ministry, and Kuhlman soon abandoned her husband to resume a solitary preaching life.

Kuhlman's rise to national—and international—prominence started almost by accident when she began to gain a reputation as a healer. In 1947, many attending her services claimed to be not only saved spiritually but also delivered from physical distress. This soon became the focus of her ministry, one she pursued with considerable energy and success. Three times a week for a decade she drew crowds of two thousand to fill Pittsburgh's Carnegie Hall. In her twenty years of preaching in Los Angeles, she packed the Shrine Auditorium. She was mobbed in Akron, lionized in London, and greeted by a parade and the mayor himself in Las Vegas. When she went on the air—at first on radio where her shows always began with "Hello! And have you been waiting for me?" and then on her television programs *Your Faith and Mine* and *I Believe In Miracles*— her fame grew by leaps and bounds. A single, divorced woman with no children who claimed not to be a preacher or a healer, this improbable aspirant to the pulpit grew to become a cultural icon.

Artman is careful to show that Kuhlman was not just a celebrity but an important motivating force in changes to American religion in the twentieth century. When the young Kathryn was beginning her career, Pentecostalism was known as the religion from the wrong side of the tracks, derided as the faith of "holy rollers," rustic rubes who were preyed upon by a legion of sleazy hucksters. "Faith healer," a label that Kuhlman always shunned, was a term of contempt. It was Kuhlman's cleverly crafted persona and appealing middle-class respectability that helped to turn low-life "Pentecostalism" into "charismatic Christianity," a spiritual approach that transcended denominational borders. She eschewed the over-the-top emotionalism and manipulative performances that had characterized earlier healing services and took no credit for any miracles that might ensue. She claimed never to have healed anyone, saying that was the work of Jesus and the Holy Spirit, and her broadcasts were notable for the absence of lengthy appeals for donations. Thanks in great measure to Kuhlman, healing ministries could move out from the canvas and sawdust circuit to become, if not mainstream, at least a publicly acceptable manifestation of American faith.

How Kuhlman managed to do this, in spite of her sex, is another important part of Artman's research. She shows how carefully and tactfully Kuhlman had to present herself; she was clearly the boss, surrounded by male subordinates, but still had to affirm traditional gender roles. Like other women before her who dared to take up sacred duties reserved for men, she told critics to raise their concerns with God himself. It was God, not her, who had called her into ministry. "I didn't ask for this ministry," she protested. "God knows I'd much rather be doing something else."

The Miracle Lady is a fascinating study in why exceptional women remain exceptions. Kathryn Kuhlman was compelled to play too many parts. To lead among men, she had to prove herself to be wildly successful at the teaching and preaching of God's word. Beyond this, she had to outshine her male counterparts with the kind of star power that could make Johnny Carson listen with a smile on his face. Without the benefit of denominational or other institutional shelter (save those she created), she had to perform the lonely work of publicity, marketing, and event management to promote and circulate her message. On top of all this, she had to master the art of spiritual deflection, explaining away her spiritual authority as being either so divine that only God could ordain it or so natural it was simply an extension of her motherly heart for her spiritual children. How else could a divorced woman without children, and without the benefit of a formal seminary education, explain her incredible authority?

The rise of Kathryn Kuhlman is the story of one woman's remarkable climb onto a national stage and the many nimble adaptations—theological, institutional, technological, and personal—she made to achieve it. But her fall into obscurity is the story of the American church, and why women's spiritual authority remains so ephemeral. Challenging the institutions that bar women from spiritual authority is impractical and often impossible for any woman, even one as formidable as Kuhlman. But failing to change institutions relegates most women to itinerancy, parachurches, and stand-alone ministries that are notoriously difficult to sustain when the founder dies. As such, the disappearance of her memory was likely inevitable. Today, the pulpits of most of the largest congregations in the United States remain closed to women; only 1 percent of the country's fifteen hundred or so megachurches are led by women. In this ministerial world, women are meteors, burning brightly until, at last, the sky settles back into a familiar darkness.

KATE BOWLER

Acknowledgments

I have spent much time with Kathryn Kuhlman over the last several years. I watched her videos, read her books, and read books about her. I talked with people who knew her and claimed to have been healed by her. I put on lint-free gloves and pored over snapshots in her few personal scrapbooks, looking with a magnifying glass for a glimpse of who she might have been before she became who she was. So my first thank you goes to you, Miss Kuhlman, as you were called. Thanks for making me think, wonder, and laugh.

Thank you to my mom and dad for the love and support that enabled me to go on this adventure without really knowing where it would take me. Thanks to you, I never had to be afraid. Thank you to my brother and sisters and their families and also to my mother-in-law for encouraging me and making me feel proud of my work. Thank you to the Billy Graham Center archivists at Wheaton College for expressing genuine interest in my research and always making me feel welcome; to Wayne Warner for your generous spirit and wealth of Kuhlman information and photographs; to Edith Blumhofer and Clark Gilpin for taking the time to read this manuscript as a dissertation and make it stronger through your insight and reflections; and to Catherine Brekus for your patience, wisdom, and guidance from graduate school to now. You once told me you never stopped believing in me. Thank you for that.

Thank you to David Bratt and all the wonderful people at the Wm. B. Eerdmans Publishing Co. for welcoming me to the Library of Religious Biography family. Thank you to Kate Bowler for the willingness to contribute a foreword that sets Kuhlman in the larger story you know so well.

Acknowledgments

Thank you, as well, to Heath Carter for your enthusiasm about Kuhlman as a biographical subject and your thorough and skillful editing. This book is much better because of all of you. Thank you to my colleagues at Missouri State University for being such a wonderful community of teachers and scholars.

Finally, thank you to my husband David. I wouldn't have started and couldn't have finished this without you. I love you.

Psalm 9:1

Introduction

O n October 15, 1974, Johnny Carson welcomed his next guest on *The Tonight Show* with the words, "I imagine there are very few people in this country who are not aware of Kathryn Kuhlman." He continued, "She probably, along with Billy Graham, is one of the best-known ministers or preachers in the country." After a few more words of introduction, Carson announced Kuhlman. Doc Severinsen led *The Tonight Show* orchestra as she stepped through the iconic curtains into one of the most famous studios in television history. The applause continued as she greeted Carson, whose attention was then drawn to the enthusiastic studio audience. As the clapping abated, Carson informed the television viewers that Kuhlman had received a standing ovation from as many as one hundred members of the live audience. After he and Kuhlman exchanged pleasantries, Carson paused, looked intently at Kuhlman, and stated in a courteous manner, "You have been called hypnotic, charismatic, hypnotizing . . ." Kuhlman smilingly protested that she was "just the most ordinary person in the world." Carson disagreed, replying, "You're not quite ordinary. I find you fascinating." Kuhlman smiled.[1]

To be dubbed "not quite ordinary" by the king of late-night television in 1974 represented a triumph for both Kathryn Kuhlman and charismatic Christianity, the brand of Christianity she represented. Since people like Kuhlman were once caricatured by the public as "holy rollers," "pew jumpers," and more recently "charismaniacs" and "Jesus freaks," Carson's interest in interviewing her was nothing short of remarkable. His wry comment that she was not "quite" ordinary—as if she could be considered even in the proximity of ordinary—was in fact a significant

1

compliment from this governor of popular culture. Charismatic Christianity, known for its emphasis on the gifts of the Holy Spirit, operated on the fringes of American religion and culture until the middle of the twentieth century. Charismatic Christians were believed by American society "to be insanely fanatical, self-righteous, doctrinally mistaken, and emotionally unstable."[2] Complaints and caricatures were common in the press. One reporter described a 1923 "Spirit-filled" service as "a mighty religious intoxication" and ended the somewhat sympathetic article with the gently sardonic statement, "And out on the street, these 'peculiar people' looked sane and normal—even as you and I."[3] A *New York Times* article from 1927 contained a disparaging portrait of charismatic forms of worship "making inroads" at Calvary Baptist Church in New York, causing the resignation of five deacons. The services were described as "a form of worship in which the members of the congregations permit themselves to enter into a state of wild excitement bordering on hysteria, some times on frenzy. Shouting, leaping, groveling, violent muscular tremors and sometimes rigidity are among its manifestations. The highest form of it, however, is an outpouring of unintelligible speech, which is considered a special manifestation of holiness." The disgruntled Calvary Baptist deacons complained of "unseemly and undignified behavior," and expressed their apprehension that "psychopathic cases would result if full bent was given to the rising tide of emotionalism at these services."[4]

Prejudices against charismatic worship, practice, and theology persisted for decades. Healing evangelist Oral Roberts, a historical cohort of Kuhlman, became a lightning rod for national discomfort with the charismatic emphasis on faith healing. Roberts biographer David Edwin Harrell notes, "In 1955, *The Christian Century* labeled Oral Roberts a 'Ringling press agent' and warned, 'This Oral Roberts sort of thing . . . can do the cause of vital religion . . . harm.'" The following year, proponents of divine healing were dubbed "racketeers" and "practitioners of religious quackery" by the National Council of Churches.[5] As late as 1963, during the peak of Kuhlman's career, the Right Reverend James A. Pike, bishop of the Episcopal Diocese of California, issued a pastoral letter "in which he admonished clergymen against participating in the growing charismatic practice of glossolalia, or 'speaking with tongues.'" Bishop Pike wrote that tongues speech, "in its most extreme forms," was "associated with schizophrenia."[6] These accounts demonstrate that the backdrop for the conversation between Kuhlman and Carson was not just the faux skyline of "lovely downtown Burbank," but also almost a century of skepticism, uneasiness, and even open hostility toward charismatic Christianity. Set against this history, the response to Kuhlman by the *Tonight Show* audience and by Carson himself revealed that a significantly positive transformation in the cultural tolerance for charismatic Christianity had occurred by late 1974.

The life and ministry of Kathryn Kuhlman provide a much-needed framework for understanding the movement of charismatic Christianity from periphery to center in twentieth-century America. At first, charismatic Christianity was identified primarily with Pentecostalism, which was rooted in late nineteenth-century Holiness, premillennial, and healing movements. "Come-outers" began to leave their Baptist, Methodist, Quaker, Mennonite, and Presbyterian congregations and draw together to form "proto-Pentecostal" congregations at the turn of the twentieth century.[7] American Pentecostals generally point to two dates as pivotal in their history. On January 1, 1901, thirty-year-old Agnes Ozman spoke in tongues while studying under Charles Fox Parham at Bethel Healing Home in Topeka, Kansas, only two hours west of Kuhlman's childhood home in Concordia, Missouri.[8] Encouraged by this "restoration of the apostolic faith" as found in the book of Acts, Parham began to travel in the United States, establishing what he called apostolic faith assemblies. He spent the autumn of 1905 in Houston, Texas, where he instructed a number of African American men who shared his interest in holiness. One of the students was William Seymour, who then moved to Los Angeles in early 1906 and established an apostolic faith assembly at 312 Azusa Street. Seymour soon distanced himself from Parham's supervision, as Parham became increasingly bitter over Seymour's successes. Parham cast caustic racial slurs at Seymour and his assembly as his own life tumbled into chaos and his influence was undercut by accusations of financial dishonesty and sexual misconduct. Due to the awkward end of Parham's leadership, history has privileged Seymour and the Azusa Street Revival of 1906 as the official starting point for American Pentecostalism.[9] The next year, Concordia became the official starting point for Kathryn Johanna Kuhlman, born May 9, 1907. The two would come of age together.

From the beginning, Pentecostals insisted upon adherence to the Fourfold Gospel, which consisted of the doctrines of personal salvation, Holy Ghost baptism, divine healing, and the Lord's soon return.[10] They established the unique requirement of an initial evidence of Holy Ghost baptism in glossolalia, or speaking in tongues. Belief in biblical prophecy also played a significant role in Pentecostal theology. Commitments such as these placed charismatic Christianity, in its guise as Pentecostalism, on the very edge of respectability. Emotional (and often loud) meetings of early Pentecostals sometimes resulted in neighborhood complaints and community disdain. Worship services were described by observers as marked by pandemonium, hysteria, and the speaking of "gibberish."[11] In a 1924 *Los Angeles Times* article titled "Holy Rollers Come to Court," a Mrs. Victoria Hottman was accused by neighbors of holding frequent meetings in her home where "It is said shouting, screams and moans create a disturbance far into the night. . . . Persons who have visited some of the meetings declare that young women and others lie on their backs on the floor, rolling, moaning, screaming and gurgling an unintelligible jargon which members of the sect characterize as 'the gift of tongue.'"[12] Accusations of "promiscuous" meetings where men and women of different races commingled were common, as were disparaging portrayals of all Pentecostals as ignorant, uneducated, and vulgar. In actuality, a large number of Pentecostals came from the stable working class, and their leadership often derived from the upwardly mobile middle class. (As only one example, Kuhlman's own sister Myrtle was deeply involved in Pentecostal ministry with her husband, Everett Parrott, by the mid-1920s. Both were educated and came from middle-class families.) Even so, the position of Pentecostals in the "theological class structure" of American Christianity was decidedly low.[13] Respected Christian leaders portrayed charismatic theology as delusion and even heresy.[14] The standard doctrines held by early Pentecostals were considered backward and ignorant by contemporary mainstream Christians and American popular culture.[15]

Pentecostalism was the primary province of Spirit-filled Christianity until the middle of the twentieth century when a new category of Christian emerged on the scene: the charismatic Christian. A charismatic Christian participated in the "charismatic renewal," a new movement that combined Pentecostal practice and doctrine with attachment to historic mainline churches. The phrase "charismatic renewal" and its derivative, "charismatic Christian," were coined and propelled into popular usage by the renewal's leadership in the early 1960s. Publishers of the influential Episcopal charismatic journal *Trinity* first used the term in a definitive sense in 1963.[16] The newly christened charismatics practiced a softened version of Pentecostal theology. Charismatics retained the emphasis on the present reality of the spiritual gifts mentioned in the book of Acts but did not insist upon the evidence of speaking in tongues to prove the presence of the baptism of the Holy Spirit in the life of a believer. This distinction made them more appealing, or doctrinally impure, depending on your adherence to classic Pentecostal doctrine.

Pentecostals participated in denominations historically grounded in classic Pentecostalism. Charismatics maintained connections with mainline denominations and did not affiliate with Pentecostal church organizations such as the Assemblies of God.[17] Charismatics came from a multitude of backgrounds besides classic Pentecostalism and remained members of their various denominations even as they participated in the movement for renewal. Kathryn Kuhlman followed this approach, maintaining her identity as a Baptist throughout her time as a charismatic Christian leader. Charismatic Roman Catholics considered themselves the answer to the prayer of Pope John XXIII at the Second Vatican Council for the Holy Spirit to "renew your wonders in our time, as though in a new Pentecost."[18] Catholics joined with Episcopal and Lutheran leaders who were reclaiming their churches' historic emphasis on prayer for healing. Organizations such as the Full Gospel Business Men's Fellowship International provided meeting places and sponsored events for gatherings of socially and financially successful charismatic Christians.[19] Even some Pentecostals who had ridden the wave of post–World War II economic prosperity began to affiliate with other charismatic Christians along socioeconomic rather than denominational lines. By the 1960s, charismatic Christianity also produced several highly visible leaders who shaped the movement's identity. Kathryn Kuhlman was one of the most influential.[20]

Kuhlman was a leader in the transformation of charismatic Christianity from a suspect form of religion to a respectable form of religiosity that was accepted and even celebrated by mainstream Christianity and culture by the end of the twentieth century. During the course of her life, 1907–1976, charismatic Christianity began to move from fringe to center, from questionable to respectable, even desirable, for a growing number of American Christians. I call this transformation gentrification. The term "gentrification" is evocative and provocative when used in reference to urban areas, and no less so when applied to the changes charismatic Christianity experienced in the twentieth century. In urban neighborhoods, as interest builds, the public perception of an area changes from being uninteresting or even dangerous to being the new "hot spot." This is "gentrification." Charismatic Christianity experienced this kind of media-driven metamorphosis; by the late 1960s, it was not just tolerable, but trendy. By the mid-twentieth century, popular culture as well as mainstream Christianity perceived charismatic Christianity as a valid, if still peculiar, religious choice. Part of this transformation involved an intentional demarcation between the designations "Pentecostal" and "charismatic" by the leaders of the movement. The new label conceived by the *Trinity* editors was used as a repudiation of the classification of the movement as "neo-Pentecostalism" by the editor of the evangelical magazine *Eternity*. The discomfort was likely due to concern over social, theological, and class associations with Pentecostalism. All the *Trinity* editors were mainline Episcopalians, except for David du Plessis, a South African, and Harald Bredesen, a charismatic Lutheran.[21] The calculated change in name from neo-Pentecostal to charismatic was an important step in the gentrification of charismatic Christianity. This was not just "new Pentecostalism"; it was a newly gentrified way of being a charismatic Christian.

During Kuhlman's lifetime and under her leadership, the designation "charismatic" Christian developed, gentrified, into something different from Pentecostal, evangelical, or mainline. In a chart of sets and subsets, "charismatic" intersected the sets of Pentecostal, evangelical, and mainline Christianity, creating a new subset in American religious history. Kuhlman was not very popular with the leadership of classic Pentecostalism because she downplayed tongues speech in her own life and in her services. Pentecostal leaders saw gentrification as a negative development, leading to the loss of authentic structures inherent to Pentecostal belief. According to these leaders, charismatic Christians might believe in the charisms of the Holy Spirit and the reality of a new Pentecost in modern times, but they were not Pentecostal. As charismatic Christianity coalesced around leaders such as Kuhlman and began to make significant inroads into non-Pentecostal churches, it achieved a discrete identity. You could, theoretically, be charismatic and consider yourself still Pentecostal. But by Kuhlman's prime time as a leader in the 1960s, it was not really possible to be a strict Pentecostal and participate without reservation in the renewal movement she led.

Evangelicalism, defined as belief in the necessity of being born again, the binding authority of the Bible, and Jesus as a personal Savior, was more compatible with charismatic Christianity. Some Baptists claimed to be "Holy Ghost Baptists," and many charismatics were comfortable being identified as charismatic evangelicals, especially as evangelicalism began to organize around the more open neo-evangelical movement led by Billy Graham. Kuhlman always maintained a strong evangelical character in her ministry. She emphasized repeatedly that the purpose of healing was to bring about the salvation of those who experienced and witnessed the miracle. Even so, not all who called themselves evangelical approved. Over time, divine healing and other spiritual gifts tended to threaten salvation as the focal point of charismatic worship. This trend made some evangelicals uncomfortable with the charismatic renewal movement. Firm dispensationalists such as Churches of Christ were as opposed to the charismatic movement as they had been to the earlier Pentecostal churches. Whether in 1906 on Azusa Street or in 1960s California, some groups still believed the spiritual gifts had ceased with the end of the apostolic age.

Its diffuse nature makes locating a center for the charismatic renewal movement difficult. In some ways the movement was everywhere, as participants in all varieties of American Christianity began to identify themselves as charismatic. In other ways it was nowhere. It was a movement without a designated leader, without a structure, without a defining identity. Movements for spiritual renewal happened simultaneously in many groups. Due to their hope for universal spiritual renewal, charismatic Christians generally chose to remain within their denominations rather than leave them and establish independent churches. Almost all brands of Christianity were affected by the movement in mid-twentieth-century America. "Charismatic" served as an adjective for Episcopalians, Lutherans, Methodists, Presbyterians, American Baptists, Disciples of Christ, and Roman Catholics, among others. The Episcopal Church was in the vanguard of mainline Protestant charismatic growth due in large part to the marketing acumen of charismatic Episcopal laywoman Jean Stone. In 1960, Stone leveraged the appeal of Episcopal cleric Dennis Bennett, the "tongues-speaking priest" of Van Nuys, California, by sending *Time* and *Newsweek* the story of Bennett's controversial self-identification as charismatic. She also headed the Blessed Trinity Society, which organized in 1961 to promote the charismatic renewal in the Episcopal Church. Lutheran churches, despite the opposition of the Lutheran Church–Missouri Synod, also contributed large numbers of adherents to charismatic Christianity, especially under the leadership of Lutheran pastor Harald Bredesen.[22]

In the early months of 1967, Catholic charismatic revivals occurred on the campuses of Duquesne University in Pittsburgh and the University of Notre Dame in South Bend, Indiana. Strongly influenced by the Second Vatican Council, Catholic lay faculty and students began to organize prayer groups and sponsor retreats where charismatic experiences were encouraged and affirmed. The press covered an April gathering of Notre Dame students and faculty numbering around one hundred, and with this media validation, the Catholic charismatic renewal was officially under way.[23] By the end of the 1970s, most major denominations in America had adopted "cautious openness" regarding the growth of charismatic practices in their congregations.[24] Given these diverse participants, "charismatic" developed into a defining term that pointed to a new configuration in American Christianity and allowed these varied movements to find each other.[25]

Kuhlman's life provides an orienting narrative, a road map for studying the gentrification of charismatic Christianity. At the time of her death in 1976, Kuhlman was at the center of a charismatic ministry known throughout the world. Attracting large crowds throughout her fifty-five years of ministry, Kuhlman preached to hundreds of thousands of people. In just one example of her drawing power, in the last ten years of her life she preached every month to capacity crowds in the seven-thousand-seat Los Angeles Shrine Auditorium. She hosted radio and television shows and headed a successful nonprofit corporation, the Kathryn Kuhlman Foundation. She authored several best-selling books, such as the collection of healing testimonies entitled *I Believe in Miracles*, which sold over a million copies. In 1975, when she came to Las Vegas to conduct one of her world-famous "miracle services," she was greeted at the airport by the mayor, who declared the date Kathryn Kuhlman Day.

Despite her successful career and remarkable popularity, Kuhlman is largely forgotten in the history of American Christianity.[26] She was a leader of a form of Christianity many believed, and some hoped, was just a fad, including scholars of Christian history. Sydney Ahlstrom offered only a footnote about charismatic Christianity in the last chapter of his sweeping book *A Religious History of the American People*. In the book, written in 1972, in the prime of the charismatic renewal movement, Ahlstrom pondered in an annotation the possible future of a movement of charismatic Christianity such as the Jesus People. "Whether they should be considered in a footnote (as here) is a question which only the future will answer." Ahlstrom included the group as one of many outgrowths of "the turbulent sixties," and expressed little confidence in its long-term viability. "Yet," Ahlstrom concluded, "surprises are the stuff of history."[27] Ahlstrom would likely have been surprised not only by the remarkable growth and perseverance of charismatic Christianity, but also by the recent proliferation of historical studies exploring it. In the last decades, noteworthy scholarship on Pentecostalism has laid a strong foundation for further exploration of Pentecostalism's descendant, charismatic Christianity.

The collections of the Kathryn Kuhlman Foundation, housed at the archives of the Billy Graham Center at Wheaton College, Wheaton, Illinois, constituted the bulk of primary sources for this project. Five hundred episodes of Kuhlman's television show *I Believe in Miracles* are preserved on VHS tape and are available for viewing at the archives. A close "reading" of these videos provided a wealth of resources for the exploration of Kuhlman and her presentation of charismatic Christianity. Kuhlman's three books of collected testimonies to divine healing as well as the many compilations of personal stories of healing published under her name gave added depth to the study of the videos. Press clippings were a valuable source of both positive and negative impressions of Kuhlman's ministry due to her popularity as a news topic during her heyday in Los Angeles and Pittsburgh. Kuhlman also recorded hundreds of thirty-minute segments for radio syndication that are preserved at the Graham Center. Selected episodes furnished additional information about her theology, doctrine, and broadcasting style. Three biographies supplied most of the information about Kuhlman's early years, with Wayne Warner's exploration of her life venturing furthest from hagiography. The Kuhlman collection at Wheaton also includes scrapbooks that belonged to Kuhlman, filled with diminutive black-and-white photographs carefully mounted. These pictures were especially absorbing, since they offered one of the only glimpses into Kuhlman's interior life. I studied the prints closely, examining her clothing and expressions and surroundings with the help of a magnifying glass. These pictures opened up an avenue to Kuhlman unavailable through the hyper-mediated sources such as the television shows. Kathryn Kuhlman as a historical figure exists primarily as a public, mediated persona. Very little private correspondence is available for research, and she rarely spoke publicly about friends, limiting her references about her family to well-used stories of her childhood and early days in ministry. She had siblings, nieces, and nephews, but they played almost no role in her public life. Her popular image during the peak of her career was often a solitary one, but the pages of snapshots carefully preserved by Kuhlman herself helped paint a richer picture of the flesh-and-blood woman who would later become "the Miracle Lady."

The careful examination of Kuhlman's life as a leader of the charismatic renewal movement affords many opportunities to add to the study of Christianity in twentieth-century America. As the single most important female leader in the charismatic renewal movement, her life intersects the study of women in religion, particularly the complex role of female leaders in conservative Christian circles in the age of feminism. Kuhlman made choices as a female religious leader that were, if not always admirable, at least understandable in the conservative context in which she operated.[28] Many of the decisions she made protected her always tenuous position of leadership and helped reinforce a ministry consistently vulnerable at the point of her gender. As Kuhlman's ministry grew in popularity, she became the preeminent woman in the new movement for charismatic renewal, a position she held through a combination of sheer hard work, political savvy, and authentic dedication to her ministry. She managed to negotiate the still-hostile environment of charismatic Christianity and successfully manipulate the oppressive structures, rules, and subtle land mines that surrounded a female religious leader within its ranks. She navigated the prejudices of her conservative Christian environment with skill.

Did Kuhlman really believe her own rhetoric about women, or was she engaging in a clever play for power, or both? These questions remain essentially unanswerable, since no private correspondence or diaries are available that could reveal Kuhlman's inner motivations. She refused to share her private life with her public. What do exist are public statements that reveal a female religious leader adept at cleverly manipulating her public identity in order to maintain her position of power. In her public pronouncements, she upheld conservative and traditional roles for women. At the same time, she was the head of a large nonprofit foundation with assets surpassing one million dollars at its height, and which employed a staff of male department heads. She served as a de facto pastor over a congregation along with her male associate minister. She traveled widely and spoke all over the world as the sole public female face of the charismatic renewal movement. She was divorced with no children. She never remarried. She lived alone, in whichever of her three residences she was in proximity to at the time. Yet she maintained an adoring public within conservative Christianity.

Was Kuhlman what scholar Kristin Kobes Du Mez calls a Christian feminist, like Katharine Bushnell before her, who "long looked forward to a new era for women, to a time when the 'new woman' in Christ would no more turn away from God and submit to man, as had Eve, but rather would remain 'loyal to God alone'"?[29] Kuhlman demonstrated her loyalty to God by divorcing her husband and spending the rest of her life and career as a single woman. Was this a form of feminism? Or was Kuhlman rather an early example of the complicated antifeminist typified by conservative celebrity Phyllis Schlafly? In his work on Schlafly, Donald Critchlow explains that she "saw history as having fulfilled the promise of womanhood by allowing women to choose to become wives and mothers in traditional families." This was a belief Schlafly espoused while crisscrossing the country on political speaking tours, running for political office, and leading a successful effort to quash the Equal Rights Amendment.[30] Like Schlafly, Kuhlman lived the liberated life while opposing women's lib. It is difficult to discern whether Kuhlman knew she was acting disingenuously or if it was just second nature to protect herself in the way she knew best. The answer probably lies somewhere in between. But in her ability to take characteristics of her life that should have been detrimental to her leadership and turn them into assets, she is fascinating to behold.

Kuhlman was a media figure, known as much for her television show as for her miracle services and her books. Her mediated existence presses the necessity of further conversation between the study of religion and the study of media. Her life and ministry engage topics of mediated religion, the effect of media on Christianity in the twentieth century, and what effect television has on the public understanding of Christianity. Kuhlman also was a bridge personality, bringing together in her ministry groups of Christians who would ordinarily never enter each other's theological neighborhoods. Her life and ministry provide a much-needed framework for understanding the movement of charismatic Christianity from periphery to center in mid-twentieth-century America.

But what about the Carson interview? How did it end? Kathryn Kuhlman held her own with Johnny Carson in Studio One. Their conversation ranged over several topics, including the recent appearance on the show of Kuhlman's harshest critic, Dr. William Nolen. "I love people," Kuhlman said with a wide smile. No one was outside of her love, she said, then paused. "Not even Dr. Nolen," she concluded, with a dry wit. Carson asked her about her talk show, and Kuhlman responded enthusiastically, but with some hesitation. "I do it from . . . is it all right? CBS!" The audience laughed; Carson clearly enjoyed the gentle dig at his home network, NBC; and then he turned to more serious topics. He asked Kuhlman why she did not want to be known as a faith healer, why some people were not healed, and presented her with the accusation propounded by Dr. Nolen that all the healings at her services were psychosomatic. Kuhlman spoke easily and candidly, often stretching her seated body toward Carson with hands clasped in front of her chest, pressed against the silver cross necklace sparkling against her dark blue dress. "I am not a faith healer," she stated. "I have never healed a person. I am not a healer. I stand there and tell people what they already know: that nothing is impossible with God." Kuhlman kept an intense and earnest focus on Carson as she spoke. Carson leaned forward, resting his elbow on his desk and his chin in his hand as he listened. "Those who preach that you cannot be healed without faith, that is cruel. I worship a God who is all-sovereign." Her voice rose and fell with emotion and emphasis as she continued. "That's the hardest thing in this ministry," she stated frankly. "I don't know why some people are healed and others aren't."

In response to Carson's most challenging question regarding psychosomatic illness, Kuhlman became brisk and confident. With sharp eyebrows raised, she admitted the possibility that some of the healings at her services were psychosomatic. "But, Johnny," she began, and reached toward him with her body, her eyes locked with his. Carson returned her gaze as she reminded him that in the opinion of most medical professionals, psychosomatic cases were by far the most difficult to cure. As she paused for effect, the audience broke into applause, Kuhlman dropped her lanky figure back into the chair, and Carson acknowledged her shrewd answer with a nod.[31]

The rest of the conversation, which lasted until the band began to play the closing chords to signal the show's end, was comfortable and congenial, but Carson never fully relaxed in the presence of his formidable and not-quite-ordinary guest. By the latter part of the twentieth century, the relationship of American popular culture and mainstream religion with charismatic Christianity was much the same as that between Kuhlman and Carson. The journey of charismatic Christianity from religious and cultural contempt to acceptance, albeit somewhat uneasy acceptance, was the narrative of Kuhlman's life and is the focus of this work.

CHAPTER 1

The Making of a Miracle Lady

O n July 20, 1973, the magazine *Christianity Today* published a pamphlet containing what it called "a wide-ranging, exclusive interview" with Kathryn Kuhlman "to dispel some of the misunderstanding that has grown up around her, or at least to present a digest, in her own words, of how she answers questions put to her by both believers and unbelievers." In the interview, Kuhlman stated, "I tell you the truth: I answer every question that is asked of me. I do not believe there is anyone in the religious field today who is more honest in answering questions than I am. That is the reason I am talking to you now. I bare my soul to you."[1] It was true that Kuhlman was always willing to answer the questions set before her by the media, but with a caveat: outside of a collection of select narratives concerning her childhood and early ministry, Kuhlman maintained a fierce silence about the majority of the first forty years of her life and ministry.

Any attempt to re-create Kuhlman's life based only upon her public pronouncements falters due to her persistent avoidance of speaking at length about the years between 1907 and 1947. She spoke of the early years only as she reminisced about her father or mother or looked back with nostalgia to her days as a girl evangelist. She chose to downplay, dismiss, or even deny most of her early education and training. Her motivation for doing this was simple: she needed to protect her preferred narrative of being a simple, untrained handmaiden of the Lord, who was "just naïve enough" to say yes to God's call.[2] With persistent repetition of carefully constructed anecdotes and a determined resistance to speaking about topics she considered closed, Kuhlman worked to control the story of her life. There were details she wanted known and others she wanted forgotten. In this she was consistent with most public figures who desire to craft a positive and edifying "birth narrative" for their life and career. But to understand Kuhlman and the charismatic Christianity she helped lead, it is necessary to look closely at these formative years.

Kuhlman was shaped by her religious background, her education, and her early career as a traveling evangelist. She developed her style and technique by observing and training under personalities such as her sister, her brother-in-law, and the healing evangelist Aimee Semple McPherson, among others. She developed an appreciation for charismatic Christianity despite the negative image "holy rollers" held in the popular culture and mainstream Christianity of the day. At first, she was not completely at ease with charismatic Christianity, as shown by her disdain for the independent healing evangelists who traveled the same circuit as she did, charismatics who represented the excess and emotionalism she rejected. The life and career of this young female religious leader were defined in many ways by the death of her beloved father and the end of her marriage. She spoke of her father's death but never reflected upon the trauma of the experience that likely propelled her into a courtship only nine months later that ended in a disastrous marriage. Regarding her marriage, she was taciturn. But an examination of Kuhlman's "silent years"[3] reveals the foundation for the popular public ministry that followed, and is vital to a full understanding of Kuhlman. In addition, her life and career between 1907 and 1947 provide a helpful narrative for an exploration of the development of charismatic Christianity during the same period. Kathryn Kuhlman and charismatic Christianity grew up together.

Kuhlman did not have the typical childhood of a future healing evangelist. She did not claim her healing ministry had its roots in a youth of sickness or trauma. Stories of her happy, energetic, and healthy girlhood in Concordia, Missouri, were common in her preaching and teaching. Kuhlman stated, "I was always healthy as a kid. I had the three-day measles that only lasted one day. I ran so fast nothing could catch up to me."[4] Although Kuhlman was a young child during World War I, she never referred to family losses due to the war or the devastating influenza epidemic of 1918. She was the third of four children, and did not mention any medical trouble in the lives of older siblings Myrtle or Earl, or younger sister Geneva. Sickness in her own life was not what led Kuhlman to a career healing sickness in the lives of others.[5]

Kuhlman was raised by father Joe, a nominal Baptist, and a Methodist mother, Emma, neither of whom had any background in divine healing. She was not raised to believe in faith healing, but other aspects of her upbringing likely contributed to her later openness to the concept. Kuhlman inherited from her parents a strong emphasis on the human ability to resist and overcome illness and suffering through plain hard work. Suffering, while a reality in human life, was never meant to define or defeat. She said throughout her career, in a variety of settings, that if you are a part of the human race, you will have troubles. But it's not what happens to you that matters, it's what you do with what happens to you that matters. Kuhlman's father taught her that human beings had the ability to prevail over suffering. Strongly influenced by her father's approach to life, Kuhlman was indoctrinated in a Midwestern approach to illness and healing. Kuhlman told the story this way: "I can always remember Papa saying something. It wasn't scientific. You won't find it in the doctors' manual. It's just good common sense. He used to say, 'Oh, just go out and work it off.' The best medicine in the world is hard work. They've got pills for everything today. We're almost pilled to death. But no one has come up with a capsule which makes people want to work."[6]

For Joe Kuhlman and his daughter Kathryn, the appropriate response to sickness was not saintly resignation, but determined action; in other words, good, hard work. This way of thinking about suffering and illness became more prevalent during the late nineteenth century, and came to full flower in the early twentieth century. Historian Heather Curtis's work notes the shift in thinking about sickness and health at the end of the nineteenth century, as advocates of what would soon be called faith healing "endeavored to articulate and embody an alternative devotional ethic that uncoupled the longstanding link between corporeal suffering and spiritual holiness."[7] During Kuhlman's childhood in Missouri, this renewed emphasis on the belief in God's desire to heal persons who were determined and bold in prayer was gathering strength in American Christianity.[8] Kuhlman was ingrained in the approach to adversity and illness taught by her father, which was similar to the ideology producing a widespread renewal of interest in divine cures.

Although Kuhlman's parents laid some of the foundation for her later interest in divine healing, it was Kuhlman's sister Myrtle, fifteen years her senior, who led Kathryn to charismatic Christianity.[9] In the summer of 1913, Myrtle attended a revival at her Methodist church in Concordia led by Mr. Everett Parrott, a young circuit evangelist from Moody Bible Institute in Chicago. Parrott was traveling in the Midwest, preaching in any church where he could find an audience. Concordia turned out in force to see the handsome preacher, and Myrtle was in the crowd. She and her friend Ora Dickey sat at the back of the church as the pews filled for the revival because "we didn't want to be seen, to associate with those types." Attendance at revivals was not common for Myrtle. She noted, "We came from high-class people on both sides. Papa's side were aristocrats."[10] Her kind of people did not go to revivals, Myrtle implied. Despite her disdain for the services, she was attracted to Parrott, and the affection was mutual. The two married October 6, 1913, and immediately returned to Chicago to finish Everett's education. Myrtle also attended classes at Moody. Everett graduated in 1914, and the couple began to travel as itinerant evangelists. For the next ten years they preached across the midwestern and western United States, visiting Concordia occasionally to see the Kuhlman family. Younger sister Kathryn was growing up quickly, and at age fourteen her life took its own dramatic turn.

Kathryn attended her mother's Methodist church during her youth, but in later years always referred to herself as a Baptist, like her father. As an evangelical, she was able to pinpoint the day when she was "born again." Kuhlman was in worship one day with her mother at their small church, and as they began to sing the closing hymn the girl began to tremble. "I began to shake so hard that I could no longer hold the hymnal in my hand.... This was my first contact with the Third Person of the Trinity, and in that moment I knew I needed Jesus to forgive my sins." Kuhlman's first experience with the Holy Spirit brought conviction and conversion, typical marks of evangelicalism. Her testimony did not mention being baptized as an infant or confirmed, the typical practices of the Methodism of her mother. The story of her conversion at the age of fourteen was one of the few stories about her youth she told repeatedly throughout her life. This experience highlighted one aspect of her early years she particularly wanted known and understood: Kathryn Kuhlman was a born-again Christian.

Kuhlman's story of her conversion at her mother's church contained not-so-subtle criticism of her childhood church home. In a somewhat damning statement about her congregation, Kuhlman added, "Since I had never seen anyone receive Christ as their savior, I did not know what to do." She recalled that new members were to go forward to be received into the church, and so she decided to do the same. She sat in the front pew, crying. "It was real, very real, and I have never doubted it from that moment to this hour. I knew I had been forgiven!" Kuhlman continued to cry. "The preacher did not know what to do with me. No altar call had been given. In fact, I doubt that an altar call had been given for years in that little church." An older woman of the church finally came and sat next to Kuhlman and offered her comfort. "She said in a whisper, 'Oh Kathryn, don't cry. You've always been such a good girl.' But even as she spoke those words, we both knew that what she said was not quite the truth for I was the most mischievous kid in town." It was a significant moment for Kuhlman. "Walking home that Sunday, I thought the whole world had changed," she remembered. "Nothing in Concordia had changed—except me. I was the one who had changed."[11]

Kuhlman soon experienced even more dramatic changes in her life. In the spring of 1924 Myrtle returned to Concordia to petition Joe and Emma for permission to take Kathryn along for a summer of touring and preaching. Kathryn's parents consented to let her go, and at age seventeen she left Concordia for her first experiences "in the field." Myrtle, who once had hidden herself at the back of the church to avoid the scandal of being seen at a revival, now associated freely with Pentecostals and supported her husband as he spoke of the baptism of the Holy Spirit and the reality of divine healing. As she lived and worked with her sister, Kathryn discovered she was not the only one who had changed.

Myrtle introduced her teenage sister to a strange new religious world. In the 1920s, adherence to belief in tongues-speech and divine healing was considered by much of American culture to be abnormal. Charismatic Christianity, primarily identified at that time with Pentecostalism, was suspect and esoteric for most mainstream Christians. The *Chicago Daily Tribune* of August 11, 1924, carried a story describing the typical image of Pentecostals. Bold letters headlined the article, "Worshipers Too Noisy, Haled to Night Court:"

> Judge Max Witkower was called from his bed to hold a midnight court in Evanston last night when the entire congregation of the Pentecostal Assembly of God at 1615 Lake Street—nine colored and three white—were arrested on complaint of William Dunfriennd who lives across the street from the church. . . . Dunfriennd and his wife complained the members of the congregation clapped their hands, sang and jumped up and down all night so they could not sleep. After being released on bond the prisoners closed their eyes, raised their right hands and began singing. The judge ordered the lights turned out.[12]

Pentecostals came under attack not just for their practices but also for their beliefs. Their emphasis on the baptism of the Holy Spirit and the present reality of the gifts of the Spirit as found in Scripture (such as healing, speaking in tongues, and prophecy) kept them on the outside of mainstream Christian belief in the early twentieth century.

Fundamentalist Baptists especially derided Pentecostals, on the basis of a dispensational understanding of biblical history that taught the cessation of spiritual gifts with the end of the apostolic age, or the age of the New Testament church. The *Chicago Daily Tribune* carried another account of an altercation over Pentecostal doctrine, this one occurring in New York City in October 1927. The headline stated, "30 Quit Straton Church; Oppose Healing Service." The pastor, respected Baptist minister Rev. Dr. John Roach Straton, held what the paper termed a "Holy Ghost healing service," one of a number of such services, at the influential Calvary Baptist Church in New York City. The services were highly controversial, causing the threatened resignation of as many as thirty members. The author of the article recorded that Dr. Straton had "laid on oiled hands" in a service held in the anteroom of the church. Stephen A. Bradford, former Calvary deacon and current member, "was outspoken against the 'divine healing' meetings." Bradford compared the healing services to those held at Calvary the previous summer, which he described as "holy roller and Pentecostal in their character." The article concluded, "Dr. Straton was likened by Mr. Bradford to a 'cuckoo,' in that he lays the eggs of strange doctrines in what is 'supposedly a baptist organization.'" The Baptist leader Bradford saw Pentecostals as dangerous, parasitic, and invasive, just like the cuckoo who lays her eggs in another bird's nest.[13] It was remarkable that Myrtle Kuhlman Parrott, a woman who once claimed to be from an aristocratic Baptist family, chose to associate with Pentecostalism in the 1920s. Myrtle's espousal of charismatic Christianity was the primary reason Kathryn Kuhlman, a born-again Baptist, was exposed to teaching about the gifts of the Holy Spirit, particularly divine or faith healing.

Early Influences

Between 1924 and 1928, as Kuhlman traveled with her sister and brother-in-law throughout the western states, she was moving in the orbit of the preeminent leaders in divine healing. The 1920s were the era of what Jonathan Baer calls the "facilitating healer," defined as one who "tried to facilitate, through teaching, encouragement, and prayer, healing faith in the Christian patient."[14] The centerpiece of this approach was the faith of the patient, not the power or heroics of the healer. The facilitating healer was to guide and direct the patient to appropriate the faith already present in him or her in order to gain victory over sickness and suffering.[15] Facilitating healing emerged out of a renewal of interest in healing in the more mainstream evangelical Christianity of the time. It represented a movement away from the more volatile and dramatic ministries of "heroic healers of incipient Pentecostalism" such as Maria Woodworth-Etter and John Alexander Dowie. Facilitating healers of this era differentiated themselves carefully from what they saw as the excesses of the new Pentecostal Christianity. "By de-emphasizing Pentecostal distinctives, especially speaking in tongues, and by softening the heavy stress on Satan, exorcism, and the evils of worldly medicine in early Pentecostal healing, [facilitating healers] appealed to a broad range of conservative Protestants."[16]

Kathryn Kuhlman entered ministry at the age of seventeen during the time of the facilitating healers, and much of her later teaching about divine healing can be traced to her exposure to them. Several figures influenced Kuhlman's understanding of divine healing: Charles Price (1887–1947), the instructor of Myrtle and Everett; Aimee Semple McPherson (1890–1944); A. B. Simpson (1843–1919); and Everett Parrott himself.

Charles Price

In 1924, as Kuhlman traveled alongside the Parrotts through the states of Idaho, Colorado, and California, she was introduced to facilitating healing through the ministries of Charles Price and Aimee Semple McPherson. In an interview taped by biographer Jamie Buckingham in the 1970s, Myrtle and Kathryn reminisced about the early days of their shared ministry. Myrtle told of going to nondenominational meetings in Albany, Oregon, with Dr. Price and receiving his instruction concerning the doctrine of the baptism of the Holy Spirit.[17] The Parrotts and Kuhlman were representative of the many who were taught by Price during his career. Price was converted at a revival meeting led by McPherson in San Jose, California, in early 1920.[18] Under McPherson's "masterful message," the Oxford-trained, British Congregational pastor was "baptized in the Spirit."[19] He began to preach what he had learned from McPherson and experienced tremendous response in his own congregation. After joining

McPherson a few times on her revival circuits, he chose to become an independent traveling evangelist with a new emphasis on healing.[20] During the 1920s Price went on to produce a series of large meetings in Oregon, British Columbia, and elsewhere in Canada. In his Canadian services, a twelve-thousand-seat ice arena was not big enough for the crowds, and people broke through windows in order to climb inside to hear the evangelist. His gathering in Vancouver alone attracted 250,000 people during its three-week run.[21] In 1926, Price began publication of the popular periodical the *Golden Grain*. Through his meetings and publications, Price exerted a considerable influence over those involved in the post–World War I revival of interest in divine healing.[22]

Under the tutelage of her sister and brother-in-law, both students of Price, Kuhlman was given the foundational instruction in healing that would come to fruition in her later career. Kuhlman's sister Myrtle openly credited Price for much of her education concerning the baptism of the Holy Spirit and other doctrinal matters. Unlike her sister, however, Kuhlman never acknowledged Price's influence, despite the evidence of his effect on her development. As one historian notes, "In several places [Kuhlman's] vocabulary and style are so close to [Price's] that it is probable she was borrowing from him."[23] Kuhlman's plagiarism, intentional or not, was a part of her total refusal to acknowledge any formal education in her early years. Price therefore remained an unacknowledged source.

Recognizing the tutelage of any major figure in divine healing was threatening to Kuhlman's preferred version of her background as an untrained innocent. The only training she chose to mention was the instruction she received from her sister and brother-in-law. As a seventeen-year-old traveling with a thirty-two-year-old sibling, Kuhlman admitted that Myrtle kept a close watch on her theological development. Sharing the stories of her sister's influence over her thinking and teaching did not seem to threaten Kuhlman. On the contrary, she enjoyed telling the stories of Myrtle's concern. "Myrtle was always warning me to keep my theology straight," she said on several occasions. If her followers knew Kuhlman was influenced by her sister, a little-known wife of an even lesser-known healing evangelist, what harm was there in that? Further, what threat was there in knowing that her sister was taught by Charles Price, once famous but now faded from the public memory? But Price's teacher, Aimee Semple McPherson, was a different story. Sister Aimee was significantly more well-known, and her influence markedly more threatening to Kuhlman's presentation of herself as an untrained handmaiden of the Lord.

Aimee Semple McPherson

The shadow of Aimee Semple McPherson (1890–1944) fell on Kuhlman throughout her career. Kuhlman repeatedly disavowed McPherson's influence on her development while endeavoring to garner whatever benefit she could from the constant comparison. It was a delicate balance to maintain. In an episode of *I Believe in Miracles* taped on February 15, 1973, Kuhlman welcomed Sister Aimee's two children Rolph and Roberta McPherson as her guests. In her introduction she dedicated the telecast to Aimee:

> I deeply regret that I never met her, but I feel as if she was known to me my whole life. Perhaps no one else appreciates Aimee more. She, too, was a woman who preached the gospel. She believed in miracles. She loved lost souls. Perhaps no one can understand her loneliness. A life dedicated to the Lord can be lonely. You can be surrounded by thousands of people, you give every ounce of strength, and then you go home . . . you wish you could have given more, you ache for those who weren't healed. I have never seen this woman, but I share the loneliness, the consecration, her fellowship with Him.[24]

Once again Kuhlman attempted the tricky maneuver of simultaneously connecting herself with and distancing herself from McPherson.

In the *Christianity Today* interview published only a few months after the broadcast with McPherson's children, Kuhlman's answer to the question of Sister's influence was more abrupt. The editors asked, "Was Aimee Semple any kind of model or inspiration to you?" Kuhlman answered, "No, because I never met her."[25] In the most basic sense, it was likely true that Kuhlman "never met her," or, in other words, did not know McPherson personally. As was often the case with Kuhlman's statements about her past, however, her assertion was incomplete. Kuhlman downplayed her relationship to McPherson in order to preserve her presentation of herself as untrained and uneducated. While Kuhlman may not have met McPherson in person, her need to distance herself from her powerful predecessor led to statements that were simply not true. On the television broadcast with Aimee's children, Kuhlman said she "never saw [McPherson]." This was almost certainly a lie. Aimee's son Rolf later told biographer Wayne Warner that he remembered Kuhlman attending services to hear McPherson preach at Angelus Temple in the mid-1920s. Warner also established a credible case for Kuhlman auditing classes at McPherson's Lighthouse for International Foursquare Evangelism (LIFE) Bible College.[26] McPherson was popular with the press and quite the celebrity, and while it was unlikely that an unknown girl from Concordia, Missouri, would have had the chance to meet her one-on-one, it was equally unlikely that Kuhlman "never saw her." When Kuhlman was traveling in the Northwest with her family in the 1920s, McPherson was coming into the height of her fame.[27] Kuhlman certainly did see Sister Aimee, and she was shaped in significant ways by Sister's approach to divine healing.

Sister Aimee's popularity was due in part to the form of healing evangelism she promoted, a form that appealed to those outside Pentecostal and Holiness circles. As a facilitating healer, she claimed she was simply teaching, offering encouragement, and praying for the gathered people's faith to be sufficient for God's power to work in their lives. During her hugely successful Denver campaign, McPherson characterized her facilitating role: "My healings? I do nothing. If the eyes of the people are set on ME, nothing will happen. I pray and believe with others who pray and believe, and the power of Christ works the cure."[28] Sister Aimee claimed that her meetings were "99% salvation and 1% healing,"[29] and regularly refused to take credit for the healings at her services. Baer explains, "[McPherson] strategically de-emphasized divine healing in her public statements, stressing salvation instead, even as she understood the power of her healing ministry to generate a following."[30] McPherson's emphasis on salvation in her public statements served to downplay the increasing role of divine healing in her campaign. For the casual observer, Sister Aimee was preaching familiar old-time revival religion. But a closer look at her salvation message revealed a deeper commitment to divine healing than she cared to publicize.

McPherson taught the controversial doctrine that healing was in the atonement of the crucifixion of Jesus Christ. The salvation message included healing, since appropriating Christ's atoning work included "the whole man." When McPherson's followers sang the hymn "The Old Rugged Cross," it was the atonement of Jesus Christ that was the "double cure" claimed in the words of the song. Atonement saved from wrath *and* made one pure.[31] The atonement included ransom for both sin and sickness, a reinterpretation of the old hymn's message of the double cure of salvation and sanctification. Jesus died not only to save souls, but also to cure bodies. His atonement was for spirit and flesh. Because healing was in the atonement, the answer to sickness was a simple appropriation of that atoning act, just as the act of accepting Jesus brought salvation. Edith Blumhofer explains, "Sister extended the invitation to salvation to all in the classic Arminian call: 'Whosoever will may come.'"[32] The same held true for healing.[33]

McPherson's ministry also included a strong premillennial worldview. Intense interest in premillennial dispensationalism filled the evangelical culture of Sister's day. Premillennialism was the belief that Jesus would return to earth to usher in a thousand-year reign signaling the coming end of the age. Scholar Timothy Gloege notes that by the early twentieth century, a "pragmatic premillennialism" held sway among most Protestants, disturbing and disrupting speculative end-times predictions with a healthy respect for the biblical mandate that "no one knew the day or hour of Jesus's return." Adherents of dispensationalism as captured in the Scofield Reference Bible of 1909 "noticed that 'essential' beliefs and practices changed over the course of human history." This was due to the effect of God's use of dispensations, or periods of time, during which "God had different ways of engaging humanity and different moral standards for believers to follow." For most dispensationalists of McPherson's time, the present dispensation precluded most if not all miracles.[34] Supernatural gifts of the Spirit ceased with the apostolic dispensation. Pentecostals were attracted to the organizing principle of dispensationalism for understanding biblical history but rejected the assertion of the cessation of "sensational" gifts like speaking in tongues and divine healing.

McPherson was more premillennial than dispensational, and saw the signs and wonders of her ministry as "last calls" in the preparation for Christ's second coming.[35] This was a motivating energy behind her ministry. Sister included altar calls in all her services, unlike her colleagues who waited until their campaigns had gained enough energy to guarantee a swarming of penitents to the center aisle, asking for salvation. This was linked with the urgency of her end-times emphasis: "time was short; opportunity beckoned now."[36] The foundational square of the four that made up McPherson's presentation of the gospel was a statement of belief in Christ as coming King. Sister proclaimed "the imminent personal, premillennial return of Christ."[37] McPherson understood the miracles of her ministry to be a part of the restoration of pure New Testament Christianity. This was the basis for her assertion that "Bible Christianity" included all the spiritual gifts given originally to the primitive church. Blumhofer explains, "When understood in this context, healing, tongues speech, miracles, and other spiritual gifts were not ends in themselves, not simply gifts to be enjoyed, but were rather locators on a map of history. The restoration came as revival, quickening and empowerment for the church, but it was far more than an ordinary revival: the revival was itself a sign."[38] The revival of divine healing was a sign of the end times.

The ministry of divine healing in Kuhlman's life was shaped by McPherson, her closest female predecessor, despite Kuhlman's denials. When the Parrotts and Kuhlman came to California, Sister Aimee was a sensation. The inheritance of influence descended directly from McPherson to Price to the Parrotts to Kuhlman. Sister's influence can be detected in Kuhlman's entire persona, including her teaching, the form of her services, and even her dress and voice.[39] It was implausible that during the 1920s Kuhlman could have lived in the Northwest, traveled in California, and ministered in Denver without being met at every step with the powerful influence of Aimee Semple McPherson. Kuhlman claimed that only the Holy Spirit taught her what she knew, but in her most formative years she was shaped by the "piety and pageantry" of Sister Aimee.[40]

A. B. Simpson

During the same period as her exposure to McPherson, Kuhlman was introduced to the teaching of Albert Benjamin Simpson (1843–1919). Official school documents show that Kuhlman attended Simpson Bible College beginning in 1924, just five years after the founder's death. She was seventeen years old, and the school accepted her into classes without requiring a high school diploma. She received A's in her four Bible training courses but did not fare as well in homiletics, which she failed.[41] Kuhlman never acknowledged this period of training, as short as it may have been, for the same reasons she dissembled about her contact with Sister Aimee. She stated, "[God] did not choose to send me to some seminary, nor to a university. I was given the greatest Teacher in the whole world—the Holy Spirit. And when He is your teacher you get your theology straight."[42] She added in another radio program, "Everything that I know, [the Holy Spirit] has taught me."[43] A. B. Simpson would have been comfortable giving credit for his teaching to the inspiration of the Holy Spirit, but the very human influence of his particular approach to divine healing echoed in Kuhlman's teaching and writing. Simpson College was deeply marked by the vision and teaching of its recently deceased namesake. In her classes Kuhlman was introduced to the thought of one of the most significant evangelical proponents of divine healing.

A. B. Simpson shared many of the foundational beliefs that flowed into early Pentecostalism. He believed that divine healing, as well as the other gifts of the Spirit, were markers of the restoration of the New Testament church, the "latter rain" of the prophet Joel.[44] These gifts had not ceased, as dispensationalists argued, but were alive and well in the church, which awaited the return of Jesus Christ.[45] Healing was in the atonement, Simpson declared, because "disease resulted from sin, and since Christ's death and resurrection overcame sin, it granted Christians who exercised faith the healing of all their afflictions."[46] He rejected the strict dispensational concept of cessationism, wherein tongues speaking had ceased due to the closing of the apostolic dispensation. He believed supernatural gifts of the Spirit were returning to the church due to the fast approach of the end times during his generation. Simpson argued that the gifts of the Holy Spirit would continue until the second advent, but never accepted the Pentecostal "initial evidence doctrine" concerning speaking in tongues. Pentecostals argued that the initial or first evidence of baptism in the Holy Spirit was the manifestation of tongues speech. While Simpson understood this doctrine to be scripturally sound, he noted that the apostle Paul did not emphasize the importance of glossolalia. He was particularly suspicious of the belief in xenoglossy, or the claim of some Pentecostals that God miraculously granted them the ability to speak in foreign languages to aid in their work in the mission field.[47] Kuhlman would have been carefully instructed in these foundational Simpson beliefs in her time at the college.

Although she spent only a short time at Simpson, much of what Kuhlman learned there is significant to her theological development due to the lasting influence of her brother-in-law, Everett Parrott. Parrott attended Moody Bible College in Chicago, graduating in 1914. Both Simpson Bible College and Moody Bible College at this time were under the influence of Keswick Higher Life teaching, which emerged from conferences in Keswick, England, in the 1870s. Based upon American Holiness teaching, the Keswick form of the "higher" or "victorious" Christian life was a life filled with power and service. Keswick advocates taught that "the relationship with the Holy Spirit required complete submission by exchanging one's will for God's."[48] Through the process of sanctification, which could occur over time or instantaneously, the Christian was filled with an "infusion of divine power," specifically a power for Christian witness and mission.[49] Sanctification was "a service done *for* you by God in exchange for oneself, fully submitted."[50] The filling by the Holy Spirit during sanctification provided the power for a higher level of Christian living.

The Keswick form of Higher Life teaching emphasized the power of God to overcome the bent toward sin in the victorious Christian without making a declaration of Christian perfectionism. This included the ability to overcome temptation but did not rid the Christian fully of the tendency toward sin. Keswick Higher Life teaching retained an emphasis on the reality of sin in the life of even the victorious Christian. The victorious life was not a sinless life. "Keswick theologians rejected the absolutizing of sanctification by the parent [Holiness] movement (during the late 19th and early 20th century) which was often expressed in terms of 'sinless perfection' by radical American preachers."[51] No matter how holy, no Christian was ever totally without sin.[52] The Keswick focus on victory, the role of submission, power for service, and reality of sin echoes throughout Kuhlman's later teaching. Her time with the Parrott revival ministry reinforced and in many ways set for life the worldview and approach to ministry she developed during her brief theological education.

Discerning the Call

Possibly due to disciplinary problems, Kuhlman left Simpson after three years of training.[53] As the twenty-year-old Kuhlman again traveled with her sister and brother-in-law, Everett would sometimes allow her to recite the testimony of her conversion experience. According to biographer Jamie Buckingham, the people gathered in the Parrott tent loved to hear Kuhlman. They enjoyed her theatrical style and her recitation of a dramatic poem at the close of her story. Pictures of Kuhlman at this time reveal an attractive and confident young woman. Tall and slender, with a big smile and glittering eyes, she was in her element in front of a camera or a crowd. Buckingham indicates the offerings were larger when Kuhlman preached, a fact that must have simultaneously threatened and interested Everett. It was uncomfortable to have the girl evangelist outshine him, but extra money in the offering plate was always welcome. One story told by Myrtle in a taped interview demonstrates the stresses for the traveling family as Kuhlman began to mature. Following a less than spectacular response to an altar call by Everett at a Parrott revival meeting (only six people came forward), Kathryn became very emotional. Myrtle remembered, "Walking to the car with me, Kathryn cried, 'I can't stand it! I can't stand it!'" Myrtle recalled that she believed her sister was distraught at the dearth of converts at the Parrott meeting.[54] Alongside an authentic concern for the "lost" in Kuhlman's outburst was perhaps equally authentic exasperation. Kathryn's cry "I can't stand it! I can't stand it!" almost certainly contained a tinge of frustration. If she had been preaching, if it had been her on the platform instead of Everett, perhaps more people would have come forward. Sitting in the tent revival, watching her brother-in-law, perhaps Kuhlman thought, "I could do that; and I could do it better."

Everett Parrott's decision to allow Kuhlman to testify to her conversion provided an entree into preaching the gospel in her own right. Kuhlman began to discern a call to preach as she shared the story of her conversion at meeting after meeting. Myrtle explained the young Kathryn felt what she and her sister called "a burden for souls." Myrtle added, "The call had been on her long before. She had a love and compassion for souls."[55] In addition, the deep connection between Kuhlman's conversion story and her sense of call was established in the Parrott meetings. By linking the proof of her call to preach with the validity of her conversion experience, Kuhlman made use of the strong tradition of subjective authority for conversion testimonies prevalent in evangelicalism. Elaine Lawless explains the role of conversion narratives in the self-validation of women preachers in conservative Christian movements: "One of the most important components of a woman preacher's spiritual life story is her conversion, which is usually accompanied by reference to a poignant moment, often a part of the same narrative, when the girl believes that she's been called to do and be something special."[56] Kuhlman certainly saw her conversion as a sign that she was called to do something special. She stated, "You can say anything you want about me, as a woman, having no right to stand in the pulpit and preach the gospel. Yet even if everybody in the world told me that, it would have no effect on me whatsoever. Why? Because my call to ministry was just as definite as my conversion. And it's just like that."[57]

Kuhlman's conversion experience, as she told it in the Parrott meetings and after, was a "lightning bolt" moment where she was struck by the power of the Holy Spirit while simply singing a hymn in church. Such stories were common and readily accepted by evangelical believers. The "born again" experience was a definite event, marked by conviction of sin and often resulting in physical manifestations such as weeping. The experience of salvation was available to everyone, male and female, young and old. Historian Ann Braude notes the connection between the experience of conversion and the call to ministry in women's lives. "Since the eighteenth century, American Protestantism has been dominated by an evangelical religious style, which encouraged Christians to focus on individual religious experience rather than on the ceremonies of the church."[58] This emphasis on personal religious experience made God's grace available to everyone, male and female, black and white. The conversion experience brought with it an unshakeable conviction that God had acted directly in the person's life. From the conviction that God would speak individually to a woman and work through her to bring about salvation, it was a short step to the dawning realization that the same God could work through a woman and grant her gifts of ministry. When the church was the arbiter of God's ordaining power, women were by and large refused access to the ministerial office. But as individual experience began to trump church authority as the foundation for discernment of spiritual matters, women began to assert their rights to ministry, based not on objective rule but on subjective experience. Braude summarizes, "The culture of Evangelicalism, and the direct experience of God's power in the conversion experience, propelled many American women into unprecedented roles of public leadership."[59]

On Her Own

At age twenty-one, Kuhlman herself was about to be propelled into a new leadership role. After five less-than-successful years working with Myrtle and Kathryn, Everett apparently tired of the arrangement. Following a series of arguments with Myrtle in Boise, Idaho, Everett abandoned her as well as Kathryn and Helen Gulliford, the revival pianist, as he traveled on to South Dakota. The women were unable to make enough to continue by themselves. Outside the Boise Women's Club where Myrtle Parrott continued to preach after Everett's departure, a local Nazarene pastor encouraged the three women to persevere. Myrtle was unwilling to continue due to the dire financial situation and had already decided to return to Everett. But the man said to Myrtle, "Let the girls stay."[60] He was the pastor of a small mission church in need of music and preaching. Kuhlman agreed, as did Gulliford. Myrtle had some apprehensions about letting Kuhlman loose from her control. "Myrtle was in constant fear that I would disgrace [her]," Kuhlman stated many years later. "I remember her telling me a hundred times a day, 'Don't cross your legs.' To this very day Myrtle is scared to death that I'll disgrace the family."[61] The steadying presence of twenty-six-year-old Helen Gulliford must have helped Myrtle's decision. Despite her misgivings, Myrtle chose to go back to Everett, and she left the two women to their independent path.[62]

Kuhlman was ready. She was an eager, enthusiastic, ambitious young woman determined to take the revival circuit by storm. Apparently undaunted by her failing grade in homiletics at Simpson Bible College, Kuhlman began to travel with Helen throughout Idaho to preach. During these first years with Helen, Kuhlman deliberately obscured her formal training in the West as she emphasized her education in the school of hard knocks. She recounted those experiences with nostalgia:

> In those early years I would wait until the farmers were finished with their milking, their plowing, their harvesting, before I held my meetings. When it was dark they would file in one by one for the services. I have preached in almost every little crossroad town in Idaho: Emmett, Filer, Caldwell. Nobody really wanted me, and I did not blame them much, but I offered my services anyway. Where the churches were closed, where they had no preacher, there is where I went and I would say, "Your church is closed and you have nothing to lose and you might gain something if you allowed me to preach." This was the start of my spiritual education.[63]

Her evangelistic meetings accompanied by Helen were met with significant success. In Twin Falls, Idaho, Kuhlman preached and Helen played to a Methodist church filled with two thousand people.[64] One participant in her Idaho services remembered that the evangelists regularly filled the Baptist churches during their two- to six-week revival meetings.[65]

Kuhlman's behavior at the beginning of her ministry career does not show signs of the standard public response to a call to ministry typical of women in conservative religious groups. Her predecessors such as Maria Woodworth-Etter and Aimee Semple McPherson both described their call to ministry by following the biblical pattern of "hearing, resisting, and yielding."[66] Although Kuhlman mimicked this language almost exactly in her later career, in the beginning she showed no resistance whatsoever to her call. In fact, her behavior was quite the opposite: she jumped at the opportunity to set out on her own.

The culture around Kuhlman was also shifting, granting to the young woman a new confidence in her right to live a professional life. It was the roaring twenties, and the reverberations were felt even in the austere environment of the American West. Women gained the vote in 1920, and the "new woman" was making her controversial presence felt in the work-place, in fashion, and in the home. All around Helen and Kathryn, women were accomplishing things not possible in previous generations. When Kuhlman turned nineteen in 1926, she might have read about another nineteen-year-old, Gertrude Ederle, who swam the English Channel in less time than any male swimmer before her. Just a few years later, in 1928, Amelia Earhart, at age thirty, crossed the Atlantic by air.[67] Women were breaking barriers and achieving new status in home and business in the years after World War I. This was the time of "first-wave feminism," when suffrage efforts united disparate groups of women across class, race, and geography. Women were asking hard questions about their roles and responsibilities in the home and in the workplace.[68] Although it was unlikely that Kuhlman was reading feminist tracts in her twenties, she was living in a country where women's roles were changing under the pressures of war, money, sex, and politics.

For Kuhlman, the twenties were roaring indeed. She was not a flap-per by any means, but she did take advantage of a religious and political world fluid in its viewpoints of female leadership. Her confidence in her ability to set out in the career of a traveling evangelist displayed her trust in herself and in her call as well as the belief that she would find a recep-tive audience somewhere, somehow. In an interview years later, Kuhlman noted, "I preached my first sermon in Idaho in the mission." The inter-viewers asked, "Did you feel comfortable?" She answered shortly, "I knew it's what I was supposed to be doing." This self-assurance also revealed a worldview that included unmarried female religious leaders serving as evangelists and making their way alone in the world, without the need for male provision or "covering." Historian Grant Wacker notes the same dynamics at work in the success of McPherson, whose "meteoric career, though hardly characteristic of anyone except herself, at least said some-thing about believers' readiness to salute a woman leader."[69]

Although biographer Wayne Warner states that Kuhlman was "thrust" into her preaching role in 1928,[70] pictures of this period do not reflect a sense of compulsion in Kuhlman's life; in fact, the pictures reveal exactly the opposite. Kuhlman kept a scrapbook of hundreds of photos of this chapter of her life.[71] It is one of only a very few personal items available for research, and as such is valuable as a snapshot of her memories of her earliest days in ministry. Pictures of Helen and Kathryn in various happy and affectionate poses obviously snapped during picnics and trips were carefully pasted in the album alongside picture postcards of various destinations. Helen Kooiman Hosier recorded several interviews with people who went to hear Kuhlman during her Idaho years. One of those who remembered Kuhlman was Freada Plating. She recalled Kuhlman as "so much fun to be with. . . . We would get together and sit on the grass or the church steps and just visit. She enjoyed going on picnics and we did have some good times!"[72] In tiny black-and-white photos, Gulliford and Kuhlman are dressed stylishly, in smart but plain suit dresses and coy hats, carefully bobbed hair curling around their smiling faces. Plating noted, "She dressed like any of the rest of us. . . . Kathryn was a very modest person."[73] Snapshots of the two convey a sense of freedom and adventure as they posed cheerfully in front of various churches or stood surrounded by young men and women, arms draped about each other, enjoying a day out.

The pictures of the various churches where Gulliford and Kuhlman evangelized capture Kuhlman's early love for promotion and celebrity. In one photo Kuhlman and Gulliford stand with a group in front of a sign advertising "City-Wide Revival." Another picture features a sign proclaiming the arrival of "Revival Evangelist Kathryn Kuhlman." One banner draped across a church entrance read "REVIVAL—Hear Girl Evangelist-Inter-Denominational." Leveraging her age as a protective device for her ministry, Kuhlman sometimes promoted herself as "the girl evangelist." While women evangelists could be considered controversial, child evangelists were popular attractions in the Pentecostal revival of the early twentieth century. During this same period, another young female preacher was in demand. Uldine Utley was eleven in 1924 when she began preaching, and she used many of the same rhetorical motifs as Kuhlman to justify her call. Historian Lee Canipe explains, "Utley refused to consider herself a preacher. 'Who ever heard of a girl preaching?' she asked. 'I had not, that was certain, and I'm sure it would have seemed even foolish, to me, to think of a little girl doing it.'"[74] Utley claimed to have been converted in 1920 at the age of seven at a meeting led by McPherson. In 1926 the young evangelist traveled to New York, where she led a series of revival meetings at Madison Square Garden.[75] The auditorium was filled with over ten thousand people eager to see and hear the child phenomenon. Canipe observes, "In a celebrity-addled Jazz Age, Utley was a star."[76] Scholar Thomas Robinson records the poignant title of Utley's unpublished collection of poetry: "Kindly Remove My Halo," revealing the dark side of Utley's success. Utley's career ended in 1936 due to a physical and mental collapse caused by the unrelenting pressures of her successful evangelistic career.[77] Kuhlman's use of the label of girl evangelist was set aside for practical reasons as she aged into her late twenties. She would have to make her way now as a grown woman.

Most of Kuhlman's Idaho services were conducted in small Baptist churches in little towns such as Twin Falls, Ola, Sweet, Notus, Wilder, Melba, Meridian, and Kuna, among many others.[78] In an interior shot likely taken in one of these churches, Kathryn and Helen stand among a group of stern parishioners, the two women carefully coiffed and dressed in white shimmering satin pulpit dresses. One photo in particular stands out as an example of Kuhlman's life during her years itinerating as an independent evangelist in the West. It was taken inside a small country church, with a cluster of about thirty people gathered in a typical group pose, expressions reflecting the seriousness of the photo. Gulliford stands to the left of center, in her white dress, gazing calmly at the camera lens. Dead center, the only person not standing, sits Kuhlman. Her lanky body is draped in a chair, elbows resting on the chair arms and hands hanging casually. Her long legs are crossed at the ankles (Myrtle would be proud), with the lustrous satin pulpit dress draped across her body, ending in soft folds just above her ankles and accenting her white high heels. Most arresting is Kuhlman's gaze. She stares ahead of her, looking up from under arched eyebrows, the hint of a smile on her mouth. It was not the beginning of an ingratiating or even sweetly posed smile. It was instead the intimation of satisfaction. This was a woman who was exactly where she wanted to be—at the dead center of attention, surrounded by admirers, dressed glamorously, clearly in control and in charge. Kuhlman would spend the rest of her career claiming not to desire the spotlight, disavowing any need for recognition, and presenting herself as a simple handmaiden of God. Those assertions were, in their own way, true. But in her twenties, flush with freedom from her family and her small town and with Helen at her side, Kuhlman was queen of all she surveyed.

Religious Obstacles

Launching an independent ministry career was a risky decision for a single woman in the 1920s and 1930s. Women in religious leadership were not common or comfortable for much of American Christianity. Like Myrtle Parrott, most women served alongside their husbands in ministry, satisfying the cultural preference for male headship in the church. The most well-known female church leader of the time, Aimee Semple McPherson, was a divorcée, but she was also a mother of two and the widow of a missionary. Kuhlman, on the other hand, was young, single, attractive, and marriageable. Many might wonder why she chose ministry over family and husband. She had to answer these questions effectively in order to justify her career. Kuhlman rested on the authority of God's inescapable call as her validation for being a female preacher. She once noted, "I didn't ask for this ministry. God knows I'd much rather be doing something else. But [God] put me in the ministry and those who don't like having a woman preach should complain to God—not to me. It's just like that."[79]

At issue was the subtle difference between a woman preacher and a woman pastor. Pentecostals were generally comfortable with women exhorting and evangelizing, especially in the nontraditional spaces of the gospel tent, auditorium, or mission field.[80] Female evangelists were encouraged to testify to what God had done for them. Female missionaries were urged to show compassion for the sick and the poor as well as instruct unbelievers in the Christian faith. Women "yoked in harness" with men were even more acceptable, and there were many Pentecostal couples in ministry in America. Establishing the delicate distinction of "founding pastor" made a single female pastor's way even easier. If she *founded* the church, rather than following a male minister in an established pastorate, the ill feeling was not so great. But there was still apprehension. Wacker explains, "What most saints doubted, at least when they sat down and began to think about it, was the right of women to speak officially, by virtue of a prescribed position. Though few if any came right out and said so, it was easy to see what the problem was."[81] The problem was when single women desired to settle into a pastorate and function as the head of a congregation.

For Pentecostals and many other conservative Christian groups, women serving as sole pastors were stepping into the biblical role of elder. According to the Bible, elders were to be the shepherds of the churches as well as overseers (1 Pet. 5:2). A woman who served in the position of elder was the overseer of all her flock, including the men. She served communion and men received it. She had the right to a voice and a vote in administrative decisions that concerned men and women. She had the right to exposit Scripture, which meant she was teaching men as an authority. Pentecostals balked at this amount of authority for women.

E. N. Bell, an influential leader in early Pentecostalism, summarized in 1914, "No woman has been known to have been appointed by the Lord as an elder or an apostle, or to any position where ruling with authority is inferred."[82]

"Ruling with authority" was the crux of the argument against women elders. Women could be in ministry, but only "as ones without authority." The role of the prophetess managed to satisfy this tricky set of requirements. Female prophets were mandated in Scripture by the words of Joel ("your daughters shall prophesy") and were acceptable in the "new Pentecost."[83] Wacker explains, "Pentecostals allowed for women to minister because the Spirit-filled prophetess was the voice of God rather than the holder of an ecclesial office."[84] Prophesying was defined as personal testimony to the acts of God in the individual woman's life. The woman was speaking only as a "mouthpiece of the Holy Spirit."[85] Prophecy was one crucial step removed from eldership: the woman was not speaking as herself, but as the carrier of the words of the Holy Spirit. Although eldership was also seen as guided by the Holy Spirit, there was definite human agency involved in leading a congregation. Elders were not just mouthpieces, but coworkers with the Holy Spirit. Elders could baptize, officiate at the Lord's Supper, and teach Scripture through preaching and Bible study. For a woman to take the reins of a congregation and serve as an elder was too much for many Pentecostal and evangelical churches in the early twentieth century.

As a leader, Kuhlman fit nicely into the historically prepared role of prophetess, although she never used that title for herself. She also was careful never to speak of herself as an elder of the church. Kuhlman used the lack of her own building as evidence that she was not trying to be an overseer of any church. In the interview about her days in Idaho, Buckingham asked Kathryn where she preached. "Never in churches?" he asked. "Never," Kuhlman replied. "Always in auditoriums."[86] This was not completely accurate. Participants in her Idaho meetings remembered that the women did lead meetings in small Baptist churches throughout the state, although Kuhlman friend Paul Ferrin recalled that Kuhlman "did not go to churches much" during this period.[87]

Especially significant in her early career and identity, Kuhlman and Gulliford established the Denver Revival Tabernacle after months of successful services in Colorado. After two years in Colorado Springs and Pueblo, the women changed their approach from itinerant ministry and settled in Denver in 1933. This was definitely a church, with Kuhlman as overseer. Kuhlman seemed ready to build a permanent base in Denver, despite the risk of receiving criticism as a female pastor. The congregation transformed an abandoned truck garage into the Tabernacle, and Kuhlman hired the Anderson Trio of sisters to provide vocal music for her services. The Tabernacle hosted church services five nights a week for five years.[88] Kuhlman was seemingly tireless in her ministry efforts. One Denver participant remembered, "She would stay at the altar and pray with [the people] until the last person, whether it be a street person or the mayor or chief of police."[89] In addition, Kuhlman expanded her ministry to include Sunday school classes, a women's society, and most importantly, a radio program.[90] In the city of Denver, as pastor of her own church, Kuhlman at last had access to the power of broadcast media. It was the beginning of a relationship that would change her ministry forever.

The Power of Radio

In 1935, at the age of twenty-eight, Kuhlman began to broadcast from Denver on station KVOD. She would go live on the air from 10:00 to 10:15 a.m. with her program entitled *Smiling Through*.[91] It was likely the realization of a long-held ambition to join the ranks of radio evangelists. Kuhlman's colleagues in independent evangelism were all clamoring to raise the necessary funds to join the radio revolution. By the 1930s, evangelistic emphases translated into an avid interest in the new broadcast technology. Evangelical Christians were thrilled by the idea of transmitting the teaching of Christianity around the nation and even the world. Their excitement rested upon the belief that anyone who was exposed to the Christian Scriptures would experience the convicting power of the Holy Spirit for conversion. Through radio, finally, all would have the opportunity to hear and believe. Historian Tona Hangen observes, "Radio served as a pulpit for evangelism on a scale impossible only decades before."[92] By 1931, more than half of all homes in the United States contained a radio, and radio listenership continued to increase in the years following.[93] A new wireless field opened up before the preachers who had spent years traveling the hard roads of the revival circuits. Evangelists who could gain access to radio broadcasting equipment could stay in one place and project their voice to more people in a fifteen-minute broadcast than in months of strenuous travel. Evangelical preachers were familiar with the capacity to communicate through print media such as newspapers and magazines, but wireless broadcasting was something new and breathtaking.

From radio's beginning, evangelists longed to learn how to harness its power. As one advocate noted, "The microphone is the door handle into the man's living-room."[94] With radio's ability to gain entrance into the heart of American homes and with wireless radio receivers in more and more residences, evangelists invested considerable effort and money in accessing the potential of the airwaves. A pioneer in this effort was Aimee Semple McPherson. McPherson built and operated KFSG, or Kall Four Square Gospel, her own radio station that began broadcasting Pentecostal Christianity in February 1924. KFSG was the third radio station to operate in the state of California and the only one owned by a religious organization. Sister Aimee's broadcasts could be heard over most of the western United States and beyond.[95] McPherson made a place on the airwaves for charismatic Christianity by presenting beliefs and practices common to Pentecostalism. She aired sermons on divine healing and prophetic teaching on the nearness of the end times. Her radio programs emphasized a personal salvific relationship with Jesus Christ and maintained a central focus on the work and person of the Holy Spirit. Radio unlocked the American home to charismatic Christianity in a new way. Previously shut out, media savvy charismatic evangelists made quick use of the new access point of radio. Whereas before, charismatic Christianity was only overheard by people passing by the local Pentecostal church, now Pentecostal worship services were broadcast into hundreds of homes. The preaching and teaching of charismatic Christianity often known only through Pentecostal newsletters and journals now radiated from one of the first large-scale radio stations in the country. Charismatic Christianity began its move from fringe to center through the power of radio broadcasting.

The strength of radio for evangelism was linked to the experience of "simultaneity" available through the broadcasting of voices over the airwaves. When radio produced simultaneity, the listener experienced an event distant in space and time as happening in the present tense. Even though a radio show was taped days previously, or was being broadcast live from hundreds of miles away, the audience felt a sense of immediacy.[96] The experience of "hearing" the voice of a distant loved one via reading a diary or a letter was familiar to twentieth-century people; to be in one area of the country and hear a live voice from miles away emanating out of a piece of furniture was something entirely new. Simultaneity was a valuable tool for creating a sense of intimacy in the potentially cold medium of radio broadcasting. Hangen explains, "Radio shrunk distances, collapsing time and space with unseen power. . . . Until television, radio was the only means for the immediate experience of a remote event, and that experience—partly because of its sheer novelty in the early years—could be jarring, epiphanic, even life-changing."[97] For evangelists used to communicating at mass meetings, the radio provided the singular opportunity to speak to thousands and have each listener experience the message "like a personal chat." Simultaneity made every listener feel as if he or she was being spoken to one-on-one by the radio preacher at that exact moment, in one's very own living room or even bedroom. Through radio, charismatic Christianity entered into the intimate confines of the American home.[98]

The services broadcast from McPherson's Foursquare Gospel Church serve as a helpful example of the effect of the simultaneity of radio. Broadcasters such as McPherson believed listeners could experience through the transmission of a charismatic worship service the present and real power of the Holy Spirit. McPherson was one of the first to teach that the power of radio extended even to divine healing. She called it "radio healing," divine healing effected without direct physical contact between the healer and the sick. Sister Aimee encouraged listeners seeking healing to kneel by their radios and place their hands on the instrument in order to receive "long-distance healing." In her church, she would lay her hands on the radio transmitter and pray, "As I lay my hands on this radio tonight, Lord Jesus, heal the sick, bridge the gap between and lay your nail-pierced hand on the sick in Radioland."[99] Broadcast media bridged the gap of space and time between radio preachers and listeners. Simultaneity opened up opportunities for charismatic radio preachers to go even beyond the conversion of their public via the airwaves to the possibility of healing. Radio audiences could certainly be "born again" by listening to evangelical radio preachers and responding to their broadcast altar calls. But by stopping the dial on KFSG and choosing to listen to Sister Aimee, they could also be divinely and remotely healed through the power of the Holy Ghost. It was a double miracle.

During this time, radio stations were required by the federal government to provide what was called sustaining time, which was public access time available for free. Churches associated with the liberal side of the fundamentalist/liberal debates received free airtime, due in large part to the powerful influence of the Federal Council of Churches.[100] While this policy seemed at first to be a likely obstacle to the success of evangelical broadcasting on the radio, it soon became apparent that evangelical radio could hold its own even in the highly competitive and expensive commercial radio realm. Hangen notes, "One study concluded that while Baptist, Gospel Tabernacle, and Holiness/Pentecostal broadcasters bought two-thirds of their airtime in the forties and fifties, more mainstream denominations such as Methodists and Presbyterians purchased a mere third, and 70 percent of Roman Catholic airtime was free. Evangelical broadcasting achieved remarkable prosperity despite receiving almost no free airtime."[101] The free-market competition forced upon evangelical Christianity in radio's beginning led to increased inventiveness and media fluency. It also led to the need for independent radio stations, large amounts of money and time, and a product that was marketable and able to vie with commercial competitors for lucrative airtime.

The phenomenon of sustained time was short-lived, however, as radio airwaves became more profitable. Quentin Schultze, scholar of communication arts and sciences, explains, "When stations began to cut back on sustaining time for religious broadcasts during the late forties, evangelicals were prepared for the commercial challenges."[102] The churches that had received sustaining time had to play catch-up in a challenging marketplace. Large operations like KFSG simply made their own way through the investment of large amounts of money and a fabulously marketable radio personality. Small-scale radio evangelists settled for reduced audiences during what cheap airtime they could garner on Sundays and during the less valuable daytime hours. Whatever the size of the audience, however, by the early 1940s evangelical Christianity dominated the religious programming across the United States, from KFSG in California to WMBI in Chicago to KVOD in Denver, the launchpad for the broadcast media career of Kathryn Kuhlman.

Coming of Age: Papa, Mister, and the Collapse of the Denver Ministry

The three years Kuhlman spent in ministry in Denver were pivotal for her life and career. For the first time she established a congregation and served as its pastor. She made her initial foray into broadcast media through radio evangelism. She also experienced two life-changing personal events: the death of her father, followed by marriage to and subsequent divorce from Burroughs Waltrip, or as she called him, "Mister." Kuhlman liked to claim the school of hard knocks as her only training ground. Denver, then, represented a series of intensive courses in her spiritual education. The stories of her short career in Colorado include Kuhlman's first personal experience of divine healing, her baptism in the Holy Spirit, and her consecration by the Holy Spirit for ministry.

Kuhlman adored her father. Joe Kuhlman took on mythic qualities in her stories of growing up, her "papa" whose indulgent love countered the stern discipline of her mother. His death was a stunning blow to Kuhlman. In an article for *Guideposts* magazine in June 1971, Kuhlman told the story of her father's accident in December 1934, when Kuhlman was twenty-seven years old. The Denver Revival Tabernacle Christmas services completed, Kuhlman remained in Denver rather than make the long trip home to Concordia. She rented a room for four dollars a week in the St. Francis Hotel, where she received a phone call on the Tuesday after Christmas. "I recognized the voice on the other end as an old friend from home," Kuhlman recalled. "Kathryn, your father has been hurt. He's been in an accident," the friend said. Kuhlman replied, "Hurt bad?" The friend said yes. "Tell papa I'm leaving right now. I'm coming home." Kuhlman drove across the ice and snow of Colorado and Kansas. "One hundred miles from Kansas City I stopped at a telephone station beside the deserted highway and called ahead. My Aunt Belle answered. I said, 'This is Kathryn. Tell Papa I'm almost home.' 'But Kathryn,' Aunt Belle said in a shocked voice, 'didn't they tell you?'" Joe Kuhlman was killed instantly when hit by a car driven by a college student home for the holidays.

By her own account, Kuhlman did not handle the death of her father well. "I was struggling with another feeling. Hate. I spewed out venom toward the young man who had taken the life of my father." At the funeral, Kuhlman reluctantly approached her father's open casket. "I reached over and gently put my hand on that shoulder in the casket. And as I did, something happened. All that my fingers caressed was a suit of clothes. Not just the black wool coat, but everything that box contained was simply something discarded, loved once, laid aside now. Papa wasn't there." She recalled the experience as transformational. "That was the very first time the power of the risen, resurrected Christ had come through to me."[103] In another setting, she added, "My belief in life after death had only been words until I came face-to-face with the reality of death. It was the first real spiritual experience I had had since my conversion."[104] She concluded the episode by asserting, "Suddenly, I was no longer afraid of death, and as my fear disappeared, so did my hate. It was my first real healing experience."[105]

After her father's death, Kuhlman returned to her ministry in Denver. At the age of twenty-eight, she was finally coming into her own as a leader of the thriving congregation at the Denver Revival Tabernacle. Soon she made the acquaintance of Burroughs Waltrip, an evangelist who came to Denver on a preaching junket in 1935. The pictures of Kuhlman and Waltrip during their courtship show a handsome and happy pair, smiling and obviously enjoying each other and their friends.[106] Waltrip was tall and slender, even a bit taller than Kuhlman, and the two began to share preaching duties in Kuhlman's Denver Revival Tabernacle and Waltrip's shiny new art nouveau Radio Chapel in Mason City, Iowa. The pair began to make the eight-hundred-mile trip between the churches a little too often for simply professional reasons. Their congregations began to suspect an affair. Such a union would be disastrous for the couple, especially for Kuhlman, because Waltrip was still married at the time, with a wife and two young sons in Texas.

Despite the danger to his ministry, Waltrip divorced his wife Jessie and abandoned his children, Burroughs Waltrip Jr. and William, in order to marry Kuhlman in October of 1938.[107] Kuhlman made the staggeringly foolish decision to accept his proposal. Why? Perhaps she was lonely; perhaps she was arrogant and underestimated the angry reaction of her followers. Perhaps she was naive; perhaps she was truly and deeply in love with the handsome and charismatic "Mister" and was willing to risk her career for him. It seems very likely that the loss of her father played a powerful role in her decision to attach herself to a male authority figure only nine months after burying her "Papa." Whatever the reason, and the reality was most certainly a complex mixture of many motivations, the marriage destroyed both evangelists' ministries. In what must have been a wrenching break, Helen Gulliford resigned her position in protest. The Denver Revival Tabernacle congregation rejected Kuhlman, and Waltrip's Radio Chapel fell apart soon after due to financial woes. Failure after failure followed the couple's descent into obscurity during the six years that followed. Faced with months of harshly critical reception as a couple, they began leading meetings independently of each other. According to records of the couple's ministerial association at the time, the Evangelical Church Alliance (ECA), Waltrip was still presenting an optimistic public face even as the two were together less and less. Waltrip made fairly regular contact with the ECA during the years of his marriage to Kuhlman. In his correspondence he reported on some of their meetings, requested renewal of ministerial licenses for them both, and gave cheery summaries of their ministry. Letters to the ECA from Waltrip and Kuhlman were often posted from separate cities. In December of 1941, Kuhlman wrote from Denver and Waltrip from Detroit. In December of 1943, Waltrip reported that he and Kuhlman were in Concordia visiting her mother. In 1944, his letter included the statement, "Mrs. Waltrip and I are enjoying wonderful spiritual blessings and good health." In April of 1946, Waltrip wrote from Los Angeles, "God is blessing our ministry in a most gracious way." In passing, he noted that Kathryn would be traveling to the East for a meeting.[108] This brief reference failed to capture the full truth: that April, Kathryn Kuhlman left her husband Burroughs Waltrip in Los Angeles, took the train to Pennsylvania, and never came back.[109]

The divorce complaint Waltrip filed against Kuhlman on February 18, 1947, in Las Vegas, Clark County, Nevada, contained his version of the causes for the dissolution of the marriage. Waltrip, the plaintiff, alleged in article 5 that Kuhlman, the defendant, "has, since marriage, been guilty of extreme cruelty, mental in character, toward the plaintiff; and the plaintiff's health was and is thereby and therefrom impaired." In the days before no-fault divorce, divorce was granted only when one spouse could prove to have been wronged by the other. The most common charges were adultery and cruelty.[110] Waltrip brought the same charge of cruelty against his first wife, Jessie Waltrip, to gain a divorce from her to marry Kuhlman.[111] Waltrip chose the same legal course with Kuhlman, but further details from the proceedings add to the story. On April 2, 1947, Kuhlman's lawyer filed an answer to Waltrip's complaint, in which Kuhlman admitted all allegations (these consisted of plain statements of fact, such as confirmation that Waltrip and Kuhlman were married in Iowa and no children resulted from the marriage). The answer denied the allegations contained in article 5, Waltrip's accusation of cruelty. Kuhlman also requested that Waltrip "take nothing by reason of his alleged course of action." In other words, if he was going to divorce her on grounds of cruelty, he should not expect to receive any money in the settlement.

On April 3, 1947, at 1:50 in the afternoon, Waltrip was sworn in by the Honorable Frank MacNamee, district judge, to give testimony in the divorce proceedings. Waltrip's lawyer, Ryland G. Taylor, walked him through a series of questions for the court and for Kuhlman's lawyer,

Thomas J. D. Salter. Kuhlman was not present. The document is pre-served as a series of questions by Taylor and responses from Waltrip.

> **Q:** You state since the marriage Mrs. Waltrip has been guilty of extreme cruelty toward you, mental in character, and that as a result your health was and is thereby and therefrom impaired. Is that true?
> **A:** Yes, that's true.
> **Q:** Will you state what these acts of cruelty consisted of?
> **A:** Largely because of her professional career. A few days after we were married she again engaged in her professional work which has kept us separated for seventy-five percent of the time of our marriage, resulting in, of course, a great deal of worry and discouragement.
> **Q:** Was this against your will?
> **A:** Yes, it was, prior to [sic] our understanding before our marriage.
> **Q:** In other words, is it true that she refused and declined to make a home for you—refused to come and join you in a home that you were living in and were willing to prepare for her?
> **A:** Yes, sir.
> **Q:** And your life was somewhat as a bachelor, notwithstanding you were married?
> **A:** Yes, sir.
> **Q:** She did that over your protests and objections, is that true?
> **A:** Yes.
> **Q:** What was her name prior to your marriage?
> **A:** Kathryn Kuhlman.
> **Q:** By the way what effect did this have on your health?
> **A:** I lost considerable weight, and it reached the place where it was al-most impossible to get sufficient rest, which resulted not only in im-paired physical and mental condition, but it affected my work.
> **Q:** Did it seriously affect your health?
> **A:** Yes, it did.[112]

After this exchange, the judge demanded proof that Waltrip had lived in Nevada the required amount of time, a mere six weeks. Nevada was famous for its liberal divorce laws, and a decree of divorce was entered by the court. "Mister" Waltrip won his suit.

No Turning Back

It was necessary for Kuhlman to separate herself from the controversy connected with Waltrip that was bogging down her career. Judging from the rapidity with which she left Waltrip to return to her work, she instantly regretted her decision to marry him. Kuhlman faced a difficult problem. To preserve any shred of her career, she had to leave Waltrip and try to start again, but such a decision could itself destroy her. A divorced female evangelist was not much better than a female evangelist married to a divorced man. In a masterful reinterpretation of her life, Kuhlman chose instead to present her decision to leave Waltrip as a difficult moment of submission, the yielding of a strong-willed woman to the relentless call of God on her life. In word and print she told the story this way:

> I can remember the day, I can remember the hour. . . . At 4:00 PM on that Saturday afternoon, on a dead-end street, I surrendered everything. . . . It was all settled. [The Holy Spirit] and I made each other promises. And some things you don't talk about, like personal things between a husband and wife. I knew in that moment what that scripture meant, "If any man would follow me, he must take up his cross." A cross always means death. . . . If you've never had that death of the flesh, you don't understand me. No one believes in the baptism of the Holy Spirit more than Kathryn Kuhlman, because I have experienced it. When you are baptized in the Holy Spirit, there will be a crucifying of the flesh. You will die. He doesn't ask for golden vessels. He doesn't ask for silver vessels or he wouldn't have chosen me. All he needs is someone who'll die. I spoke in an unknown tongue as he took every part of me. I surrendered everything. Then, for the first time, I realized what it meant to have power.[113]

Kuhlman ended her story with the words "That afternoon, Kathryn Kuhlman died."[114]

Kuhlman chose to present the decision to leave her husband at the first possible moment as an act of sacrificial atonement for her defiance of God's will. She obliquely indicated throughout her career that she had realized her decision to marry Waltrip separated her from God and from her call to ministry. As she told it, the sacrifice of her marriage was necessary for her final consecration as God's instrument. Kuhlman's only references to her marriage and divorce are couched in these terms. It seems certain that she did experience genuine sorrow at the decision to end her marriage and was led to the action in part by a conviction that she was outside of God's will for her life.[115] She represented this moment as one of consecration, where she was baptized in the Holy Spirit and set aside for what would become a ministry of miracles through the Holy Spirit.

Kuhlman's presentation of her "death to self" was simultaneously a powerful image of sacrificial submission and a brilliant manipulation of her persona. If the divorced Kathryn Kuhlman was dead, then critics had little to work with. As she told it, she was no longer the disgraced divorcée, but a chastened, sanctified, and consecrated vessel for God's Holy Spirit. With this reinterpretation of her identity, she was able to move beyond what should have been a career-ending mistake and even turn it to her own benefit. Kuhlman used this imagery throughout her life with remarkable success.[116] But in 1946, Kuhlman didn't yet know she would make it past this personal and professional disaster. Alone in Franklin, Pennsylvania, she was a forty-year-old female evangelist who had just left her husband. She had no ministry, few friends, and a questionable reputation weighing her down. It would take a miracle to turn her career around.

CHAPTER 2

The Beginning of Miracles

Kathryn Kuhlman moved to Franklin, Pennsylvania, in 1946 in order to begin a new career far from her mistakes in the West. One year after her move, Kuhlman marked "the beginning of miracles," a turn in her ministry toward the realm of divine healing.[1] Divine healing became the central focus of her services, and from 1947 onward she was regularly identified as a "faith healer," a label she resolutely rejected. When asked why she didn't like the designation, Kuhlman once replied, "I do not put myself in a class with faith healers."[2] Kuhlman claimed she was not just *different* from others who led healing ministries; rather, she was in a different *class*. All the possible interpretations for her declaration about class are applicable: Kuhlman considered herself more educated, more socioeconomically advantaged, more intelligent, more sophisticated, and more respectable than others known as faith healers at the time. She was especially determined not to be counted among the primarily Pentecostal deliverance evangelists who were seen and heard in towns across post–World War II America. These Pentecostal faith healers were perceived by the culture as back-hills preachers in perspiration-soaked shirts, grappling people's heads in their hands as they bellowed out rebukes to demons and sin sickness. Kuhlman did not want to be branded with a term that conjured up these kinds of images.

Kuhlman's disdain for faith healers was shared by most of America during the first half of the twentieth century. As she led her own healing ministry, Kuhlman worked to present a more refined image of charismatic Christianity and its most public practice, divine healing. Kuhlman's presentation of faith healing distanced her from the images of rural faith healers at work in dusty tent revivals across the country. Her miracle services were calmer and less emotional, which aided in the gentrification of charismatic Christianity. But the path to respectability was not smooth. Kuhlman was also the object of criticism and controversy during these years and received her fair share of the derision directed toward any advocate of charismatic Christianity in mid-twentieth-century America. Between 1946 and 1953, Kuhlman leveraged the growing popularity of healing ministries, minimized controversy by refashioning charismatic practices to make them more palatable to the broader culture, and reestablished herself as the leader of a well-known and respected ministry. In the course of seven years, she revived a career that should have been beyond resuscitation.

A New Home in Franklin

Kuhlman came to Franklin, Pennsylvania, at the request of Matthew J. Maloney, owner of the Franklin Gospel Tabernacle. The fifteen-hundred-seat Tabernacle was well known for its dynamic services (evangelist Billy Sunday filled the pulpit in a series of meetings during the 1930s). Kuhlman found a receptive audience in the town. Immediately after beginning evangelistic services, Kuhlman naturally sought out a radio station. Because of her loose affiliation with the Baptist denomination and her status as an independent healing evangelist, she could not access sustained time. Instead, she purchased airtime from WKRZ in Oil City.[3] Kuhlman biographer Wayne Warner states, "During the summer of 1946, northwest Pennsylvania and parts of eastern Ohio wildly accepted Kathryn, and the Franklin Gospel Tabernacle was bursting at the seams even before she was well known for her healing ministry. A weekend radio broadcast over WKRZ of Oil City soon went to a daily program. Then WISR of Butler picked up one of Kathryn's broadcasts."[4] By the summer, Kuhlman's radio broadcasts from Oil City were popular enough for her to add a Pittsburgh radio station to her small network, with the signal still issuing from Oil City.[5] Kuhlman's radio career was off to a new and successful start.[6]

Kuhlman's style was particularly suited to her postwar working-class listeners. Her background in preaching to hardscrabble farmers in the West gave her a style and language that translated well. As Warner observes, "Kathryn could strike a responsive chord in her radio audience with what she called Missouri corn bread—down-to-earth, practical Christian living."[7] Her *Heart to Heart* radio talks were often about simple topics such as "nerves" or "perseverance." Kuhlman shared the message of a "can-do" approach to Christian daily life. She repeatedly asserted, "there is no such thing as a defeated Christian," and emphasized qualities such as gumption and hard work. Her ability to move easily from chitchat to serious Bible teaching to life application of Scripture made her shows accessible and entertaining.

The war-weary radio audiences of the late 1940s were in the mood for shows that brought lightness, hope, and a message of stability. Kuhlman gave her listeners a comforting combination of solid teaching, personal advice, loving guidance, easy laughter, and a heartfelt altar call. "[Kuhlman's] effervescent greeting and her frequent chuckles projected a conversational style in her *Heart to Heart* [radio] talks that gave the listener the feeling that she had just dropped in for a visit."[8] Kuhlman would open her radio program with her trademark greeting, "Hello! And have you been waiting for me?"[9] Wayne Warner recorded the words of one listener to WISR in Butler, who said, "By golly, you were waiting for her, because we all are waiting for someone, a person out there who will understand how we hurt and who will care."[10] Warner continued, "Critics called Kathryn's opening strictly corn."[11] It was corn that connected with her audience, and Kuhlman knew it.

The First Miracle

For almost a year, Kuhlman broadcast her radio program and held her services at the Franklin Gospel Tabernacle and experienced gratifying success. Then, in April 1947, everything changed. It was in Franklin that Kuhlman received the first testimony to a miracle of divine healing at one of her services, a miracle she pointed to all her life as signifying the beginning of her healing ministry. Divine healing was nothing new for Kuhlman, but it had not been a major part of her primarily evangelistic services. Kuhlman remembered attending a divine healing service shortly before the first testimony of miraculous healing occurred in her own ministry. She may have seen well-known healer William Branham himself at a service in Cleveland, Ohio.[12] Whether it was Branham or another of the new healing evangelists leading the service, Kuhlman did not like what she saw. "I remember well the evening when I walked from under a big tent where a Divine Healing service was being conducted. The looks of despair and disappointment on the faces I had seen . . . would haunt me for weeks."[13] In another account, she recalled her deep disappointment:

> In the early part of my ministry, I was greatly disturbed over much that I observed occurring in the field of Divine Healing. I was confused by many of "the methods" I saw employed, and disgusted with the unwise performances I witnessed—none of which I could associate in any way with either the action of the Holy Spirit, or, indeed the very nature of God. Too often I had seen pathetically sick people dragging their tired, weakened bodies home from a healing service, having been told that they were not healed simply because of their own lack of faith. My heart ached for these people, as I knew how they struggled, day after day, trying desperately to obtain more faith, taking out that which they had, and trying to analyze it, in a hopeless effort to discover its deficiency which was presumably keeping them from the healing power of God.[14]

Kuhlman indicated that this event clarified her own understanding of divine healing:

> I understood that night why there was no need for a healing line; no healing virtue in a card or a personality; no necessity for wild exhortations to "have faith." That was the beginning of this healing ministry which God has given to me; strange to some because of the fact that hundreds have been healed just sitting quietly in the audience, without any demonstration and even without admonition. This is because the Presence of the Holy Spirit has been in such abundance that by His Presence alone, sick bodies are healed, even as people wait on the outside of the building for doors to open.[15]

Kuhlman seemed to imply in this account that her healing ministry began as she rejected the practices she deemed offensive and as God revealed to her a better way. Perhaps she truly was inspired to craft an alternative approach to divine healing. In all other versions of the beginning of miracles, however, everything began with a surprise announcement at a Tabernacle service in Franklin.

In one of her *Heart to Heart* talks, Kuhlman stated, "One of the very first questions that almost every reporter asks me is, 'Kathryn Kuhlman, just how did these miracles begin happening in your ministry?' I try to answer the question the best I know how, even as I shall try to answer it for you."[16] After recapping her years in Concordia and Idaho, skipping the years in the West and leapfrogging over her marriage and divorce, Kuhlman laid out the story as she would tell it throughout her life. Her account of her development of an awareness of the healing power of God rested on her devoted study of the Bible and a progressive revelation from God. Typically, she did not credit any early training or influences. "I preached salvation throughout Idaho to everyone who would listen. Gradually, however, I began to realize there was someone besides the Father and the Son—there was this Third Person of the Trinity. I felt compelled to know more regarding Him, and as I began searching and studying God's Word, I could see that divine healing also was in the atonement. You cannot study the Word of God without realizing that healing for the physical body, healing for the whole person, is in the Bible." She quoted the classic text for this doctrine, Isaiah 53:5, "He was wounded for our transgressions, he was bruised for our iniquities . . . and with his stripes we are healed." Kuhlman stated, "[Jesus] not only died for our sins, he died for the whole person."[17]

Kuhlman claimed to have "discovered" that divine healing was in the atonement and maintained that God gave her this revelation based solely on her study of the Bible. "These things are only spiritually revealed," she stated, "and that is why sometimes the most uneducated person knows more about the deep truths of God's Word than someone who has spent years attaining knowledge through much education."[18] Guided by divine instruction, she began to preach about the Holy Spirit to her congregation in Franklin. She painted these days as a time of waiting for God to reveal the secret to unlock his promises of divine healing. "And then it happened!" Kuhlman declared. "As I was preaching on the Holy Spirit, sharing with the people the little that I knew about that Third Person of the Trinity, a woman stood up and asked, 'Kathryn, may I say something?' I answered, 'Of course you may.'"[19] The woman spoke. "Last night while you were preaching, I was healed."[20] Kuhlman's message the previous evening had concerned the person of the Holy Spirit but was not a sermon about healing and did not contain a call for divine healing.[21] "I was shocked," Kuhlman recalled. "I asked, 'How do you know?' The woman replied, 'Because I had a tumor that had been diagnosed by my doctor. While you were preaching something happened in my body and I was so sure that I was healed that I went back to my doctor and had it verified today. He could not find a tumor!'" Kuhlman summed up, "That was the first healing that took place in this ministry."[22]

Post–World War II Healing Revival

The advent of miraculous healing in Kuhlman's ministry was in line with an overall revival of interest in divine healing in shell-shocked America in the mid-twentieth century. Many factors contributed to the appeal of healing during this period. Despite the joy of victory in World War II, Americans faced the cruel reality of approximately four hundred thousand casualties of war.[23] The world faced for the first time in atomic bombs the possibility of complete annihilation. The dawning evidence of the atrocities of the Holocaust emphasized the powerful presence of evil in human character. Within five years of D-Day, America was again involved in armed conflict in Korea, and certainly the growing tension of the Cold War affected American culture as a whole. It was for many a time of stress and disorientation.

Cultural turbulence contributed to a renewal of interest in divine healing in America at large. Within Pentecostalism, however, it was a perceived *lack* of tumult that gave energy to the revival. The fervor of many adherents to early Pentecostalism was settling into well-ordered denominationalism. Pentecostal churches such as the Assemblies of God began to join with the evangelical mainstream. The Assemblies of God participated actively in meetings throughout the 1940s that led to the organization of the National Association of Evangelicals by decade's end. While these centripetal forces were at work in the organizations where divine healing was well established, a small but powerful subculture was uncomfortable with what was perceived as a dampening of revival fires. By the end of the 1940s, many of the great leaders of the post–World War I healing movement were gone. McPherson died in 1944 at the young age of fifty-four, Charles Price and Smith Wigglesworth in 1947. With the loss of the powerful independent evangelists and the rise of the denominations, some Pentecostals began to chafe. In particular, "Latter Rain" proponents expressed a deep discontent with the direction of Pentecostalism. Many believed the revival had lost its way. "The rhetoric of Latter Rain advocates closely resembled that of early Pentecostals: they coveted a restoration of apostolic Christianity. They considered Pentecostalism a step in the direction of restoration but indicted the movement for organizing and 'quenching the Spirit.'"[24] The time was ripe for a new revival.

Into this spiritually fertile environment came a new wave of independent healing evangelists. As Wacker explains, "in the late 1940s and early 1950s a new group of shaman-like healers skyrocketed into national prominence."[25] The post–World War II healing revival, as historian David Edwin Harrell Jr. has called it, was gaining momentum under the leadership of healers such as Oral Roberts and William Branham. Roberts began his healing ministry in 1947. As his career blossomed, diseases from headaches to terminal cancer were reported healed. Quoting Roberts, Harrell explains: "Roberts felt a 'manifestation of God's presence in his right hand' which supplied a 'point of contact' between the believer and the healing power of God. This gave him 'an assurance that resulted in the healing of thousands of people.'"[26] Roberts claimed the ability to serve as a "circuit" between the available healing power of God and the ill. This circuit could be completed at any time, as long as Roberts was available to act as the conduit. Healing through the laying on of hands or through a "point of contact" was another mark of those who adhered to the "Latter Rain" doctrine prevalent in the 1940s. In this doctrine, spiritual gifts, such as the gifts of faith and healing, were received instantly through direct physical contact. This was in opposition to the idea of "tarrying," or waiting until the Holy Spirit chose to come and heal. Laying on of hands took the agency for the healing action of the Spirit and placed it, literally, in the hands of the healer. The afflicted no longer had to wait upon the unpredictable working of the Holy Spirit, but instead could be guaranteed access to the power of God through the healer's actions. No more "tarrying" for these healers; God's power was available on command whenever they reached out to touch the sick.

Kuhlman's portrayal of what happened to her and her ministry in the Franklin years reveals continuity with the approach of her colleagues in other healing ministries as well as important adaptations. Put simply, she did not heal by laying on hands. At times she would touch people as she prayed for them, but this action was not connected with their healing. Sister Aimee and Charles Price both held to the standard practice of healing lines and laying on of hands. Roberts used a point of contact. As noted earlier, McPherson, Simpson, and Price were all "facilitating healers," who brought about healing in their followers through teaching and praying with them and for them, "facilitating" the action of the Holy Spirit to heal. Kuhlman was in some ways a version of a facilitating healer, because she did pray with and for the people who came to her. Where Kuhlman differed was in the method by which divine healing manifested itself in her ministry.

From the very beginning of miracles in her ministry, Kuhlman described her role as surprised onlooker. She regularly abstracted herself from the healing work of the Holy Spirit in her actions. The woman in Franklin healed of a tumor "shocked" Kuhlman with her testimony. This was a notable shift of emphasis away from the healer, demonstrated again in her account of the second healing credited to her ministry, the restoration of sight to Mr. George Orr. Just days after the first healing, Orr received healing of an eye injury. In a twist, Orr was healed during the car ride home from a Sunday Kuhlman service. Kuhlman recalled, "No one had laid hands on George Orr. No one had prayed for him. I was not there. But something glorious had happened! Mr. Orr came back to the service the next night and told what had happened. His face was shining, and he did not need anyone to tell him that physical healing was real—he could see!"[27] Regarding the moment of Orr's healing, Kuhlman said tellingly, "I wasn't there." This small adaptation of the facilitating role was very significant in the development of Kuhlman's career as a healer who regularly claimed not to be one.

Moving On

By 1948, Kuhlman had fought her way back to success. Despite the fertile field offered by Pittsburgh, Kuhlman kept her center of operations in Franklin. She felt a loyalty to the people of Franklin because they accepted her despite her divorced status. But Franklin soon became a center of controversy for Kuhlman. Matthew J. Maloney, owner of the Gospel Tabernacle, where Kuhlman had enjoyed such success for two years, accused Kuhlman and her followers of financial misdealing. The dispute was over the contractual agreement regarding the percentage of offerings Kuhlman had to pay the board of trustees of the Tabernacle. As the offerings to the Tabernacle increased, Maloney and the other trustees demanded additional revenue. They threatened to fire Kuhlman and shut down the services if she did not comply. In a story dated June 19, 1948, the *Pittsburgh Press* reported, "There won't be any services in Franklin Gospel Tabernacle tomorrow because of two well-filled collection plates. Miss Kathryn Kuhlman, a blond Missouri evangelist, is forbidden to preach inside. Trustees of the temple claim they have been short-changed on $20,000 raised by Miss Kuhlman's evangelism."[28] Judge Lee A. McCracken granted a preliminary injunction against Kuhlman, which prevented her from holding services. The drama grew as Kuhlman countersued, and increased further as her supporters broke the locks off the doors of the Tabernacle in order to conduct a miracle service in defiance of the injunction. The local newspapers covered the battle, which included accounts of noisy courtroom debates as well as accusatory articles and advertisements exchanged between Kuhlman and Maloney supporters. Wayne Warner summarized the resolution of the conflict: "Maloney had the law on his side. But the court could rule only on who should have the building, not on where the people were to attend church. So after the attorneys argued their cases, Maloney wound up with the nearly empty Tabernacle, and Kuhlman kept the people."[29] Taking her loyal followers with her, Kuhlman moved the ministry to Sugar Creek, three miles outside Franklin. There she preached in a renovated skating rink christened "Faith Temple." Her ministry was doing so well that her close associates began to encourage her to expand. In 1949, she extended her ministry into the Pittsburgh area at the urging of her friend and administrative assistant Marguerite "Maggie" Hartner. Kuhlman began to hold a regular round of services in rented space in the Carnegie Auditorium on Pittsburgh's North Side and the Stambaugh Auditorium in nearby Youngstown, Ohio.

In Sugar Creek, Pittsburgh, and Youngstown, Kuhlman began to develop the style of "miracle service" she would use for the rest of her career. In these services, after a musical introduction, Kuhlman would preach on the Holy Spirit and related topics until she began to feel the "anointing" of the Spirit guiding her to call out healings already occurring in the room. Just like her first miracles, Kuhlman argued, she simply preached and the Holy Spirit did the healing. In recognition of the challenges her gender presented for her ministry, Kuhlman established her persona as a healer without agency, as simply a "yielded vessel" for God's healing power. Taking this standard claim of most faith healers to a new level, Kuhlman claimed to have no part in the healings at all. All she did was show people how big God was, and it was up to them to apprehend that goodness for themselves. Healing occurred when a person took hold of the power of the Holy Spirit, which was available to everyone, not just one lone healer.

Kuhlman laid a strong emphasis on human agency in her preaching and teaching about healing. In print and on the radio she told a witheringly critical story about a man who spent day after day "resting," never

53

working, never putting forth any effort, never achieving anything with his life. "That man was my brother," Kuhlman declared. "My brother has spent his life 'resting.' He has no gumption."[30] For Kuhlman, having no gumption was the great failure of the Christian life. Not disease, not suffering, but refusal to "put feet to your wishes" was the ultimate disappointment.[31] "God has not time for lazy creatures. . . . God believes in work."[32] "James 2:26, faith without works is dead. Faith without works, without gumption, is dead," she paraphrased. "It takes more than faith and wishing to achieve success. Nothing will happen until you put forth the effort and do something about it."[33] Action or "gumption" was the work of the human being in refusing to be defeated, continuing to put forth effort, no matter what may come.

Kuhlman's emphasis on the importance of human activity in divine healing tapped into the popularity of "positive thinking" during the middle of her career. Positive thinking was an heir to New Thought theology, a cousin to Christian Science, and a cohort of the new interest in psychology and psychotherapy after World War II. Scholar of American religion Kate Bowler describes New Thought in the late 1800s as "the era's most powerful vehicle of mind power." Christians who adopted New Thought saw "'salvation' not as an act imposed from above by God, but rather an act of drawing out humanity's potential." Christian Science rode the same mind-cure wave as New Thought, its founder Mary Baker Eddy declaring, "Jesus came to save the world, not through his divinity, but by demonstrating right thinking."[34] This way of conceiving spiritual power had a long and varied history in American religion.

Post–World War II positive thinking was most closely associated with the work of Dr. Norman Vincent Peale (1898–1993).[35] Peale scored a national best seller in 1952 with his book *The Power of Positive Thinking*, which topped the best-seller list for two years. Over seven million copies had sold by the end of the twentieth century. This work was preceded by two volumes, *The Art of Living* in 1937 and *A Guide to Confident Living* in 1948, the latter also a best seller. Through his publishing house, Foundations for Christian Living, Peale printed the popular *Guideposts* magazine, an influential periodical in American Christianity.[36] With his wife as cohost, he presided over a short-lived advice show on television from 1952 to 1953 called *What's Your Trouble?* and also helmed a popular radio program in the years prior to television.

The success of *The Power of Positive Thinking* revealed a deep desire in American society in the post–World War II years for wholeness and redemption, the same currents that fed the healing revival. One chapter of the book was titled "How to Use Faith in Healing." Religious Studies scholar Craig Prentiss explains, "Peale wrote in one of his earliest books, *The Art of Living*, that 'essentially the function of the Church is that of the General Electric Company—to release power.' The power of God existed for the service of 'the individual and society.' This divine power was 'inherent in the world and freely offered to those who want it and will take it.'" [37] Positive thinking was "quintessentially American," with its "belief that one's health, happiness and prosperity are contingent on the attitude and will of the individual."[38] In his analysis of self-help and religion in America, English scholar Roy Anker argues that Peale and others like him "promulgated the belief that mind and belief together conquer all of life's woes, whether physical illness, emotional distress, or plain bad luck."[39] Peale was influenced by nineteenth-century American psychologist and philosopher William James, who espoused the outlook of pragmatism and its doctrine of the ability of the human will to overcome negative experiences. Peale's wife would later say he quoted James more than he quoted Jesus.[40] R. Laurence Moore notes, "[Peale's] listeners didn't suffer from sin . . . but from unawareness of the practical power of faith. They believed in Christ, but they did not know how to use him to construct prosperous lives for themselves and their families. Faith, prayer, and scripture, Peale said, existed for one thing—to help individuals overcome their feelings of insecurity and inferiority."[41] This was the true power in positive thinking.

Peale was not without his critics. The theologian Reinhold Niebuhr found Peale's theology lacking, calling it "easy religion." Other detractors delighted in the motto "Paul is appealing and Peale is appalling."[42] Peale's approach lacked a sufficient appreciation for the power of sin at work in humanity, his critics continued, and overemphasized human ability to the detriment of divine sovereignty. If God was so radically immanent, then the transcendent, prophetic, sovereign God had no place. For many, this was an uncomfortable elevation of humanity's abilities and threatened the orthodox declaration of God's sovereignty.[43] It was doubtless true that a positive attitude could make anything better. Taken to its extreme, however, this attitude turned the sovereign God into a holy vending machine, dispensing miracles at the whim of the human race.

The tension between God's sovereignty and human agency had a long history within divine healing ranks. If the suffering person was granted no agency, then all that was left was despair, or a stoic resignation to valorized suffering. If the suffering person was made the entire focus of the healing act, then when healing did not occur the conclusion was inevitable: there had been no faith, or at least insufficient faith. Peale and his followers claimed to have found the answer to this dilemma. The solution was the power of positive thinking.

Positive thinking was at work in the culture around Kuhlman, and she sometimes flirted with this type of teaching. She often stated, "The only limit of God's power lies in the individual," or in more direct address to her audience, "The only limit to God's power lies in YOU!" She said, "Prayer is the voice of the soul. But it's faith that walks up to the throne of God and unlocks the storehouse."[44] Faith walked, faith acted, and in this activity there was power, even for physical healing. On her radio program she said even more. "Listen. There are no limitations to what you can do. There are no limitations to what you can be. The first step is faith; then all reservoirs of power from God himself are open to you. But hear me: God won't do anything to bring it to pass until you get up out of that chair and do something about it."[45] Kuhlman proclaimed that human beings could make a difference, and human determination or "gumption" was important for those seeking healing and restoration.

Kuhlman handled the tension between human initiative and the sovereignty of God in the healing of sick bodies in a way that tapped into the same broader cultural interests that Peale did, but with a Calvinist twist. In contrast to "positive thinking," Kuhlman did not state that Christians would not, or even should not, experience suffering. She stated, "If you are a part of humanity, you will suffer." The response she advocated to illness and other forms of suffering in the human life was again tied to her concept of "gumption." The ill believer should "never go down in defeat." She taught that life for a Christian was not free from trial, but should be free from despair. "There is no such thing as a defeated Christian," she declared many times. In her interviews on her television show, she invariably asked the testifier, "Were you ever discouraged? Did you ever want to give up?" As the guests confessed their discouragement, Kuhlman would emphasize that they had never been defeated. "If you have faith, nothing shall be impossible to you. Faith is such a powerful force that when taken into the soul and lived by, it can see you through anything in life."[46] Kuhlman espoused the belief that the power of the Holy Spirit, available to all believers, was sufficient to overcome any circumstance, from cancer to depression to debilitating pain to drug addiction to the loss of a child. For Kuhlman, defeat, not disease, was the unpardonable sin.

Although different in its conception, Kuhlman's approach shared some of the dangers of positive thinking. The demand for "gumption" pressed the sick and dying somehow to live "the victorious life" without acknowledging the reality of despair caused by illness. Kuhlman's teaching placed almost as heavy a burden on her followers as blaming an illness on lack of faith or lack of positive thinking. In her presentation, the sick person is not blamed for a lack of healing, an admirable caveat in the standard playbook of divine healing. But that same person could be held responsible for allowing illness and suffering to bring discouragement and despair. Kuhlman's teaching about the embarrassment of defeat in the Christian life was potentially problematic for many of the same reasons levied against positive thinking.

Praise and Criticism for the Preacher Lady

As Peale's *Guide to Confident Living* climbed the best-seller list and added to the cultural interest in healing, Kuhlman threw herself into the work of her growing local ministry. Many of her congregants were people who had witnessed or experienced physical or spiritual healing through the Kuhlman ministry and returned again to her services and Bible studies. Those people brought others, who came hoping for miracles and expecting Bible teaching. The men and women who attended Kuhlman's services considered her a minister, and often claimed her as *their* minister. In 1949, the *Pittsburgh Press* featured an article and picture of Kuhlman with a well-dressed couple. The caption underneath read "WEDDING."[47] The article was about a New Year's ceremony celebrating the dedication of Faith Temple in Sugar Creek. As the copy indicated, the ceremony reuniting John F. Ott and Hazel V. Ott was the "highlight" of the day's festivities. The multitude of contradictions and conflicting images contained on this one page of newspaper demonstrated the complexity of Kuhlman's role at this point in her career.

Kuhlman was not dressed in ministerial robes, but instead wore a simple dress and corsage. Her hair was curled, makeup just right. Her position relative to the couple in the picture signaled her role as minister, as did the small open book held in her hands, which likely contained the words of the ceremony. The backdrop was an auditorium-type environment, not a traditional church setting. The couple and Kuhlman were smiling at each other, the bride in an attractive suit dress with matching flowers on her lapel and hat, and a demure dark veil securing the hat to her head. The man was in a simple suit and tie. Kuhlman was looking at the man, seemingly in "midvow," as the photographer snapped the picture. Any image of a woman performing a religious ceremony in 1949 was significant, and this picture captured Kuhlman in her uncommon role as a Pennsylvania pastor.

The imagery of Kuhlman as officiant was perhaps not as startling as it would have been in a high-church setting, with the blushing bride in white and the smiling groom in a tuxedo. A renewal of vows did not require Kuhlman to be a legal officiant. She was not performing a legally binding wedding but was providing a ministerial presence at a ceremonial event. However, the celebration was important for her role as a pastor. Kuhlman in the picture was clearly serving as a pastor to the couple at her side. They requested her presence and authority as a minister to renew their wedding vows. In this they were reinforcing her role as pastor. In addition, Kuhlman's image was featured in a prominent place in a Pittsburgh newspaper. This was not an accident. Kuhlman was adept at the use of media, and the picture was clearly not a candid "snap" of an unaware Kuhlman in action. It was a carefully staged photo, even revealing stage management in the positioning of the three in a way that in "real life" would be awkward, but which made for a good shot for the press. The couple and Kuhlman either willingly agreed to pose for publication or the Kuhlman organization provided the picture to the press. This newspaper image of Kuhlman as pastor did not draw upon traditional markers of ministerial authority such as a robe or a high-church setting. Her dress and her hair were "ladylike," drawing upon comforting imagery of traditional femininity. The book in her hand, her place of authority relative to the couple, and the caption crediting her as officiant clearly marked her as "pastor." Kuhlman in this picture was presenting herself as the complex image of "preacher lady," as she would throughout her ministerial career. The traditional marks of a pastor are teaching the Word and presiding over the sacramental life of the congregation, including communion, baptisms, weddings, and funerals. Press releases, clippings, and testimonials of her parishioners attest to Kuhlman's performance of pastoral roles during the late 1940s through the 1950s. As one parishioner said, "We love her. That's putting it mildly. We thank God for her."[48]

Not everyone was grateful for Kuhlman's presence in Pittsburgh. Divine healing was as controversial in the 1950s as it had been in Kuhlman's early days, perhaps more so as it grew in influence with the post–World War II revival. The independent healing evangelists were attacked by representatives from the religious Left who saw only profiteering and fraud in the healing revival.[49] Representatives of Baptist congregations and Churches of Christ were particularly vitriolic in their condemnation. Churches of Christ, dispensationalists determined to show that the gift of healing had ceased, took out advertisements offering cash rewards for any proof of actual healing by the evangelists.[50] As healers became more prevalent and more popular, those who found charismatic Christianity disturbing or even heretical continued to be harshly critical. The conflict between "holy rollers" and "nonrollers" even became violent. One 1946 newspaper article from Oklahoma City was titled "Admits He Shot Preacher over 'That Ranting.'" The story focused on a "bewhiskered recluse" named Isaac Coker, age seventy-five, who interrupted a Pentecostal Holiness church service with a shotgun full of buckshot. Coker "broke up a prayer meeting next to his home Friday night by shooting the preacher with a shotgun." The man said "he acted in desperation because he 'couldn't stand that ranting.'" The shot was deflected by the Bible held by the young preacher, who was only slightly wounded in the chest and shoulder.[51]

Kuhlman worked to distance her ministry from "ranting" Pentecostals and the more extravagant independent healers, but she, too, was the object of criticism in Pittsburgh. Not all local pastors were happy to welcome the Miracle Lady to town, and tempers ran high. A series of articles in the *Pittsburgh Post Gazette* of December 11, 1948, told the story of an altercation caused by Kuhlman's ministry. The lead headline read, "Baptist Deacon Resigns in Tiff over Evangelist." Details followed: "The chairman of the Board of Deacons of the Sandusky St. Baptist Church, North Side, yesterday resigned in disagreement with his pastor over Evangelist Kathryn Kuhlman. Herbert R. James, 626 Warrington Ave., who held the office about two years, said he did not believe the Rev. Peter E. Boyko should 'pick on' Miss Kuhlman. Mr. Boyko and about 20 others touched off neighborhood excitement Thursday night when they passed out cards criticizing the evangelist after her meeting in Carnegie Music Hall. Yesterday, the pastor challenged her methods and the validity of 'healings' which reportedly occurred at her meetings." Other accounts of the evening reported "a near riot" halted by police.[52]

Rev. Boyko persisted in his criticism of Kuhlman, and the disagreement escalated. The December 30 paper featured a picture of Boyko with the heading "Pastor Attacked during Services: Minister Blames Ex-Parishioners." "A religious controversy on the North Side flared into violence last night," the article began. "The disturbance started during services at the Sandusky St. Baptist Church and apparently was between followers of Kathryn Kuhlman, an evangelist, and members of the Sandusky Church. Rev. Peter Boyko, pastor of the Baptist Church, said several men 'started swinging at me, but missed.'" Boyko requested police protection and was afraid to return to his residence "because he thought further violence was planned."[53] Boyko's statement to the press stopped short of explicitly attacking Kuhlman, but he made clear that the rioting and violence were a direct result of the conflict and controversy surrounding her ministry. As much as Kuhlman tried to place herself in a different class, in the minds of local pastors such as Rev. Boyko, she was no different from any other suspect healing evangelist. Well, she was no different except for one distressing fact: she apparently was not going to move on. Kuhlman had found her place in Pittsburgh, and she intended to stay.

As the 1940s drew to a close, Kuhlman maintained her home in Franklin and her services at Sugar Creek as her ministry grew more broad-reaching. One 1949 newspaper article summarized her intensely busy weekly schedule, consisting of services six nights a week at Carnegie Hall in Pittsburgh as well as two services each Sunday at the Faith Temple in Sugar Creek. She was firmly established and thriving. If the roof of the Faith Temple auditorium had not literally caved in under the weight of a late November snowstorm in 1950, Kuhlman would likely have kept her home in Franklin for the rest of her ministry. Even before the fateful snowstorm, Kuhlman had been encouraged to change venues by Hartner, her closest friend. Hartner pressured Kuhlman for over two years to move her base of operations to Pittsburgh. Eve Conley, Kuhlman's housemate in Franklin, also supported the relocation. When Kuhlman made the transition to the new ministry site, Conley purchased a house in Fox Chapel, a suburb of Pittsburgh. After the setback at Sugar Creek and buoyed by the encouragement of her friends and followers, Kuhlman settled her ministry in the Steel City and her home in Fox Chapel.[54]

In a press release dated 1953, a Kuhlman associate noted the celebration of Kuhlman's five-year anniversary of ministry in Pittsburgh. The language of the release was exuberant due to the promotional bias of the writer, but the copy pointed to the robust condition of Kuhlman's career:

Kathryn Kuhlman, nationally known Lady Preacher, will conduct a day-long service in Syria Mosque Temple, Oakland, Pittsburgh—Sunday August 16 commemorating the completion of five years of ministry in this city. Miss Kuhlman has been preaching and conducting divine healing services in the North Side Carnegie Hall since July 1948 and attracting over-flow audiences twice and sometimes thrice weekly since coming to Pittsburgh. Every Sunday, she travels to either Cleveland or Youngstown, Ohio where the crowds are so large she has found it necessary to hold two services, beginning the first to a jam-packed Theatre or Auditorium at six thirty A.M. and a second service, following a brief rest period starts about ten thirty A.M. to another capacity crowd. [After the "preaching and divine healing service"] there will be an intermission of an hour and a half. At 3 P.M., with the assistance of two hundred men of her staff, Miss Kuhlman will administer Holy Communion to all in attendance who desire to participate. On the mammoth stage of the Mosque where the world's foremost artists of Concert and Stage have appeared, it will be an inspiring sight to see spread on this stage the Lord's Table with the bread and wine which will be served to the communicants representing all faiths, race and color. [A handwritten note in the margin reads "Insert: This symbolizes the spirit of Miss Kuhlman's ministry."] Six thousand individuals will be used in the service which will no doubt be the largest service of its kind ever held in Pittsburgh.[55]

From disgrace to honor, in the space of seven short years; Kuhlman succeeded in fighting her way back to success.

Between the years 1946 and 1953, Kathryn Kuhlman overcame her past missteps and established herself as a media presence, a pastor, and a significant participant in the revival of divine healing in American Christianity. While most of the independent healers faded into obscurity after the 1950s, historians identify Oral Roberts and Rex Humbard as the primary leaders who went on to make the transition to the charismatic renewal movement they helped foster.[56] Kuhlman also deserves a place in this cohort of leaders. The 1950s represented a time of success and development for Kuhlman as she built a ministry as significant as that of Roberts or Humbard. Kuhlman's highly visible and flourishing ministry of the 1960s did not emerge out of thin air, but was the result of determined effort. What did emerge out of thin air was the next bold advance in Kuhlman's career: evangelism via the airwaves, using the new technology of television.

CHAPTER 3

Televising Testimony

At every stage of her career, Kathryn Kuhlman was "on the air." In the 1940s, her radio show entitled *Heart-to-Heart* reached beyond Pittsburgh and Franklin, Pennsylvania, to Ohio, West Virginia, Maryland, and Washington, DC.[1] But by the mid-1950s, the people of Pittsburgh were rushing to get their hands on the hot new thing for the up-to-date family: a television. Kuhlman, always eager to embrace the next available broadcast medium, quickly expanded her reach to include the cutting-edge technology.[2] She once said, "The greatest combination is television and radio . . . together they form a combination that is unbeatable."[3] Accounts of Kuhlman's ministry career date her entrance into television as 1967, beginning with her talk show *I Believe in Miracles*.[4] Kuhlman in actuality made the move to television much earlier, launching a show called *Your Faith and Mine* in the 1950s. Her show thus becomes even more significant due to her presence at the birth of both television and televangelism.

On one episode of *Your Faith and Mine*, Kuhlman welcomed Harry Stephenson, who had come to tell of his miraculous healing from cancer of the tongue. "Come here, Mr. Stephenson," Kuhlman said as she waved him on to the screen. "You can tell it far better than I can. It's one thing to read of divine healing, but it's something else to see the person themselves."[5] This dual insight formed the foundation for Kuhlman's highly successful television career. First, "You can tell it far better than I can." It was vitally important that the healed persons speak for themselves and offer their own subjective authority for the validity of their claim of supernatural healing. Second, "It's one thing to read of divine healing, but it's something else to see the person themselves." Truly seeing a person who claimed to be divinely healed was different from, and superior to, reading the person's testimony, or even hearing the person speak on the radio. On *Your Faith and Mine*, Kuhlman merged her knowledge of the persuasive power of personal testimony with her evangelism skills, a combination she knew to be effective from her years on the revival circuit.[6] In the earliest days of the development of charismatic Christianity, Kuhlman's televised testimonies broadcast images of average people speaking freely about divine and spiritual healing into hundreds of homes in the Pittsburgh area. This public witness on the most public of technologies began the dissemination of a gentrified form of charismatic Christianity into the homes, lives, and minds of people previously unexposed.

Any attempt to understand the gentrification of charismatic Christianity in the twentieth century must take seriously the primary forms of media used to disseminate that category of Christianity into the larger culture of America. This requires regarding broadcast media such as radio and television as legitimate repositories of historical information. For many years, broadcast media did not elicit much historical interest. As media historians J. Emmett Winn and Susan L. Brinson argue, "Radio and television lurked among the 'inconsequential' subjects of study, dismissed by the cultural elite as simply the opiate of the masses and cultural pollution. Even within historical work on other media, broadcasting was ignored. Until the mid-1960s . . . the history of radio and television remained largely unresearched and unwritten."[7] Cultural historians have spent the last decades making the case for the significance of broadcast media for historical research, with increasing success.[8]

Broadcast media and American Christianity share a long history. Evangelical Christians in particular quickly made peace with using the latest forms of media to communicate the gospel. Quentin Schultze observes, "Evangelicals have always kept the faith partly by giving it away through every available medium."[9] American evangelicals pursued media fluency because of their belief that salvation through Jesus Christ was the most important message the world ever received. It was a crucial announcement that must be communicated to as many people as possible, as quickly as possible, so that all might be saved before the return of Jesus and his judgment. But the relationship between evangelicalism and television was not always cozy. Television was first connected in the evangelical mind with the stage and film, forms of entertainment classified as "worldly" and off-limits.[10] Over time, however, the prospect of being able to package the old, old story of Christianity in the latest technology irresistibly appealed to those strains of American Christianity that emphasized communication of the gospel of Jesus Christ as the primary duty of all believers. When the main objective of a Christian group is dissemination of information, innovative media becomes a primary emphasis.

New Medium, New Challenges

Despite the strong theological impetus, from a business standpoint the addition of television to Kuhlman's radio and print enterprises was not as self-evident a move as it may seem. As television came on the scene in the late 1940s, media producers were not completely convinced of the new technology's viability as a competitor for radio.[11] Television sets were expensive enough to be a significant investment for working-class families. Even as manufacturers worked to lower the cost, the purchase of a set "still required a sizeable portion of the family paycheck [$250–$300], and therefore involved a deep commitment to the new medium."[12] In contrast, few people in America in the late 1940s needed to invest in a new radio. Radio was firmly established in the American living room; over 95 percent of homes had a receiver.[13] Radio was a successful medium that required no additional cost to the consumer and had firmly established audiences for advertising.

Yet Americans invested in television at an extraordinary rate. As media historian Bernard Timberg notes, "From 1948 to 1953, television-set ownership exploded from 1 percent of the population to 53 percent. By the end of the 1950s, the American household was saturated with television, reaching 90 percent."[14] Media historians look to several factors to explain the "ripening environment" for television during this time, including a rise in marriage rates, the baby boom, the revitalization of the nuclear family, and the prefab suburban home, "so affordable that young middle-class couples, and at times lower-middle-class, blue-collar workers, could purchase their piece of the American dream."[15] In a surprisingly short time, television replaced radio in the homes of the working class. Newly expendable income was happily expended on television sets in homes throughout the Pittsburgh area. Television, despite its slow start, had begun its journey to media dominance.

Kuhlman's audience was made up of this lower-middle-class demographic, a group with more income available in the post–World War II years than had been common earlier. The Korean War also created a mini-"boom" in Pittsburgh in the early 1950s and kept the city's mills humming at 100 percent of capacity or better.[16] Pittsburgh in the early 1950s was flourishing. The modernization demanded by World War II positioned the city for success in the postwar domestic economy.[17] The city "was back to business as usual, evidenced by the smoke and hum of the mills which were in high gear producing steel for domestic markets. Now instead of supplying steel for tanks and ships, U.S. Steel and other companies were rolling out steel for everything from automobiles and appliances to nails and bridge girders."[18] The Allegheny Plateau of western Pennsylvania, southeastern Ohio, and northeastern West Virginia was the home for Kuhlman's ministry, the population made up of workers in coal mines, steel mills, foundries, metal shops, metal fabricators, and glassworks.[19] The entire area gathered its resources from industrial manufacturing, and "steel was the largest employer and engine of the [Pittsburgh] economy."[20] This working-class area was the socioeconomic environment of Kuhlman's ministry, and as her followers snapped up televisions, she pushed ahead to add television broadcasting to her repertoire.

Evangelists who wanted to add television to their ministries faced tremendous financial obstacles. The same issues surrounding sustaining time that plagued evangelical ministries in the early days of radio played out in television. Powerful radio networks ABC, NBC, and CBS gained quick control over prime-time slots on television, and sustaining time was handed primarily to mainline ministries.[21] Evangelicals "found themselves struggling against a triple disadvantage. In most cases, they could not buy television time. When they could, it was much more expensive than radio time. And they had to pay expensive production costs as well."[22] Paradoxically, the church groups affiliated with the Federal Council of Churches and granted the bulk of sustaining time did not initially find television a worthwhile technology, much less a suitable avenue for ministry. The *Christian Century*, a periodical associated with the mainline churches, ran a series of articles in 1946 titled "Can Protestants Win America?" Managing editor Charles Clayton Morrison deplored the advent of television in a piece with the heading "Protestantism and Commercialized Entertainment." Morrison wrote, "No number of sustaining or public-service hours for religious programming on radio or television could offset the destructive influence of everyday commercial entertainment."[23] Television itself was not worth much in the eyes of the more liberal churches, wrapped up as it was with boorish popular entertainments. The editors of the *Christian Century* in the mid-1950s had this advice for their readers regarding television: "Turn it off."[24]

In sharp contrast, the lure of television for the post–World War II healing evangelists was irresistible. As David Edwin Harrell writes, "Every minister dreamed of launching a national television program. 'The people that's on radio and television,' said old-timer W. V. Grant, 'is the ones that's getting the crowds.'"[25] But Kuhlman's association with Pentecostals and healing evangelists connected her with the side of Christianity still considered fringe and suspect in 1950 and therefore not eligible for sustaining time on TV. The high cost of producing television programs was a daunting challenge. For many of Kuhlman's colleagues, the answer to the money question was clear, as Harrell states: "The need for funds was endless; the competition was fierce. Hard-sell financial appeals were often the price of survival."[26] Both Oral Roberts and Pat Robertson sought dedicated sponsors for their productions. Roberts initiated the "Blessing Pact" concept: in return for sponsorship, Roberts "pledged to enter into a 'prayer-pact' . . . asking 'that God will especially prosper you in your job, or your business, or your profession.'"[27] Robertson took a similar approach in 1960. Historian John Wigger states, "Robertson came up with a scheme to ask seven hundred viewers to pledge ten dollars a month and *The 700 Club* was born."[28] Kuhlman managed to support her television ministry without constant appeals for money during her show. Direct requests for funds were extremely rare. Her media ministries, both radio and television, were supported by dedicated offerings during her various services. Without "stumping" for financial support over the air, Kuhlman established herself in radio and television while fellow evangelists resorted to pushy on-air fund-raising or simply faltered due to lack of money.

As the postwar healing revival began to wane in the latter part of the 1950s, finances became a major issue for all the evangelists.[29] Kuhlman's contemporary Oral Roberts launched a television ministry in the 1950s and felt the draining effect of television's financial demands. Harrell states, "Oral struggled with the financial burden the television series imposed; the new medium proved to be the financial graveyard of many aspiring evangelists."[30] Major figures such as William Branham, widely acknowledged as the founder and leader of the healing revival, struggled to make ends meet. Harrell adds, "When even William Branham suddenly found it difficult to meet expenses in 1955, the future looked dim indeed for lesser figures."[31] Meanwhile, Kuhlman managed to maintain her daily radio show while adding weekly television broadcasts. This was no small accomplishment for any evangelist of the time, and especially significant for a recently divorced female making her way in the male-dominated world of radio and television ministry.

Kuhlman succeeded in establishing a television ministry in the early 1950s while many of her male contemporaries failed. One way she prevailed in the high-cost world of television was through the use of syndication. Syndication was a proven method for newspapers and radio, and it quickly became a frugal option for television. Broadcasters had long recognized the value of locally syndicated programs for radio. Erickson states, "Larger [radio] stations in major metropolitan areas were able to develop their own talent to fill the dead air around network broadcasts . . . but small-time outfits with weaker signals needed to fill their air time with something more than the birth reports and the hog futures. So, just as small-town newspapers relied on syndication to fill in the blanks, so did small-town radio outlets."[32] For these same reasons, syndication was useful for early TV stations. "Just as in radio's heyday, local TV channels had schedule gaps to fill, and could not make do with test patterns and recorded music forever. What was needed was new, quality product."[33] While the developing television networks placed their emphasis on the more lucrative evening hours, cost-conscious syndicators produced shows in their own studios and sold them to independent stations for lower prices than network productions.[34] Network affiliates could use these less expensive syndicated shows to fill off-peak hours, hours that included weekdays and slots on Sunday not set aside for sustaining time.[35] Coming to the fore in the 1950s, syndicated television shows were convenient, of decent quality, and, most important, *cheap*.

Decisions by the federal government also made syndicated shows appealing to local programmers. In 1952, the Federal Communications Council (FCC) lifted its freeze on new television station licenses. Imposed in 1949, the freeze stopped the distribution of licenses while the FCC studied emerging issues for television, which included "the qualifications of the applicants, the potential of television's Ultra High Frequency band (channels 14–83), and the future of colorcasting."[36] The latter consisted of overcoming the difficulties of broadcasting a color picture over black-and-white televisions. Since almost all early televisions were black and white, this was a significant obstacle for the new colorcasting technology. NBC developed a colorcasting technique that worked with all televisions, which helped obviate wholesale conversion to new televisions with color reception. Such a conversion would have slowed television's growth considerably, as viewers slowly switched over to new, expensive, color-ready televisions. Access to the ultrahigh frequency channels also offered new opportunities for broadcasting outside of the increasingly network-controlled programming found on VHF stations. With the lifting of the FCC restrictions, syndicators all over the United States had access to increasingly open airwaves, the ability to broadcast to all televisions, and a market in need of programming for the "dry" daytime hours and Sundays. As Erickson summarizes, "Once the freeze was unfrozen, brand-new television channels bred like rabbits."[37] Taking advantage of the new market for syndicated television, Kuhlman began producing her own show in the 1950s.

Kuhlman was not the only religious leader expanding into television at this time. Billy Graham's *Hour of Decision* began in 1950 on ABC. In 1953, Rex Humbard made the switch from radio to television and began transmitting programs from his Calvary Temple in Akron, Ohio. For one short season in 1952–1953, Norman Vincent Peale and his wife presented *What's Your Trouble?*, a show consisting of "filmed words of advice."[38] Bishop Fulton Sheen also ran a syndicated show in the late fifties, from 1958 to 1961. Pat Robertson purchased a "defunct 'hillbilly' television station" and launched the Christian Broadcasting Network in 1961.[39] Whether on national networks or locally syndicated, religious programming became a regular part of early television, just as it had been a staple of radio before.

Kuhlman's television ministry is also historically significant for two reasons: the head of the ministry was a woman, and the charismatic Christianity presented on the program was different from the Christianity of any of her contemporaries. Kuhlman was the only female healing evangelist to make the transition to television in the 1950s. Her leadership of a media ministry at the very beginning of television's ascendancy is significant, and her conspicuous absence in the standard narrative reveals a larger problem in media studies. As Lynn Spigel points out, "Women . . . are systematically marginalized in television history."[40] Kuhlman's most well-known television contemporary was Oral Roberts, and most historians of American religion and television privilege Roberts's broadcast career over that of Kuhlman. To a degree, it is right to place Roberts in the forefront of evangelical television ministries during the 1950s. Erickson explains, "Most of the '50's 'electronic evangelists' were strictly local acts. Oral Roberts was one of those few whose weekly sermons achieved national distribution."[41] Kuhlman biographer Wayne Warner offers an evenhanded summary of the evangelists' relative positions. "Some will argue that Kathryn Kuhlman can be listed behind Oral Roberts as having the greatest impact among healing evangelists. Others will put her first place. I think Oral had the greater impact into the 1960s, but then Kathryn Kuhlman charged to the front and maintained that appeal until her death a decade later."[42] Warner's evaluation is fair regarding the relation of Kuhlman's overall ministry to Roberts's in the 1950s, but Kuhlman's early television ministry deserves much more attention and respect. She did not have a national audience, as Oral Roberts had, but she was a major figure in the significant metropolitan area of Pittsburgh. She played an important part in the development of a television presence for independent healing evangelists after World War II. The dearth of references to her in the history of the broadcast ministries of the postwar healing revivalists is an unacceptable oversight.

Kuhlman also offered a unique presentation of charismatic Christianity on her television program. Although her healing ministry was gaining attention all over the Pittsburgh area, she deliberately chose not to record her miracle services on film, as her male contemporaries did. The television programs produced by her male colleagues often received considerable criticism. Roberts's first efforts at television were not well received by those outside Pentecostal circles. "Without a grotto or apparitions, Roberts had come up with an American version of Lourdes. The critics came down hard."[43] Erickson gave a disparaging summary of Roberts's first television attempt from 1955 to 1967, stating that the evangelist's "weekly programs during this decade were heavy into spectacular (and to the critical eye, not altogether convincing) acts of faith-healing." A. A. Allen, another leader in the healing revival, also created friction with his television broadcasts. "Allen's program was even more outrageous than Roberts', and the very few television channels that picked it up usually dropped it in a hurry amidst an avalanche of viewer complaints."[44] Some evangelists, Allen and Roberts included, resorted at times to broadcasting from across the border in Mexico when American stations refused to show their tendentious programs.[45] Roberts chose simply to film and telecast his healing services, with all their attendant Pentecostal fervor. The show was filmed in Roberts's huge tent, "filled with Pentecostal worshipers expressing their enthusiasm and delight."[46] American audiences were not used to the kind of charismatic worship found on Roberts's show, and the program stirred controversy throughout its run.[47]

Kuhlman chose a more refined approach to televising divine healing. Rather than film the actual events of miraculous healing, Kuhlman featured people testifying to spiritual and physical healings that had taken place previous to the telecast. Her choice to present testimonies to miracles rather than the miracle services themselves was wise on many levels. As Roberts, Allen, and others had discovered, watching a miracle service could be threatening, disconcerting, even frightening for the uninitiated in charismatic worship and theology. But seeing regular people telling stories about what had happened to them at a healing service was less challenging. By gently exposing the television audience to divine healing through the method of personal testimony, Kuhlman offered a comfortably mediated experience of charismatic Christianity. This was new, and it would have a significant effect on charismatic Christianity, starting small in Ohio and then spreading nation-wide.

Projecting an Image

Kuhlman made her first foray into the new and wide-open frontier of TV broadcasting with *Your Faith and Mine*. The show was recorded at the site of Kuhlman's Sunday services in Stambaugh Auditorium in Youngstown, Ohio. The service drew upon Kuhlman's established following in western Pennsylvania and the Pittsburgh area as well as from the Youngstown population. Youngstown was about an hour's drive from the north side of Pittsburgh, and was also a working-class, steel-oriented town in the Allegheny Plateau. Stambaugh Auditorium was an impressive building with columns inside and out, a large main floor, and wraparound balconies. The shows followed a very standardized format, with almost no deviation from episode to episode other than the identities of the featured guests and their testimonies. The stock opening consisted of taped footage of the auditorium filled to capacity, with the music of an organ playing church bells. As the camera continued to sweep the audience, the superimposed head of a young Kathryn Kuhlman floated across the screen, a side view at first of the preacher lady with a serene expression, hair neatly curled, eyebrows plucked and lined, lipstick carefully applied, and a long attractive neck lifting out of a tidy collar. As the visage of Kuhlman floated down across the room, it turned to look at the television audience as the male announcer intoned, "Here she is, Kathryn Kuhlman, the young woman whose widespread ministry has brought faith and hope to thousands" (later "millions").

In an unnervingly bad edit, the camera at this point awkwardly shifted from the beatific face of Kuhlman to the platform, where the action was already in full swing. The platform contained a small lectern, but was dominated by the large double microphone on its stand, placed in the middle of the stage. A giddy Kuhlman lifted her hand to direct the audience in the singing of a chorus, perfectly aware of the position of the cameras, her distance from the microphone, and the placement of each person around her on the platform. From the very first moment of the show, Kuhlman was center stage, in charge of the service and the clear authority in the ministry.

Kuhlman was aware of her vulnerability to criticism as the female head of a ministry as presented on the television show. With subtle skill, Kuhlman presented her image as a woman very carefully and consistently on the program. Her dress was professional, restrained, and refined. In all twenty-two episodes, she wore a version of a white suit dress with a demure skirt that hit below the knee. Her flair for style and a little "sass" was shown in her choice of white high-heeled ankle-strap shoes, shoes that showed off her long legs to good advantage. She wore little to no jewelry, and only occasionally added a large white corsage to her lapel as decoration. She looked modern, stylish, "normal." Dressed like most of the women in her audience, Kuhlman presented herself as an average 1950s woman who just happened to be leading a television ministry.

As further visual validation of her role as leader, Kuhlman filled the stage with men, all dressed in suits and ties, lined up in ranks behind her. These men provided unequivocal imagery of male support for her leadership. Joining her in songs, the men were the early form of Kuhlman's beloved "Men's Chorus." (By the first episodes of her subsequent television show *I Believe in Miracles* in 1967, the Kathryn Kuhlman Men's Chorus would be hundreds strong.) Kuhlman was almost always the only female on the platform until the testimonials began, although a few episodes included women in the chorus behind her. Her organist, Charles Beebee, and pianist, Jimmy Miller, were both male, and like many of the great evangelists before her, Kuhlman had her soloist. On *Your Faith and Mine*, the featured singer was Lem Stroud, an attractive man who sang the gospel hymns with emotion and restraint. The voice that announced her show was also male. Men were present everywhere in the images and sounds of the show, but always in supporting roles. Surrounding Kuhlman on her television show were visual and aural affirmations of her role as a religious leader by the male adherents in the auditorium.

Kuhlman was exhorter, choir director, and presiding pastor all in one as the opening worship sequence continued. She moved back and forth on the platform, gesturing toward the off-screen audience while shouting out (due to her distance from the stationary microphone), "Turn now in your songbook to number twenty-three, sing that grand old hymn of the church, 'Onward, Christian Soldiers,' and on the chorus while you're finding the number, LIFT IT!" At this point in the show, under her direction, organ, piano, and audience burst into music, with Kuhlman directing and mincing to and from the large microphone on its stand on the toes of her high-heeled shoes. She sometimes sang in a deep alto, sometimes shouted over the hundreds of voices things such as "That's MAHVELOUS," or "Oh, the feeling's wonderful in the auditorium today," or even calling for a repeat of a chorus with "Do it again, I just love it!" The entire auditorium was under her control as Kuhlman's skilled musicians followed her every lead. Obviously trained in revivals and a polished professional at launching a worship service, Kuhlman demonstrated skill in directing the beginning burst of song and praise.[48] Her status as leader was unquestionable, and her ability to fortify that position for the viewing audience through nonthreatening visual reassurances was impressive.

Kuhlman and her production team demonstrated sophistication in the staging of the opening worship sequence, using "tricks of the trade" to offer the most engaging imagery possible. The presentation of the audience was particularly engineered for best effect. The audience was an important presence throughout the shows, as they were heard singing, coughing, responding, and laughing while the camera was focused exclusively on the platform. This mainly unseen company of Kuhlman followers was glimpsed only at the beginning of the show, where in every episode the auditorium appeared to be completely filled. As the cameras switched back and forth from the platform to the audience, every seat was filled on the floor and in the two upper balconies. This was the first impression of her ministry for the television viewer; Kuhlman would not have wanted to show a less than packed auditorium. Empty seats were not her style. This probably contributed also to the occasional use of looped footage on the show. In several episodes, the film of the people singing hymns in the auditorium did not sync up with the sound track. In one episode, the hymn that is heard by the television audience is "I'll Be There." What the looped footage reveals, however, is an audience mouthing the words to "Leaning on the Everlasting Arms."[49] This extended even to the occasional looped footage of her organist and pianist playing out of sync with the notes heard on the track. The program opening often combined new footage of the platform with looped stock film of the auditorium or musicians. Through the magic of editing, Kuhlman consistently stood on the platform in front of a full auditorium as her program broadcast images of a packed house each episode. It is impossible to know if the auditorium was truly filled each episode, but in the mediated and manipulated world of television, Kuhlman's services were always overflowing.

In addition to enhancing the presentation of Kuhlman's ministry, using stock footage for the opening sequences also was a cost-saving measure. Filming the audience every episode would have been cumbersome, with the necessary movement of cameras, microphones, and equipment. Since financial issues were always at play, the looping in of an earlier audience was much cheaper than producing new film each episode. The real reasons for the stock footage probably lay somewhere between good theater and good business.

Film of the *Your Faith and Mine* audience also revealed some of the demographics of Kuhlman's 1950s following. The audiences were mostly white, although some African American and Asian worshipers were always in the crowd and sometimes on the platform. The races were not separated, with African American participants seated next to white. These brief glimpses of an integrated gathering revealed a progressive approach to race for a ministry of the 1950s. Although the group was skewed female, there was a significant male presence. The group wore their "Sunday best" to the service, with all men in suits and ties, women in dresses, often wearing hats and even gloves. It is difficult to estimate the average age since the clothing was so standardized across the age groups at the time, but the group seemed to be predominantly middle-aged and older. When the people rose to sing, many raised one hand during the choruses, a marker of charismatic worship style. In the 1950s, charismatic Christianity was still considered eccentric and even aberrant by mainstream America, and yet Kuhlman's television show featured well-dressed, average people worshiping in a charismatic style that was calm almost to the point of being staid. Combining the professional appearance of Kuhlman with the clean-cut and respectable look of her audience, *Your Faith and Mine* brought to the airwaves a new vision of charismatic Christianity.

The Testimonial

With a revival preacher's skilled touch, Kuhlman's opening worship prepared the room for the next attraction: testimony. In her use of testimonies about healing, Kuhlman was in line with the other healing evangelists of the post–World War II healing revival as described by Harrell: "For the first ten years of the revival the lifeblood of the deliverance ministries was the healing testimonials."[50] Harrell was referring primarily to written testimonies, but for the few early television pioneers like Kuhlman, testimonies were spoken aloud and broadcast to a small but growing viewership. Presenting stories of divine healing each and every week served not only as proof of God's reality but also as proof of the accessibility of God's power for anyone at any time. As Kuhlman repeatedly asserted, "What God did for this person, he can do for you." The testimonies were examples of "your faith and mine," faith in the accessibility of God's miracle-working power as proven by the real-life experiences of everyday people.

When Kuhlman brought her guests to the microphone to testify to their encounters with God's miracle-working power, she was standing in the long history of Christian testimony and its place in revivalistic worship services. Historical patterns of testimony shaped how the stories were told—how they began and how they inevitably concluded. Kuhlman drew upon her days on the revival circuit in the West and her deep familiarity with traditional forms of evangelical and Pentecostal testimony as she carefully directed the stories through skillful prompting. The construction of her show around the testimonies of those who had been spiritually and physically healed revealed a deep connectedness to the radical evangelical/Pentecostal understanding of the applicability of personal testimony.[51]

A comparison of Kuhlman's testimonial pattern with that of her Pentecostal predecessors reveals continuities with classic charismatic Christianity as found in early twentieth-century Pentecostalism.[52] A careful study of the two also points to the changes already occurring in charismatic Christianity by the 1950s, as one branch began to develop into a new and discrete movement. It is interesting, therefore, to examine where the testimonies found on Kuhlman's television show were consistent with Pentecostal precedent, where they varied, and how these variations pointed to the development of distinctive "early charismatic" practices. One important continuity was the simple act of privileging testimony within the worship service.[53] *Your Faith and Mine* was a thirty-minute program, devoid of any advertising. Of those thirty minutes, the first ten were devoted to the highly produced spectacle of worship at the Kuhlman service. The remaining twenty were dedicated to the testimony of the featured guest, where the camera served to create a sense of intimacy as Kuhlman and the testifier came into close-up. During those twenty minutes, Kuhlman's training led her to spotlight the stories of people who had been healed, emphasizing the mediated testimony of God's power rather than raw footage of the Holy Ghost in action. What she presented was the whole story, narrated by the one who experienced it, rather than unmediated images of the Holy Spirit at work, available for interpretation (or, more likely, misinterpretation) by the untrained viewer. The "mysteries" of God revealed in the miracle services needed to be interpreted for uninitiated observers, a role Kuhlman took on as the interviewer of those who had been healed.[54]

No guest on *Your Faith and Mine* was allowed to come up on the platform, grab the microphone, and just begin talking. Kuhlman kept a close narrative rein on the testimonies presented on her shows by directing the speakers through precise prompting, questions, and summaries, carefully overlaying the typical testimonial narrative on the television guest's individual story. The narrative structure of early Pentecostal testimonies was often problematic due to its rigidity. Often, the individual's story was constructed according to, and constricted by, the narrative requirements of the testimonial form. Much the same can be said for the testimonies of those on *Your Faith and Mine*. Kuhlman was strict in her direction of the men and women who testified on her show. She was guiding her guests in the narrative form she had been trained to understand as reflective of the true path from sin to redemption, from sickness to health. Kuhlman helped shape the oral spiritual autobiographies of her guests. Quoting Peter I. Kaufman, Grant Wacker explains, "Autobiography involves an artful arrangement of the narrative to make things come out right." It was part of Kuhlman's job as host and testimonial "emcee" to make sure everything came out right.[55]

Each testimonial segment on *Your Faith and Mine* began with Kuhlman's dramatic summary of "how they got here." Through this, Kuhlman established her control over the story. She determined the parameters of the testimony and then invited the guest to come and "flesh out" the basic narrative she established. Everything was carefully controlled and followed a set pattern. Often it was obvious that Kuhlman knew the people testifying; they were current members of her ministry in Pittsburgh or Youngstown, and their stories were as familiar to her as to themselves. Later in her career Kuhlman would emphasize the "unrehearsed testimony" of her guests. But at this time, most of the guests and testimonials were derived from Kuhlman's own worship services. A genuine affection between Kuhlman and her guests was often evident as well. The men and women did not seem to resent Kuhlman's omnipresence as they told their stories, but often seemed reassured and encouraged by her guidance. Many stood rigid and nervous in front of the television cameras as Kuhlman gently and deftly helped them tell their story. Some were given more freedom to speak, but it was quickly apparent that the "freedom" was granted because they had memorized their story in advance. It was likely that Kuhlman had heard their testimony before, perhaps in another miracle service, and was therefore able to retreat somewhat from her controlling stance. Whether memorized or freestyle testimony, Kuhlman was there, always there, moving and shaping the stories through word and action, pacing the show to fit smoothly into its time slot, skills learned in revivals and radio studios.

One testimonial segment concerned the redemption of Johnny Stake, called "Two-Gun Johnny." With the organ music following her every emotion, Kuhlman set up the testimony of the guest. She told a story of "a young wife in battle, her husband leaving, her children in jeopardy. The husband threatened the young wife's life."[56] As Kuhlman spoke, she leaned into the microphone. Her wide, unblinking eyes swept the auditorium, then rested on the camera. She told of receiving a letter from this young wife, and then quoted the letter from memory, her eyes never leaving the camera. "Will you, Miss Kuhlman, Sunday, preach—preach like ya never preached before. It's the only thing that will save our family, our home." After this rendition of the dramatic cry for help from the young wife, Kuhlman told of her own effort to reach Johnny. "Sunday night, I preached a one-man sermon. Only God knows how I put every ounce of strength in that sermon. All I could think about was four children. I was fighting for four little children!" Her voice rose and faltered according to the emotion of the story. The auditorium, filled with hundreds of people, was perfectly quiet. "When I gave the altar call, I pled for the soul of that man. . . . Before I finished, I saw that man move. But not forward; instead, he turned around and walked out of that auditorium." Kuhlman sat back on her heels, curled her arms around her torso in a typical pose, and paused before continuing. "Hard. I'd never seen a man quite that hard." At this point, the story of "Two-Gun Johnny" was already filled with pathos and emotion, and he had not even been seen. Enough was known of the typical plotline of the testimony to assume Johnny would be redeemed, and that he was even in the auditorium at the time. Kuhlman skillfully continued the story to its inevitable, dramatic climax: "Johnny came back, at the very next service. He came back, and dropped to his knees, sobbing."

Often after the dramatic setup, Kuhlman would call the name of the person in a way that implied she did not know where the person was in the auditorium. In this episode, she called out across the auditorium, "Johnny, are you here, Johnny? Where are you, Johnny? Come on up here and talk to me!" The sounds of the audience clapping and Kuhlman's encouraging "That's right, come on, that's right" gave the viewer the sense of the testifier's approach and the excitement it was creating in the room. As Kuhlman called out for them, the entire family of "Two-Gun Johnny" walked on to the screen from the right. The group consisted of the surprisingly small and tidy Johnny, his wife (who was never named), and their four children, all attired in dresses and suits. Of course, Kuhlman was not truly unaware of the whereabouts of the people she featured on the show. This was good theater; she was creating a sense of expectancy and excitement. But she also was taking a risk. She could potentially undercut her integrity with a television audience unfamiliar with the more theatrical style of charismatic testimonies. Kuhlman's artificial naïveté ran the risk of disturbing the suspension of disbelief necessary in a television show. In other words, the audience could catch on. This could generate one of two responses in the viewer: either the viewer would enjoy being in on the game, as Kuhlman claimed to know absolutely nothing about her guests and their stories, or the viewer would find the ploy disingenuous or simply irritating and turn the set off. With charismatic Christianity's tenuous place in American religious culture in the 1950s, including a stereotype of hucksterism, Kuhlman's seemingly harmless manipulation of reality ran the risk of alienating the very viewers she was hoping to attract.[57]

Despite its risks for the gentrification of charismatic Christianity, the emotional buildup to the testimony was typical of *Your Faith and Mine* episodes. Kuhlman often shaped the testimonies on the show by controlling who spoke and when. In the instance of "Two-Gun Johnny," as Johnny was slowly overshadowed by his garrulous spouse, Kuhlman directed the testimony by shutting down the talkative wife and drawing the attention back to Johnny. At one point, as the wife was talking, Kuhlman stopped her, saying, "Now, honeybunch, you wait and let Johnny tell that." The wife seemed unable to contain herself, however, and Kuhlman then physically pulled her to the side and placed Johnny at the microphone. (In another episode, Kuhlman's voice can be heard off-screen prompting under her breath a Mrs. Kichline to "Speed it up, speed it up.") This was in part skilled interviewing with a sharp sense of how much time was available for the testimonies in a thirty-minute program. Kuhlman had an excellent sense of momentum and pacing, expertise learned in radio and revivals. She also had a strong will to direct the speakers to the end she desired, and was unafraid to exert her authority to keep things moving.

As Johnny Stake continued his story, he confessed to an addiction to alcohol that almost destroyed him and his family. He then testified to being delivered from liquor. His speech was blunt and simple as he said, "I kept trying to pull myself up, didn't think of the Lord. You can't do it yourself." Using this statement as a segue, Kuhlman turned to the camera and began to speak directly to the television audience. She said she was addressing "a young man out there." "You're a slave to sin, bud," she stated flatly. "You're weak." She encouraged her viewers to "slip to their knees," to confess their faith in Jesus Christ, and to be saved from sin and delivered from alcohol. It was a classic evangelical altar call. At this point in her career, Kuhlman was still primarily an evangelist, with the miracles of divine healing serving as means to an end, the end always being salvation of the individual. She was trained by evangelists whose religious background was radical evangelicalism, with its emphases equally distributed between salvation and healing.[58] Although she was teaching and preaching divine healing by 1950, her ministry was still strongly tied to bringing about the "new birth experience."

Changing Perceptions

At the same time, Kuhlman's career was changing. She was becoming known as much as a faith healer as she was as an evangelist. She began most of the testimonials on her show with a tale of intense longing for God's action, a pattern she likely learned in her early ministry. The testimonies of classic Pentecostals also began with the same expressions of deep desire for what they called "an endouement [endowment] of power."[59] This was the first step of the three that made up the blueprint for classic Pentecostal testimony, the pattern Kuhlman drew upon and modified on *Your Faith and Mine*. Using the Pentecostal template she knew by heart, Kuhlman shifted its perspective and guided the testimonies on her show toward a different end. For her guests, the "endouement" that was sought was physical or spiritual healing. This was different from Pentecostal testimonies. The Kuhlman testimonies did not speak about a desire to witness, or to heal others, or to exorcise—all typical endowments of power coveted by early Pentecostals. The yearning of the Kuhlman testimonies was not for the baptism of the Holy Ghost. There was little to no emphasis on the baptism of the Holy Spirit as such, and almost no reference to the evidentiary sign of speaking in tongues. Baptism in the Holy Spirit as a vital part of the process of salvation and sanctification quietly dropped away. The new-birth experience also played only a supporting role in most of the testimonies. Kuhlman stated throughout her career that the greatest miracle was a transformed life, a life marked by "the new-birth experience." Although this may have been declared the greatest miracle, it was almost always eclipsed by divine healing in the dramatic stories featured on *Your Faith and Mine*. By shifting the emphasis to divine healing and away from Holy Ghost baptism or being "born again," Kuhlman helped define divine healing as the central desire and endowment of power in the testimonies of charismatic Christians.

One episode of *Your Faith and Mine* contained a particularly powerful account of one man's yearning for physical healing.[60] The story of Carey Reams also became one of the chapters in Kuhlman's best-selling book *I Believe in Miracles*. The show opened as usual, with singing and prayer. Then, with organ music swelling beneath her, Kuhlman began to recount the basics of the story of Carey Reams. "I shall never forget that day," Kuhlman stated. She told of a man who had read an article about her in *Redbook* magazine, and because of that article made a pilgrimage to one of her miracle services. Continuing her standard dramatic introduction, Kuhlman remembered the service drawing to a close as she gave the benediction. Suddenly, she recalled, she stopped, and looked out into the wheelchair section, where she saw a man staring up at her. "I walked off the platform to him and said, 'Stand up.' He said, 'I can't.' He stood up with the crutches, and I said, 'Hand me the crutches.' He bowed his head and asked God to be merciful. I said, 'Sir, he will be merciful—look up, don't look down; Jesus is up, not down!' And then he began to walk." While Kuhlman spoke, a tall, dark-haired man in his late forties, dressed in a suit and tie, walked on to the platform and stood quietly next to her.[61] It was immediately apparent that this healthy and strong individual was the man in Kuhlman's story. Kuhlman brought the audience into this testimony at its most dramatic moment, the moment of divine healing. Having set the testimony in motion toward this conclusion, she retreated from the picture and allowed Reams to begin to speak for himself.

Carey Reams was soft-spoken and gentle in manner. He told how he suffered a grave injury in World War II. On January 5, 1945, he was in a truck in Lausanne, Switzerland, that was blown up. He recalled, "My back and neck were broken in the explosion, and I was unconscious in a military hospital for thirty-one days. I was paralyzed from the waist down for six years, and went through forty-one operations. After my last operation, the doctors gave me very little hope. I was hemorrhaging. Then friends sent me a copy of the *Redbook* magazine with the article about Kathryn Kuhlman's healing ministry inside." Faced with no hope from the medical community, he concluded his background story in a soft voice: "I realized my only hope was God." Reams decided to make the trip to Pittsburgh, not knowing exactly what would happen. "I got on the bus. Either I'll be healed or I won't make it back. It didn't make any difference."[62] He had begun the search for divine healing, an endowment of God's miracle-working power.

The next step in the testimonial pattern is facing what Grant Wacker calls "the Terrible Test."[63] Reams was convinced by his doctors that there was no medical hope after his last operation. On December 26 he left his home in Florida, alone on a bus, in a final effort to make it to Pittsburgh for a miracle service. He arrived in Pittsburgh on Friday, but was too late to make the evening miracle service at Carnegie Hall. "My heart sank," he said. On Saturday, he had a hemorrhage "that almost took me away." Despite his desperate physical condition, Reams discovered Kuhlman was going to hold a service in Butler, Pennsylvania, the next day. He was determined to go. Unable to walk on his own, Reams enlisted the help of two men to get him into a cab to make the journey. After an excruciating trip, Reams arrived at the service in Butler. He described his experience: "Over fifty men gave their heart to Christ that day. That impressed me much. A worker asked me if I wanted to give my heart to Christ. I said yes. Healings began. You [Kuhlman] said you didn't intend for healings that day, but they started." Kuhlman often held evangelistic services at this time that were not focused upon physical healing. She concentrated her healing ministry in the Friday night "miracle services" in Pittsburgh, which Reams had missed. Reams continued, "I was sitting near the front. My hopes began to rise by the moment. And then the meeting went on, and you was closing the service, Ms. Kuhlman, and . . . [up until this point

Reams had been staring slightly down at the floor, and now he looked up at Kuhlman] . . . I wasn't healed. I was disappointed." Kuhlman gently replied, "Were you?" At this point in the autobiography, Reams had come to the end of his options. He had made his final pilgrimage and faced the Terrible Test in hopes of being endowed with divine healing. He had not been healed.

Carey Reams had, however, received salvation. Reams's testimony followed the standard formula of salvation followed by healing. This was the typical format for testimonies on *Your Faith and Mine*, where salvation received a nod as the story rushed forward to healing. Reams continued: "But you called my name." Reams's voice broke as he looked at Kuhlman. With a teary voice, the big man said, "You told me to stand. To look up." He looked over at Kuhlman at this point. "I've been looking up ever since." An emotional Kuhlman whispered, "God bless ya." Reams passed the Terrible Test and received his "endouement" of power. "Miss Kuhlman, I can walk. I haven't had a hemorrhage since. The next day I bought a truck, drove back to Florida unaided. I opened a business, and I still have it today." Kuhlman had him bend his legs, and he said, "Oh, I can bend them—I can pick you up and carry you across the platform!" he said, laughing good-naturedly, and the audience laughed with him. Kuhlman narrowed her eyes with a smile and said, "You better not try!" "I know that, Miss Kuhlman!" Reams said, and the auditorium was filled with laughter and applause.

Carey Reams bore witness to divine healing, the centerpiece of the testimony of charismatic Christianity, with deep roots in its Pentecostal ancestry.[64] Divine healing gave classic Pentecostalism life;[65] it gave charismatic Christianity a center. Divine healing became one of the most important orienting beliefs for charismatic Christianity, although it never reached "evidentiary" status in the way tongues did for Pentecostalism. In charismatic Christianity, the baptism of the Holy Spirit resulted in healing: spiritual, physical, or both. This was distinct from Pentecostalism, where the Holy Ghost baptism brought tongues as the first sign, or non-Pentecostal evangelicalism, where the sign of the Holy Ghost was being "born again." This shift in perspective gave early charismatics an important organizing belief. The testimonies of divine healing on *Your Faith and Mine* helped charismatic Christianity develop its own understanding of healing, in continuity with but distinct from its Pentecostal forebears.

Raw Testimony

Kuhlman's early television show also included the sometimes unrefined details of physical restoration. Early Pentecostal testimonials had set a pattern of unvarnished honesty about describing the effects of the Holy Spirit.[66] During the post–World War II healing revival, that tendency toward frankness was retained by the early charismatics in the free sharing of earthy details of physical healing, details that were sometimes bizarre. Harrell found this gritty testimony in his research:

> For the first ten years of the [post–World War II healing] revival the life-blood of the deliverance ministries was the healing testimonials. Hundreds of thousands of testimonials were published—frequently in indelicate detail. Evangelist LeRoy Jenkins recorded a typical description of a cancer healing: "The next night the Lord spoke to me and told me she had a cancer. He told me to have her bring a jar to church and she would spit up the cancer. After [three nights of] prayer, she was healed. She spit up a bloody cancer which had long roots on it. She had a terrible time as it almost choked her to death while it was coming up."[67]

Testimonies of cancers leaving the body in graphic ways were found on Kuhlman's show as well. A Mrs. Turner told of her cancer of the liver, stomach, gallbladder, and "pankrees" (pancreas) that had been confirmed by five doctors. After exploratory surgery, she remembered that the doctors "sewed me up and sent me home to die." The family sent in a prayer request to Kuhlman's ministry. Mrs. Turner commented, "Before daylight my bowels started to move, and they moved for thirty-six hours, every ten minutes." Obviously interested and not the least discomfited, Kuhlman asked for more details: "What was passing from your body?" Mrs. Turner replied, "Poison, and the cancer." Mrs. Turner then followed up with a quick note that her husband had also received a healing, and "had vomited up a piece of something—green, purple and everything."[68]

It is surreal to watch these carefully coiffed women in hats and gloves speak calmly about what should have been embarrassing details of bodily functions. But for these people, and for Kuhlman, the particulars of the Holy Spirit's work in their bodies were details of life-saving miracles, things to be celebrated. In addition, the rough features added authenticity to the stories. These are not pretty little tales of magical mending, but sometimes coarse testimonies of purging, cleansing, and healing of sick bodies. In one episode, a grandmother and granddaughter shared distressing aspects of the little girl's horrific eczema.[69] The grandmother stood next to Kuhlman, who lifted up a beautiful little curly-haired toddler on to a chair so the camera could fit all three in the frame. The child shyly gazed into the camera as Kuhlman twisted her curls around her finger and listened to the grandmother. With a thick eastern European accent and misshapen teeth, the woman spoke of her granddaughter as "all raw, just like raw meat." Covered with scabs, "she was so ugly, you just couldn't love her no more." She was afraid the disease was going to eat the little girl's ears off. "The scabs was in her head, too," she offered. Sickness can be an ugly thing, and these testimonies did not shy away from the grotesque.

The men had their share of coarse testimony as well. Harry Stephenson told his story of cancer healing, an account also made into a chapter in the book *I Believe in Miracles*. Stephenson began by explaining he had cancer of the stomach and bowels for ten years. The doctors dismissed him. Nothing else could be done for him, and he went home to die. "The odor from my body was so bad I had to live outside in a shed," he shared.[70] Then there was Harold Suttles, who was told by his doctors he had cancer of the tongue, and "we can use radium or we can cut your tongue out."[71] Mr. Suttles wrote Kuhlman, and upon receiving a letter from her, was converted to belief in Christianity. He said, "The cancer come out; it backed up out of my tongue like a fishin' worm." In Kuhlman's later television career, these types of earthy testimonies were not as common, replaced by stories of much more sanitized healings. However, in the early days, she shared with her television audiences the raw data of raw lives. The people featured on *Your Faith and Mine* lived working-class lives filled with struggles. A few details about bowels didn't seem to faze these folks at all.

Other aspects of traditional Pentecostal testimony appeared in the episodes of *Your Faith and Mine*. Classic Pentecostals often included in their stories the negative and positive motivations for their pursuit of the "endouement" of power. Converts pointed to financial disasters, relationship problems, even tragedies such as the loss of a child as factors that motivated them to begin their spiritual search in earnest. Some observers interpreted stories like these as "compensation narratives," where the person was given Holy Spirit power as repayment for tragedy or suffering. But even as they acknowledged distressing and even devastating experiences in their testimonies, Pentecostals resisted framing the subsequent reception of Holy Spirit power as "God's reimbursement."[72]

83

One particular episode of *Your Faith and Mine* stands as a prime example of the nuanced approach to compensation models of divine healing charismatics inherited.[73] The episode focuses on the story of a young woman named Maxine. Kuhlman set up the story with all the vivid details of her standard introductions. She told of the day when one of her office workers received a phone call. "A young woman called. She was blind due to trying to kill herself, and had only been blind for nine weeks. She was twenty-nine years old, and had a six-year-old daughter. She listens to the radio broadcast in Canton, Ohio. She doesn't even know what I look like!" While Kuhlman spoke, a male usher led a young woman into the picture and placed her next to the evangelist. The woman's eyes were tightly closed, and all around the eye sockets the skin was darkened and appeared bruised. Her hair was shorn short. The young woman smiled as Kuhlman took hold of her and stated, "I'm going to promise you something; one day you will know what I look like!" The audience applauded loudly as Maxine's smile widened and she nodded in agreement.

Maxine told Kuhlman, "I thought to myself, I should get a gun and shoot myself." Kuhlman replied, "You thought death would end everything." Maxine periodically opened her eyes, which rolled slowly and unseeingly as she spoke. Kuhlman placed her arm around her, and it remained around the woman's shoulders throughout her testimony. As Maxine spoke, Kuhlman prompted and guided with questions and restatements. Maxine continued, "I just heard a blood-curdling scream, and then I realized it was my voice. The bullet went clear through my head and came out on the other side." At this, there were audible murmurs from the auditorium. Kuhlman kept her arm around Maxine's shoulder and with her other hand took Maxine's chin and turned her head so that the small, dark, round scar from the wound was visible to the audience. "The people who found me couldn't find a pulse," Maxine added. Kuhlman released her chin. "The coroner came, he found a little pulse, and they operated on me. I was moved into a new hospital room with a seventy-four-year-old lady with a broken back. I heard her praying, and I was, 'Oh! Did they put me in with someone like that?'" People would come to visit the woman, and "they would talk and talk. Then I began to listen. They talked about salvation." Kuhlman interjected, "You never went to church?" Maxine replied, "I'd go on Easter if I had a new hat, y'know." There was laughter from Kuhlman and the audience. Maxine resumed, "I never prayed, or I forgot how to pray. I never read the Bible." She told how a minister began to come and read the Bible out loud to her in her hospital room. "The minister asked me if I ever listened to Kathryn Kuhlman. I began to listen to you, and I decided I wanted to go." Maxine continued her story, explaining that her traumatic near-death experience and subsequent blindness led her to Kuhlman, and through Kuhlman to salvation. Through Kuhlman's ministry, Maxine received salvation but not the divine healing of her blindness.

In conclusion, Maxine declared, "I'll tell you one thing—if this is what it took, then it's worth it. I have found God. I can't smell, I can't taste. If God wants me to be blind, it's all right." The compensation of salvation was presented as sufficient for the loss of her sight. Kuhlman did not challenge Maxine's statement implying God's willingness to blind the young woman to bring her to salvation. With tears streaming down her face, Maxine smiled as she said, "I'm completely happy. I have peace." Testimonies such as Maxine's are troubling because of the interpretation of abject suffering as pedagogical. Critics harshly denounced this tendency in the ministries of faith healers. At the same time, Maxine's testimony of spiritual healing was compelling precisely because of her triumph over her tragedy. These types of testimonies form a continuous, unsettling line from classic Pentecostalism to charismatic Christianity, revealing both admirable courage and disquieting theology in adherents all along its course.

A final type of healing testimony featured in both Pentecostal history and *Your Faith and Mine* is the spiritual autobiography of the recovered "drunkard."[74] Kuhlman featured the story of a man called "Paddy" and his boss, Mr. Wilson.[75] Mr. Wilson was a long-suffering employer during Paddy's days of terrible drinking. Kuhlman called them on to the stage, wiggled between them, and bent into the microphone to say, "Tell the folk." Paddy began to talk; he had one tooth missing, an Irish accent, and a face that showed years of hard living. He said he spent many years either drunk or in jail, until one day his employer's wife, Mrs. Wilson, asked him to go to Stambaugh Auditorium to see Kuhlman. "Mrs. Wilson asked me if I wanted to quit drinking," Paddy remembered. "I didn't have any place to go, and Mr. Wilson's wife invited me to their house. I looked terrible. I was half liquored up at their house." Mrs. Wilson went out, and Paddy got drunk. "I said it was going to be my last drink." He had been in the city jail twenty-two times in one year. Coming back around to the question that had started his testimony, Paddy said, "No, I didn't want to drink." He went on to say he had since quit drinking, and the audience applauded enthusiastically. Mr. Wilson added, "Pat is a model employee now." Kuhlman wrapped up the testimony by saying, "It's not willpower, it's the power of God. The power of sin—you're helpless; only One can break that power. When you come to him, he'll set you free. It's real, believe me, people, it's real!"

Kuhlman guest Nick Harden, a recovered alcoholic, exemplified the Pentecostal testimonial trope that divine healing from alcohol addiction resulted in practical changes in the recipient's everyday life, yielding improvements in family, marriage, and work.[76] Kuhlman began her typically dramatic introduction by stating, "You can verify everything at the police department of Warren, Ohio." This show featured the story of the Harden Gang, a "gang" consisting of Nick Harden and his brother, both of whom were converted through the Kuhlman ministry. Harden told of a friend asking, "Nick, you coming to work?" and his reply, "No, I'm too busy gettin' drunk." After his experience with Kuhlman's ministry, "The desire [for alcohol] instantly left me. My eighteen-year-old nephew had never seen me sober until my conversion." Harden told of all the new things he bought with the money that used to go to liquor. Kuhlman added, "He is through being plastered and is now a plasterer!" In an emotional moment, Harden's young son and daughter came on to the platform to join him. "My son has never seen me drunk," he said with pride, and teared up as he looked at his children. The son said, "My daddy's a Christian daddy." Conversion to charismatic Christianity took on very utilitarian functions in these testimonies.[77]

Perhaps the most interesting and entertaining episode concerning deliverance from alcohol was the show featuring Mrs. Kilgore, her husband, and friends.[78] A group of unsmiling, awkward men and women in Sunday dress shuffled on to the platform with Kuhlman as she began the testimonial segment. Kuhlman introduced Mrs. Kilgore with the lead-in, "She was a waitress in a tavern. One day, while she was serving beer to four men, she overheard a conversation about Kathryn Kuhlman the preacher." Mrs. Kilgore took up the story. "They was talkin' about the healings." After this, Mrs. Kilgore began listening to Kuhlman on the radio, but her husband wasn't interested. The following Sunday, Mrs. Kilgore, along with the cook at the tavern, the cook's husband, and a waitress, went to the Kuhlman service. Kuhlman laughed, "The whole outfit got converted." Kuhlman began to ask questions of each of the members of the group of converts. George, Ruth, and Floyd told of their respective conversions. They then revealed that despite these conversions happening all around him, Mr. Kilgore did not convert until a year later.

Kuhlman threw up her arms and called Mr. Kilgore forward with a rousing "Come here, you old rascal!" ("Rascal" was a favorite epithet for the rough men who became an active part of Kuhlman's ministry.) The man stepped forward, grinning sheepishly, but obviously enjoying the attention from Kuhlman and his chance to be on television. He stated, "I was a drinking man for twenty years. I think I could float a battleship. I went to church drunk." Kuhlman interjected, "You must have been something." He spoke for a moment about praying that he would stop drinking. Kuhlman asked, "How did you pray?" He replied, "Dear Jesus, deliver me from liquor . . . but I hope you don't." The audience broke into laughter, as Kilgore beamed. Becoming serious, he then stated that he was "six years sober." Kuhlman declared rhetorically to the audience, "Wanna know whether these healings last?" For the finale, Kuhlman told the audience that now the Kilgores' daughter had converted. "Far more wonderful than a physical healing," Kuhlman ended with her constant refrain, "is the transformation of a human life."

Wrapping Up

Each episode ended with a passionate altar call to the viewing audience. Fading from Kuhlman's final prayer, the image of her hands closing a Bible washed over the screen. Closing credits overlay a tree in the sunset as the announcer intoned his good-byes. From worship to testimony to altar call, *Your Faith and Mine* was a unique presentation of old-time evangelical revivals and classic Pentecostal testimony, with a twist. Kuhlman harnessed the advantages of technological innovation in media with skills learned on the sawdust trail. She was a leader in the post–World War II healing revival, where she was the only female leader of note who made the difficult and expensive transition to television ministry from radio. Kuhlman carefully constructed her image, and presented that image effectively on a program dedicated to the tried-and-true power of first-person testimony. With her strong evangelical optimism about media technology, Kuhlman made a brave first leap into the realm of television ministry.

Your Faith and Mine exists today in only twenty-two episodes. Although there may have been more, the show does not seem to have been a smashing success. It would be almost a decade before she again televised her ministry at Stambaugh Auditorium in a new Technicolor talk show called

I Believe in Miracles. In the early black-and-white days of *Your Faith and Mine*, she created a unique format of televised testimony that set the stage for her highly successful sequel. Before the television show *I Believe in Miracles*, however, there was the best-selling book by the same name, which began Kuhlman's rapid rise to cultural celebrity and leadership in the growing charismatic renewal movement. Her future faced just one inescapable obstacle: she was a woman.

CHAPTER 4

Leading Lady

"Why aren't there more women preachers?" The editors of *Christianity Today* did not sidestep the issue of gender in the 1973 interview with Kathryn Kuhlman. "You will just have to ask God," she replied. "I don't know. I really don't know; but I wouldn't wish this job on any woman, I'll tell you that. If you think it's easy try it."[1] Kuhlman was correct; establishing and maintaining authority as a female religious leader in the charismatic renewal movement was anything but easy. Charismatic Christianity in mid-twentieth-century America was a conservative environment for women's religious leadership. It was a diffuse movement that drew from a variety of streams within American Christianity, none of which were enthusiastically supportive of women commanding a ministry. With roots in Pentecostalism, the divine healing revival of the 1940s, and still-conservative mainline churches, charismatic Christianity was dominated by male leaders. It was no easier for a woman to make her way as a leader in the charismatic renewal in the 1950s and early 1960s than it was in contemporary Pentecostalism or evangelicalism. The same rules applied. Organizations where women's leadership was already defined and denied provided what little structure there was in the renewal movement. Because of this, the movement did not experience the common first phase of new religious movements where a lack of structure and organization makes room for the leadership of women. Its ready-made tradition was derived from long-established groups with long-established prejudices against female leadership. Even though women came into the charismatic renewal movement from a changing culture where second-wave feminism was taking shape, inside the auditoriums of charismatic worship services, women were not welcome in positions of authority.

In her challenge to the editors of *Christianity Today*, Kuhlman stated concerning ministry, "If you think it's easy try it." She seemed oblivious to the fact that many women in fact *did* want to "try it," and were contending for equality in all aspects of their lives, including ministerial opportunities. Especially as women in the culture and in churches all around her were struggling for equality, Kuhlman could have offered her voice in support of their efforts. Kuhlman chose not to support women's efforts at equality in female religious leadership. Although she succeeded in her own right, she failed to use her leverage to help dismantle the oppressive system that placed obstacles in the way of female religious leaders like her. The significant influence she garnered through her media presence and her privileged position as the only public female leader in the charismatic renewal movement placed a burden of responsibility upon her to speak on behalf of women's religious leadership, a responsibility she chose to disregard. Instead, she spoke in support of the conservative system she herself was flouting.[2]

Domesticating Her Image

In the late 1950s and early 1960s, the popular cultural definition of postwar womanhood "retreated into domesticity."[3] Kuhlman had an innate sense of the importance for her leadership of embodying roles defined by this domestic sphere she did not in truth inhabit.[4] As a woman living a life contrary to the one her audience revered, she worked diligently to present a manipulated image that was reassuring and safe. Kuhlman was a divorcée without children, but understood the power of the domestic images of wife and mother for her own ministry. Stories about her parents gave Kuhlman the opportunity to reinforce the uneven power relationships in marriage she herself rejected. She described a folksy hierarchy where the woman gained power through manipulation of the man. Her father Joe was the mayor of Concordia, and in Kuhlman's words, "Papa was mayor, but momma ran the town," or in other words, "Papa did the work, and Mama ran Papa without Papa knowing it. It was a beautiful situation."[5] Kuhlman promoted this type of unhealthy relationship between husband and wife with a smile and wink while simultaneously retaining complete control over her entire ministry and life. Mama may have run

Papa, but Kuhlman ran her life on her own and by her own rules, despite her kitschy rhetoric.

Kuhlman's divorce was a black eye in her presentation of herself as a paragon of average womanliness. Although she rarely spoke publicly about Burroughs Waltrip, her time as a married woman was fairly well known among her followers. If for some reason they didn't know, they soon would, since her divorced status was a favorite weapon opponents trotted out against her. In 1952, the newspapers in Akron, Ohio, followed what they dubbed "The Battle of the Pulpits." Asked to participate in huge healing meetings led by Rex and Maude Aimee Humbard, Kuhlman waded into a mud-slinging controversy with Akron's fundamentalist Baptist minister Dallas Billington. Billington attacked Kuhlman as a fake healer, an unscriptural female preacher, and basically just a poor imitation of Aimee Semple McPherson. He also denounced her as a divorcée.[6] Billington offered to pay Kuhlman $5,000 if she could prove even one person had been healed at her meetings. Kuhlman offered to give the money she would certainly win to a local charity, and began to gather followers to testify to Billington. This set off a back-and-forth war of words between the two, carried gleefully by the local newspapers, which ended in an impasse. Billington upped the ante by demanding that the Kuhlman ministry present a person healed by Kathryn's prayers. Kuhlman explained that she did not believe her prayers were the means by which anyone was healed. (Touché.) After a few more rounds in the press, Billington withdrew his offer, and Kuhlman returned to the Humbard tent meetings. The "battle" was a draw,[7] but the specter of the "disgraced divorcée" was raised again.

In another example of Kuhlman's vulnerability to criticism based on her divorce, a Mr. Edgar L. Dickson sent a typewritten letter to the *Pittsburgh Press* from Denver, Colorado, to make sure Kuhlman's marital past was remembered. Accompanied by what must have been a disparaging article that appeared in the *Denver Post*, Dickson wrote on July 12, 1954:

> Dear Sir: You don't know me, of course, but since Kathryn Kuhlman is such a well-known figure both in the Pittsburgh and Denver areas, I just thought that possibly you might find the enclosed article on the evangelist Kathryn Kuhlman interesting. . . . If you are further interested in the facts about this controversial and sensational "evangelist," the full facts are available either through The Denver Post or through me. The facts include how her Denver congregation left her after she wooed one

of her visiting evangelists away from his wife and two children in Texas, married him, and then later divorced him also, making this her second divorce. This man's name was Burroughs Waltrip.

Kuhlman was incorrectly accused by Dickson of being a divorcée twice over; once apparently wasn't enough. Dickson also had information about "How she got into serious difficulties in Mason City, Iowa. How she aided her old sister Myrtle Parrott to get a divorce from her preacher husband of 25 years in 1951." Then the writer added what was likely the whole point of the letter: "How she destroyed my own ideal marriage of 13 years through her evil domination of my wife." With a final flourish, Dickson concluded, "If you want more information, I have a complete and chronological report of her less public activities, with full proof of everything stated. Hoping to hear from you soon. Sincerely yours, Edgar L. Dickson."[8] Dickson's efforts revealed the threat Kuhlman's divorce presented throughout her career.

Kuhlman lived a busy life as a divorcée, but knew her audience was not comfortable with divorce as a life choice for their leader. She would have been familiar with McPherson's divorces and how her ministry had survived the dissolution of the marriages, but Aimee was different: Aimee remarried. Despite her own background, or perhaps because of it, Kuhlman did not choose to advocate for the validity of life as a single woman. Publicly, she never dated and never allowed herself to be connected romantically with any man. Marriage was consigned to her past, a past she often described as characterized by naïveté, recalcitrance, and stupidity. Kuhlman wanted her marriage and divorce to be seen as missteps made by a young woman too young and dumb to know better and too willful to listen to God's warning. Even more, she just wanted to avoid the topic completely.

Kuhlman's lack of children presented another public relations challenge for her domestic image. With her typical acumen, she attacked this weakness in one way by presenting her public the poignant and effective picture of "a mother who could never be." On one episode of *Your Faith and Mine*, Kuhlman welcomed a young couple with their baby on to the platform. The family was obviously well known to Kuhlman and must have been part of her Pittsburgh or Youngstown congregation. Kuhlman told a favorite story as the couple came on to the stage concerning how disappointed her mother was when she was born without any hair—"just red fuzz." In the background tinkling music played, evoking an infant's music box. Kuhlman took the child from the mother's arms. "You act as though I don't know how to hold babies," Kuhlman said, smiling. "I'm not too good at it. I'm always afraid they'll break." In vignettes like this one, Kuhlman was able to use her lack of children to create a sympathetic image of a devoted woman of God who had given up motherhood for a larger purpose.

"This is a mighty special day," Kuhlman continued as she held the infant. With this, she offered a prayer for the baby and the parents, dedicating the baby in the tradition of denominations that do not perform infant baptisms. "Take this life and make it a power in your service," she prayed over the child. Kuhlman continued to hold the baby and talked about what kind of "mama" she might have been. "If there should ever come a time when you don't want her," she said softly to the parents, "I'll take her."[9] Kuhlman emphasized her childlessness when dedicating babies in her services, a role clearly associated with being a pastor. It was necessary for Kuhlman to destabilize her function as minister in the baby dedications in order to avoid controversy about her role. She used the more acceptable role of the "wistful woman without children" as a protective overlay to diffuse the threatening imagery of pastoral authority connected with the dedication of infants.

Kuhlman's spin on her motherly side was different from her predecessors in religious leadership. These women leveraged their actual motherhood to enhance their authority. Well-known early Pentecostal evangelist Maria Woodworth-Etter, sometimes called "Mother Etter," suffered the loss of five of her six children to illness, leaving a single daughter who lived to adulthood. McPherson was mother to two children, Rolph and Roberta, and often used mothering imagery in her leadership of the Angelus Temple. Sister Aimee was seen as nurturing and compassionate by her followers because of her work with poor children. "Her adoring crowds believed she had a mother's heart for children everywhere."[10] McPherson offered healing services for children where her maternal side was emphasized. She often gave sermons on home life and the family, messages in which she underscored the important role of the Christian mother. In comparison, Kuhlman emphasized the importance of motherhood while sidestepping the fact that she chose not to have children of her own in her brief marriage.[11] She also did not remarry in order to have a family. By the time Kuhlman came into the prime of her ministry, she was in her early fifties and possibly not able to have children naturally. But twenty-odd years separated the end of her marriage from the peak of her celebrity; by her choice, those decades did not produce another marriage or children.

Kuhlman's own prejudices concerning the role of mother were sometimes revealed in episodes of her television series *I Believe in Miracles*. The show on December 8, 1971, began with Kuhlman's standard opening address to the television audience in which she told a story about her "papa." It seemed "Papa" held the wry opinion that only teachers and old maids had "perfect" children. She then introduced "the mother of four teenage girls," Shirley Boone, wife of Pat Boone. The young and attractive Boone was dressed in a pink and white miniskirt outfit with white knee boots and sported sizable blonde hair. The women sat next to each other in large wicker chairs on a stage decorated to look like a garden. "I'll live and die never knowing what kind of mother I might have been," Kuhlman began. Her manner was brisk. "You think it never disturbs me? I sort of envy you. All I can do is come to you and say, 'What constitutes a good mother?' We're going to talk about the nitty-gritty." Boone explained she had given birth to four girls in three and a half years, all while her husband Pat was traveling. Kuhlman asked how she handled discipline in the home, adding, "I was brought up by an old-fashioned mama," a mother who believed in spanking and firm punishment.[12] It was apparent from this conversation and others that Kuhlman's mother was the disciplinarian in their home, at least where Kathryn was concerned. Boone noted that she was forced into the head-of-household position due to Pat's travels. She did not desire the role of disciplinarian and spiritual head, but saw it as her duty. "I believed that God had given me this position as mother," Boone said, but "The man is the head of the house—this is order."

After discussing all that Boone did as a mother while her husband worked on the road, Kuhlman commented, "I feel I've missed so much." At the end of the exchange, Kuhlman again referred to her mother's strong hand in her childhood. "I would like to thank my mama, to kiss my mama's feet. [In heaven] I am going to thank my mama for discipline. She molded my life; she taught me the difference between right and wrong."[13] Kuhlman defined a mother as a woman who ruled her household with a firm hand and submitted to her husband when he was in his proper role. If the man of the house was absent or unable to handle the child (such as Kuhlman's indulgent father), the role of disciplinarian fell to the woman. If a man wouldn't do the job, then a woman had to. This bedrock understanding of domestic roles colored many aspects of Kuhlman's life as a female religious leader. Just as her mother took over when Joe Kuhlman abdicated his responsibilities as disciplinarian, Kuhlman presented herself as one who stepped in as the head of the ministry where a man had refused. She stated, "I'll tell you something confidentially, the true conviction of my heart. I do not believe I was God's first choice in this ministry. . . . I believe God's first choice for this ministry was a man. His second choice, too. But no man was willing to pay the price."[14] Although Shirley Boone did not want to usurp the position of head of her home from her husband, the circumstances dictated her decision. She was "called by God" to the role. Kuhlman was also called by God to take on a role she publicly declared suitable only for a man. Her ability to hold her conventional and conservative domestic views while living the life she did was grounded in this expedient concept of the role of male and female in the home.

Momma Kuhlman

Kuhlman understood and sometimes wielded the power of maternal imagery for the sake of protecting her leadership. Even so, she did not care to be seen as a mother figure. Kuhlman was still working to present herself as young, healthy, and less a mother than perhaps a sexy and vivacious aunt. But by the 1960s, the youth culture had exploded into American consciousness, and the Kuhlman ministry needed a way to relate to this new audience called "teenagers." Always quick to spot the next opportunity, Kuhlman recognized that the charismatic revival among the youth was important. She needed a way to access what was happening among teens and people in their twenties, a group not largely involved in her current radio, book, or television ministry. Kuhlman chose to use maternal imagery, a proven path to success for female religious leaders before her, albeit one she had resisted. By this time Kuhlman's ministry had expanded to include services in California, and she added "youth only" services at the Hollywood Palladium, a venue more associated with rock concerts than with healing services. Kuhlman claimed the worship was so exciting that an upper age limit had to be enforced at the services to keep adults away.[15] "Have you ever had three hundred kisses in one day?" Kuhlman asked at the beginning of one telecast. "I have had [the youth at the services] say thank you for loving us, for helping. At the meeting at the Palladium, [one youth] brought me two dozen long-stemmed red roses, 'just because we love ya.' They've ruined every white dress! They cry on my shoulder, hug me. They want somebody to understand them. They want understanding. They want love."[16] Kuhlman was not motivated purely by motherly affection; she knew she needed to connect with the youth culture for the future viability of her ministry. She also didn't turn to "virtual" motherhood easily, as evidenced by some hedging statements about teenagers such as "I'm not quite sure what my image is to them, whether I'm a sister or a mother."[17] Considering Kuhlman's age, the youth likely saw her as a grandmother. She was willing to turn to maternal imagery to further her career, but identifying herself as "Granny Kuhlman" was still entirely out of the question.

Despite her reluctance to completely domesticate her image, comments Kuhlman made in various places indicated that her interaction with the youth at the Palladium services helped her truly to enjoy the "kids" of the day. She began actively to exploit the role of "mother" to the teenagers of the sixties and seventies. To that end, Kuhlman became involved in the ministry with youth in California led by Chuck Smith. Called the "Jesus People," this group was the focus of a series of episodes of Kuhlman's television show *I Believe in Miracles*. The voice-over at the beginning of each of the telecasts featuring the Jesus People intoned, "The show today is dedicated to youth, showing that the touch of faith is a vital and contemporary encounter."[18] The phrase "the touch of faith" was a standard reference to Kuhlman's ministry; it now needed to be shown that the "touch" was still alive and relevant. Kuhlman was fighting the aging of her ministry and herself. Although she was at the peak of her career, younger ministers such as Ralph Wilkerson and Chuck Smith were drawing the next generation of charismatic Christians in ways Kuhlman wasn't. Wilkerson opened a successful ministry at Melodyland Christian Center in 1969, holding worship services in a refurbished theater. Chuck Smith founded Calvary Chapel in the same period and filled it to capacity with converted "long-haired hippies."

The episodes with the Jesus People, filmed in 1971, captured the most "motherly" imagery Kuhlman ever presented. In her interactions with these "Children of the Day," as one of their music groups was called, Kuhlman moved into a persona of "earth mother" extraordinaire. On these telecasts the production of the show was altered, an extremely unusual action for Kuhlman. The episodes were shot in a studio with a live audience sitting in rows of seats surrounding a central stage. As the show began, rather than the standard organ and choral music, the sound of youthful voices singing the Kuhlman theme song, "He Touched Me," accompanied the opening credits. As the camera panned the studio, it revealed a packed room of young people, most in their teens and twenties. The women wore peasant blouses and jeans or long, loose dresses, their hair often waist length. The men were dressed in tight shirts with wide collars, faded jeans or shorts, and sandals. Impressive sideburns, long flowing hair or bushy Afros on white and black men were typical. On the main stage, situated "in the round," the youth sat cross-legged on the platform, crammed in around three figures seated on chairs in the center. One of the three was a beaming Chuck Smith, minister to the Jesus People, strangely formal in a suit and tie. Seated next to him was Duane Pederson, another leader in the charismatic renewal movement among the youth in California. He was also dressed in a relatively conservative jacket and pants. Kuhlman was the most striking, as she exchanged her trademark flowing sequined gowns in these episodes for a purple and red country print "granny dress," with a high neck and blouson sleeves. "Oh bless ya! I never dreamed that the day would come when I'd be wearing a granny dress!" she laughed at the beginning of one episode. "But I love it! I just love it!" Later in the same show she opened her long arms wide in a gesture to the room full of youth and stated, "I've never been a mother, and now all these wonderful children!"[19]

The shows were marked by a breezy, informal style, with young people rising from their places on the floor to testify about their rejection of drugs, alcohol, and "free love." The show moved easily from testimony to musical performances, as several artists performed the anthems of the movement such as "Come to the Water." The rising star of the Jesus People movement, Lonnie Frisbee, engaged in a lighthearted conversation with Kuhlman, calling her "Kathryn," a privilege rarely taken (or allowed) on the television show. Throughout the free-flowing telecast Kuhlman directed and clapped and laughed from her seat in the center of the mass of hippies. She called to speakers by name, asking them to tell their story or sing a song. Throughout the show, she leaned forward, taking the faces of various young girls in her long fingers, tucking their hair behind their ear and cooing to them about how they shared the love of their "wonderful Jesus." The girls would smile up at Kuhlman as she spoke. In these episodes, Kuhlman nurtured, caressed, and "mothered" the Jesus People. In a self-description not repeated in any other source, she explained to the television audience that the Jesus People referred to their beloved minister Chuck Smith as "Daddy Chuck," then added, to great laughter from the group, "Just call me Momma Kathryn!"[20]

Domestic Misery

Despite her public support of conservative roles for women, Kuhlman once welcomed a guest to her television show who inadvertently revealed the agitation that existed below the surface of women's lives as career and motherhood clashed. This episode emphasized the prevalence of the "restlessness" in women by 1975, a dissatisfaction so pervasive it even infiltrated the carefully controlled and crafted *I Believe in Miracles*. Kecia Fluevog was a successful young model from Finland who had appeared on several magazine covers and in many fashion spreads, and Kuhlman proudly featured her on several episodes of *I Believe in Miracles*. Fluevog credited a Kuhlman meeting with bringing her a new life of faith. On some shows she conversed with Kuhlman and gave her testimony, on others she sang somewhat painfully while awkwardly accompanying herself on the guitar. On these shows Kecia Fluevog was bright and beautiful and happy. On the final show featuring Fluevog, Kuhlman invited her back after a few years' absence from the telecasts to talk about her new role as a mother.

As the camera panned over magazines filled with glossy photos of the beautiful Fluevog, Kuhlman began the conversation. "You are still one of the world's top models." Fluevog did not respond to Kuhlman's assertion, but noted, "I modeled for the magazine *Elegance*, and I had photo shoots in Paris, Mexico City, Tangiers." "Do you enjoy it?" Kuhlman asked. "Love it, love it. Now more than ever, since I've had a break from it." Fluevog left modeling to give birth to a son. She was returning to her career when she visited with Kuhlman. It was not an easy transition. "I am not too thrilled with being a mom," Fluevog confessed. "You're completely at a loss when you have your own child. He is not a placid, relaxed child." Kuhlman asked, "Was it a time of frustration for your life?" Fluevog replied, "I sometimes thought God had abandoned me, that he had put me on the shelf. I found myself really, utterly incapable." Kuhlman gave her standard response: "I've often wondered what I would do with a baby," then quickly redirected the conversation to Fluevog's earlier days and her testimony. The young woman recounted her conversion story, emphasizing the travel, the hard work, and the busy schedule of modeling. "I spent a lot of time on myself," she noted. Kuhlman added, "It was more or less a very selfish life." As Fluevog continued to speak, she began to cry. "God has put restrictions on me. He has wanted to keep me safe." Fluevog seemed to see her forced retirement from modeling due to her pregnancy as God's way of protecting her from the self-serving nature of her career. She struggled to appear thankful for these "restrictions," but was visibly unhappy. "My son makes me tired. I have to pray for patience. I don't have much time to think with Jonathan around." Rallying at the end, Fluevog added, "We are to mature in [God], in marriage, with a child."[21] Despite her final words, Fluevog seemed miserable as a mother, dissatisfied with the domestic life, and acutely nostalgic for her earlier days as a career model. Despite her efforts to rationalize her unhappiness as an opportunity for spiritual growth, her statement that she had been "put on the shelf" revealed frustration at the interruption of her once-bright career. Kuhlman directed the conversation away from Fluevog's struggles and offered a less than helpful response by characterizing Fluevog's career days as "selfish." This was particularly ironic considering Kuhlman's own decision to remain unmarried and childless due to her own career. Kecia Fluevog brought on to Kuhlman's soundstage the very real trials of motherhood, and the Miracle Lady had no healing word for her.

Miss Kuhlman

Kuhlman's image as a female religious leader included maternal aspects, but it was not the persona she preferred. Because of her former marriage, Kuhlman could flirt with her identity as a sexual being: a woman who had been a lover at one time but was now celibate.[22] After her marriage, she was not romantically linked to any man at any time during her career. Her relationship with her young and handsome piano player, Dino Kartsonakis, did attract some attention, but no allegations of impropriety concerning him were proven during Kuhlman's life, or have emerged since.[23] It was undeniable, however, that at least in her public role Kuhlman enjoyed the company of men and men enjoyed being around her. She was supremely confident in her dealings with men on her television shows, especially the stock of recovered alcoholics, drug addicts, and "tough guys" who peopled her ministry in Youngstown and Pittsburgh. On a series of episodes at the very beginning of the run of *I Believe in Miracles*, Kuhlman focused exclusively on the stories of her beloved "Men's

Chorus." Filmed in 1967 on the stage at Stambaugh Auditorium in Ohio, the Men's Chorus stood rank upon rank, consisting of approximately two hundred men, young and old, black and white, who called Kuhlman's ministry their church and Miss Kuhlman their pastor. These episodes reveal preacher lady Kathryn Kuhlman at her coquettish, irrepressible best.

The episodes began with a medley of hymns sung in rousing style by the chorus, "Faith of Our Fathers" being a favorite. As the singing ended, Kuhlman would cry, "This is my reward!" or "I give my life for this!" as she waved her arm to indicate the beaming men behind her. She asked every man who was "delivered from alcohol" to raise his hand, and arms shot up everywhere. Kuhlman then began calling individuals down from the chorus to talk with her. It was obvious she knew each man and his story personally. "Every man on this stage is a living miracle," Kuhlman declared. "I was there when they were born again. Some of these men will say that I pounded them on the back, that I have more strength in my hands than they'd ever seen." Kuhlman's physical presence was a factor in her interactions with the men. She often stood shoulder to shoulder with even the tallest and was just as likely to loom over them due to her high-heeled shoes. Her hands were large and powerful, and she often draped an arm around the men as they spoke with her. Her manner was confident, jovial, and strong. She was in charge, the men knew it, and they respected her for it. "We have everything up here on this platform," Kuhlman said proudly. "There are rich men, there are poor men. There are fat men, there are thin men [she chuckled]. There are plumbers and railroad men and steel employees. I think we have, oh let me think, at the last count over fifteen different nationalities, and one thing I can tell you they all have in common, they are children of the King, heirs of God and joint heirs of Christ Jesus. They are worth fighting for. They are worth giving your life for."[24] Kuhlman's genuine affection for and dedication to the men were plain to see.

The episodes with the Men's Chorus were filled with laughter and mutual delight as Kuhlman called the men down to share stories of deliverance and redemption. Kuhlman used a variety of designations to introduce the men. "Come down here and talk to me, you old rascal!" was a favorite. On one episode she told a tale about "two good-lookin' men" she had come across in her ministry and called forward "Ace," an African American man who was now a part of Kuhlman's ministry, along with his son. After telling the story of his redemption from stealing and alcohol, Kuhlman placed her arm around him and said, "I don't believe any case is hopeless. You were an old reprobate, you know that. And now, you're a son of God." Ace nodded in agreement, a serious look on his face. Kuhlman managed to maintain a careful balance with the men in her ministry, moving easily from a more nurturing persona to a more unabashed and bold deliverance evangelist. Several of the men spoke of her pounding them on the back as she prayed for them, or commanding them to "Let go! Let go!" as they struggled to free themselves from addiction. "Miss Kuhlman," as they called her, was a commanding presence, committed to rescuing the men from their sins.

Kuhlman established a powerful leadership role in the men's lives by tapping into the old and respected role of woman as rescuer and redeemer. At the same time, she reinforced traditional male roles by praising the men for reclaiming their positions of loving father, wage earner, and responsible husband. She reminded Ace, who had eleven children, "No man is without his influence." Ace agreed, telling the television audience to remember, "Your children are watching." This "domestication" of men was a tradition in evangelical revivals. Wacker explains, "Historians of nineteenth-century religion have shown that when evangelical men gave their hearts to Christ, they readily relinquished brawling, drinking, swearing, gambling, and philandering. They proudly replaced, or at least tried to replace, those habits with stereotypically female ones of gentleness, peaceableness, sobriety, and fidelity."[25] Kuhlman managed to domesticate the men in her ministry while allowing them to claim their bygone "rascal" days as proof of their latent "worldly" masculinity. She summarized her opinion of the men in one episode after finishing an interview with the formerly dissolute Micky brothers. She turned to the camera and proclaimed loudly, "It's real! These are men who've lived! These aren't sissies!"[26] In Kuhlman's conversations with "Red" and "Kilgore" (she almost always used nicknames for the men), she said they were "Saints of God now, but both of you were rascals in your day." Red agreed, and Kilgore offered further proof. He claimed that he had always supported his wife coming to the Kuhlman services. "I seen that she got there," he stated. Kuhlman responded with appropriate surprise, and Kilgore added with a big grin, "Gave me more time to go out and drink and do what I please!" The Men's Chorus erupted in laughter; Kuhlman shook Kilgore's arm and declared, "Oh! You men are impossible!" Kuhlman's flirtatiousness with the men of her chorus established an engaging and effective persona. She was able to maintain authority with the men in her ministry by playing coy when necessary, but she also seemed to have a genuine connection with them. They understood each other. The men all had a "past" they had left behind, and so did Kuhlman. Kuhlman's tough love approach made her ministry accessible to tough-living men. She was proud of them, and they were proud of her. Although there is a maternal tint to her interactions with the men, Kuhlman was not so much a "proud mama" as a leader pleased to say, "These are my men."

Women's Work: Miracles and Mystique

Kathryn Kuhlman excelled at navigating successfully in worlds ruled by men. Her career as an author was no different. In the first part of the twentieth century, book publishing was controlled by a select cadre of men who published primarily for others like themselves. The female audience was not considered worth addressing until the 1960s, when readership of magazines such as *McCall's*, *Ladies Home Journal*, and *Redbook* reached the millions. Catching this new wave of female readership, the Kathryn Kuhlman Foundation published *I Believe in Miracles* in 1962. A collection of testimonies concerning healings connected with the Kuhlman ministry, the book was a best seller, with two million volumes sold. One year after, Betty Friedan's seminal book *The Feminine Mystique* hit the market. The book sold a million copies and put feminism in the public eye. Both titles tapped into adaptations in publishing connected with the changing role of women. Women consumers became an attractive demographic for purveyors of books due to their increased buying power. Historian Patricia Bradley explains, "It was not just that women were a large part of the mass media audience—that was not new—but that women were coming into the workforce in ways that gave them independent buying power. . . . Women between the ages twenty-five and fifty-four were on the cusp of exploding into the workforce, a group that increased 45 percent from 1962 to 1975 according to the U.S. Department of Labor."[27] Even then, women readers were seen as a gold mine primarily for the purchase of paperback books and "popular culture" publications, offerings not considered to have intellectual merit. Booksellers assumed the new suburban woman was only interested in cookbooks and would not be enthusiastic about "higher literature."

Feminist scholars have examined this tendency in American culture to feminize the popular forms of media. Sue Thornham summarizes the identifications as "serious/differentiated/critical/masculine, versus trivial/undifferentiated/consuming/feminine." Citing Celia Lury, Thornham notes, "The high-culture/low-culture divide is a thoroughly gendered one, corresponding to a division between mainstream cultural activity and public professionalism on the one hand, and a critically marginalized, privatized, and less 'original' form of production on the other." In other words, low culture is gendered female, high culture is gendered male.[28] So long as literature was considered elite and intellectual, it was gendered male in American culture. Certain types of books remained gendered male, books that were "serious," meaningful, geared toward professionals and the educated elite. Books that were available for the right price and for all audiences became gendered female, and trivialized.

But in the post–World War II market, any book that would sell became a book worth publishing, banal or profound. The 1950s also saw a boom in the mass production of paperbacks, which made books cheaper to publish and more available to the average person. As publishing began to be controlled by profit-minded businesspeople, any and all new audiences were mined as potential markets for books.[29] Publishers took a new interest in titles such as *Mystique* and *Miracles*, books that seemingly held little attraction for the male intelligentsia and whose content appealed to new populations of readers made up primarily of women.[30] Thornham explains, "The desire to meet the demands of the postwar generation prompted commercial underwriters of mass media to seek an inclusive audience, which led to some expression of emerging ideas. [It was] a mix that aimed to please and to please as many as possible."[31] In the case of both *Mystique* and *Miracles*, a book published with the intention of making money by pleasing a trivial and consuming female public instead caused serious engagement of the elite and intellectual, both female and male, and eventually aided in the transformation of the consciousness of women and the gentrification of charismatic Christianity.

The combination of new interest in marketing techniques in publishing and a largely untapped audience of postwar suburban women produced a vital incubator for both second-wave feminism and charismatic Christianity. Many scholars credit Betty Friedan's work as the first expression of second-wave feminism and the inspiration for the women's liberation movement of the 1960s. She defined a restlessness, a sense of dis-ease among suburban women in the 1950s as "the feminine mystique." Friedan's book put feminism in the public sphere and gave a voice to the many women who were dissatisfied with their lives and with society's proscriptions concerning femininity. Bradley notes, "Beginning with *The Feminine Mystique*, mass media brought feminism to millions of women who otherwise might never have been connected to the movement at all."[32] The year before, Kuhlman's best-selling *I Believe in Miracles* hit the booksellers' shelves. In a way similar to *Mystique*, mass media brought the charismatic renewal movement and its main female leader Kathryn Kuhlman, in Bradley's words, "to millions of readers who might never have been connected to the movement at all."

Both Betty Friedan and Kathryn Kuhlman first gained national attention through women's magazines. The popularity of *The Feminine Mystique* can be partly attributed to Friedan's background in magazine journalism. Bradley listed the types of evidence readers of women's magazine articles had come to expect and trust, evidence both Kuhlman and Friedan used to their advantage. These included "the professional voice of the advice columnist, the anecdotal and other 'proofs' of the nonfiction articles, the small but achievable steps presented by the self-help articles, and the epiphanies that routinely climaxed romantic fiction."[33] *I Believe in Miracles* contained many of the same journalistic characteristics as *Mystique* because it was ghostwritten by reporter Emily Gardiner Neal.[34] Kuhlman likely selected Neal because she wrote a glowing article about the evangelist for *Redbook* magazine in 1950, a feature that put Kuhlman in the public eye. Under Neal's influence, *I Believe in Miracles* read very much like the popular magazine journalism of the day. As a result, the readers of Kuhlman's first book were exposed to charismatic Christianity, and to Kuhlman, as interpreted through the talented pen of a professional journalist who was trained in the nuances of magazine writing for a female audience. By using a talented ghostwriter, Kuhlman further polished her public image as well as that of her ministry, and also managed to put charismatic Christianity on the best-seller list.

Kuhlman and Friedan both chose to use domesticated representations of their lives in order to communicate their messages to the American public. Sociologist Ruth Milkman explains, "[Friedan] presented herself as a suburban housewife and mother whose insights into the social subordination of women were forged in the isolation of her kitchen. In fact her personal experience of housewifery was rather minimal, some would say nonexistent."[35]

Friedan herself admitted that her life was not what *The Feminine Mystique* implied. She was asked by an interviewer what she was doing when she wrote *Mystique*:

What was I doing? Well, I was, technically, a housewife in Rockland County, suburban New York, with three kids. I had been kind of free-lancing for women's magazines after I'd been fired from a newspaper job for being pregnant with my second child. And what I later called "The Feminine Mystique" was filling me full of guilt for working. Even though my husband had been in the theater and then starting in advertising, we needed my paycheck, but I'd been feeling so guilty. Now I'm fired. You couldn't look for a job with your belly out to here, pregnant, then— you know, not in those years—well, not now, too. So I was technically a housewife, but I couldn't quite get rid of the itch to do something so I was free-lancing for magazines, mainly the women's magazines, like secret drinking in the morning, because none of the other mothers in that suburb were working then.[36]

Friedan concealed her less-than-average life as a working journalist in order to publish a best seller to suburban housewives. Kuhlman denied her successful pastorate in order to communicate effectively with the conservative charismatic Christian women who made up the bulk of her audience. Both women succeeded in achieving positions of leadership based upon media-created domesticated personas.[37]

Woman Leader but Not Women's Liberator

The celebrity brought on by the publication of *I Believe in Miracles* presented Kuhlman with many opportunities, but also many challenges. In 1962, increased visibility for a woman religious leader carried new pressures to advocate for women's equality. There was a new landscape for female religious leadership in America. Before the 1970s, less than 3 percent of ordained clergy were female. During the 1960s, the peak of Kuhlman's career, second-wave feminism spread into the mainline churches, where battles over female ordination began to rage. Women and men throughout the United States mobilized to support female ordination. Historian Ann Braude underscores the broader implications of women's ordination: "It is perhaps difficult to recapture the symbolic impact of women's entry into the male preserve of the ministry. The priest or pastor represented both social and divine order when he stood before his congregation. . . . The idea that a woman might assume this role represented a shocking reversal of traditional roles, one that is still objectionable to many Americans."[38] Kuhlman did not offer support for the "shocking reversal" represented by women's ordination, even though many of the mainline denominations with which she interacted began to move toward the ordination of women.[39] Despite her close contact with leaders from these denominations, Kuhlman chose not to use her influence to raise up other women leaders. She employed many women in the Kuhlman Foundation as secretaries, ushers, and administrators, but her only associate minister was male.

Kuhlman's reluctance to advocate for female religious leadership was particularly curious considering that she was ordained by the Baptist-affiliated Evangelical Church Alliance of Joliet, Illinois, sometime in the 1930s. She never made much of this. Being ordained, or "getting her papers," as it was often called, had its risks. By choosing to acknowledge the authority of a church body to ordain, Kuhlman was undercutting in some ways her own defense of the call to ministry she received. Kuhlman argued that her original call to preach came directly from God through the Holy Spirit and was not mediated through the ceremony of ordination of any church. The authority for a woman to preach was available only on a case-by-case basis per the sovereign will of God. God chose her, and therefore her right to preach was unassailable. God could choose other women, but the choice was up to God, not humans, to ordain women for ministry. In contrast, by pursuing ordination Kuhlman was acknowledging the possibility that a woman could decide for herself to become a minister. Biographer Jamie Buckingham softened the importance of Kuhlman's decision by stating that "the young evangelist" was persuaded by the Evangelical Church Alliance that she "needed" to be ordained.[40] In response to a question about her ordination, Kuhlman stated, "I am a Baptist. I still belong to a Baptist church. I was ordained by the Evangelical Church Alliance in Joliet, Illinois, years and years ago when I went there for a meeting. They were the first to ordain me, and I have continued to hold papers with them."[41] Kuhlman omitted one glaring fact: as a Baptist woman, she could not be ordained by the denomination she called her own.

Provided with a bully pulpit through her television and radio shows, Kuhlman could have helped other women religious leaders in their efforts to gain equality. She chose instead to discount the movement for women's liberation and speak out in support of the traditional domestic model that she in practice rejected. Kuhlman's presentation of herself as antifeminist made her acceptable to the conservative side of charismatic Christianity, with its resistance to women's leadership outside of the governance of a man. One important voice for charismatic Christianity concerning the role of women was Kuhlman's former talk show guest Shirley Boone. Boone's 1972 book, *One Woman's Liberation*, reinforced the antifeminism of charismatic Christianity. "So-called Women's Libbers militantly object to the place in society God has ordained for their sex," Boone wrote. "But, by so doing, they lose much of the precious liberty the Lord intended them to have." The liberty Boone spoke of was the liberation through submission propounded by conservative Christianity in response to feminism. Boone added, "Though I know it—and I really do know it—that I've found new happiness and freedom through this Divine Order, I must frankly say that submission doesn't always come easy. . . . However, I've prayed regularly for an obedient and submissive heart, and one day, as I prayed, God gave me the insight I needed. 'Shirley,' His answer came, 'you only have to be obedient. Pat doesn't have to be right. Continue to pray that you learn obedience, and trust Me to deal with your husband.'"[42] Shirley Boone wrote and spoke for a charismatic Christianity that was not ready for the liberation of women from traditional, domestic roles.

Operating against this backdrop, Kuhlman was fearless in her inconsistency. She blithely stated:

One day in Los Angeles a representative of women's lib called to ask if I would appear on a television program for women's lib. I laughed. "You won't want to hear what I have to say." You see, I'd give anything if I could just be a good housewife, a good cook. Oh, I'd like to be a good cook. I'd like to have about twelve children. Sometimes I feel like the mother of the world now. I've got so many spiritual children I don't know what to do. I worry about them. I mother them. I love them. I care for them. It would be so nice to have a man bring in the paycheck. I would just love to have a man boss me. It might not last long, but for a little while it would be just great! So when it comes to women's lib, I'm still as old-fashioned as the Word of God. I still think that the husband should be the head of the family. I know how it was at our house. Papa was always the head of the family, and if Papa said it, it was just as though God had said it. We never had any women's lib at our house, but we had a mighty happy family.[43]

This pronouncement by Kuhlman contained the many contradictions and ironies that characterized her career-long determination to maintain a singularly nontraditional life as a female religious leader while simultaneously criticizing the feminist movement that made her lifestyle possible.

Kuhlman often emphasized that her authority should be understood within the context of being "a lady." She stated, "I tell you the truth. I am a woman, I was born a woman, and I try to keep my place as a woman, and I want to say to the women here in this auditorium, please, whatever you do, don't try to be a man. We were born women. I recognize the fact that I am a woman, and with it I try to be a lady."[44] Kuhlman made a point to emphasize her traditionally feminine appearance on her television shows, wearing elaborate gowns, never pants, as well as fashionable jewelry and carefully coiffed red-dyed hair. In her miracle services she wore a long, flowing white "pulpit dress," with a high neck and high heels, formal attire that identified her as the "lady" she wanted to be. The sixties and seventies were decades when clothing and hairstyle became signs of identification along the cultural continuum. Countercultural leanings such as support of women's liberation and the hippie lifestyle were signaled by fashion. Women began to wear pants more often, men grew their hair long, and the media capitalized on the imagery of feminists as sullen, drab, and shapeless. Kuhlman's flamboyant femininity, considered against this framework, might in fact have appeared comfortingly traditional and nonthreatening to her audiences.

Defending Her Ministry

Kuhlman was equally careful to wrap her rhetoric concerning her leadership in traditional garb. As a divorced woman minister, Kuhlman made use of the Holy Spirit to provide a much-needed "covering" for her ministry. She referred to the Holy Spirit continually as a male personality who was essential and integral to the success of her ministry. "I can only tell you my relationship with [the Holy Spirit], that's all," Kuhlman said in one message. "Have you really gotten acquainted with him? Do you know him as a person? Not just having spoken in tongues, really knowing a person?"[45] The power of her preaching did not come from her own authority, she explained, but from the Holy Spirit. "I'm absolutely dependent on the power of the Holy Spirit," Kuhlman said in a radio show about speaking in tongues. "The Holy Spirit convicts the sinner of his sin. You may have the greatest minister in the world, but he cannot, he does not have the power to bring conviction on anyone. Unless the Holy Spirit is present, nothing I do will convict. I could preach my head off, [but unless the Holy Spirit convicts, I can't do anything]."[46] Her ability to discern healings occurring in the miracle services was also attributable to the Spirit. "I have no healing power. No man has. Remember that. No person has. It's his power. It's the presence of the Holy Spirit who heals these bodies."[47] Kuhlman was not unusual in the ascription of her preaching and healing ability to the Holy Spirit. Most ministers credited the Spirit of God with the ability to bring about conversion in listeners. As a female minister, however, this rhetoric served a further purpose by abstracting the authority to preach and heal away from Kuhlman to a Holy Spirit represented as male.

Kuhlman's language regarding the Holy Spirit was personal and ardent. In her messages, the Holy Spirit was more than an intangible, invisible source of power. "He," as she called the Spirit, was her partner, even her husband. According to Kuhlman, her first attempt to co-minister with a male partner had gone terribly awry because she left behind her true companion, the Holy Spirit. In the emotional message given toward the end of her life where she recounted her decision to leave Burroughs Waltrip, Kuhlman explained this choice brought about a deep moment of intimacy with the Holy Spirit.[48] She told the story with unusually sensual language about the action of the Holy Spirit, stating, "I spoke in an unknown tongue as he took every part of me."[49] The imagery Kuhlman used in this message was close to a mystical representation of the Holy Spirit as husband and lover. It was atypical language for her and does not appear in her other messages or writings about the Holy Spirit. In this one lone emotional discourse, she presented the powerful image of her partnership with the Holy Spirit as a marriage covenant consummated in spiritual union. This partnership served to protect her authority from questioning by the conservative charismatic Christians she was leading.

Kuhlman's highly visible leadership in the inherently conservative charismatic renewal movement demanded careful defense and management. She knew she faced first the challenge of certain Scriptures in the Bible. After quoting 1 Timothy 2:12, King James Version, "But I suffer not a woman to teach, nor to usurp authority over the man, but to be in silence," Kuhlman launched her argument. "So what do we do about Paul's command for women to keep silent in the church?" Kuhlman asked. "Look at the situation. In the synagogues of that day, women would sit in the balcony. . . . The women would speak so loudly that the rest of the people could not hear the speaker. Women are just the same as they were then. I can just hear John's wife calling down and saying, 'John, do you re-member? Did I turn the stove off?' Or maybe they were doing a little voting and Elizabeth would call down and say, 'Abe, say no, say no, you know I don't like him, don't put him in office.' They talked so loudly no one else could hear. They just couldn't keep their mouths shut. So Paul said, 'Let the women be quiet.' "[50] Kuhlman's description of the women of Corinth was less than flattering and served to promote stereotypical images of church women as officious, nosey, and controlling. Many who rejected Kuhlman's leadership would have used her own argument against her. But Kuhlman presented herself as different from your typical woman of the church, one who deserved the role of leader. This was her answer: Paul simply wasn't talking about someone like her.

Kuhlman also maintained her position as female religious leader by regularly rejecting the titles "preacher" and "minister," designations associated with a pastoral role in the church. In the introductory comments of an interview in *Christianity Today* in 1973, she was named "the best known woman preacher in the world today." She replied, "I do not consider myself this. I have never used the term reverend for myself. I do not consider myself a woman preacher. I'm just somebody who loves souls. I love people. I want to help; and it's just that simple."[51]

Defending Her Call

While repudiating the title "preacher," Kuhlman staunchly defended her right to engage in the act of preaching. She argued:

> If all the forces of hell defied me regarding my call to preach the Gospel, it's as real as my conversion. It's something I've got to do if I have to stand on the street corner and do it. It's something I've got to do if I have to live on bread and water. If ever you've been called of God to preach the Gospel, you've got to. If your call is genuine, if your call is of the Holy Ghost, you'll preach if you have to live on bread and water, you'll preach it. I have never questioned my call.[52]

Kuhlman stated that she had received an overpowering call from God to preach. Kuhlman's forerunners Maria Woodworth-Etter and Aimee Semple McPherson argued the same point. In her famous "From Milk-pail to Pulpit" sermon, Sister Aimee recounted her conversation with

God: "Lord I never heard of a woman preacher. They're all men. I don't know why. Why wasn't I a man? I'd like to be a young man so I'd go out and preach. Lord said, 'Hold your peace, now.'"[53] For McPherson and Kuhlman, the call from God to preach was irresistible. Preaching was not something Kuhlman chose to do; it was something she *had* to do. She made her defense in words her predecessors would have applauded: "A lot of people seem to think that being a woman in the ministry means I have two strikes against me. I've never felt that way. I just lift my chin a little higher and act like I don't hear the insults. I didn't ask for this ministry. God knows I'd much rather be doing something else. But He put me in the ministry and those who don't like having a woman preach should complain to God—not me. It's just like that."[54] By invoking this pedigreed distinction, she was able to assert both her authority as preacher called by God and her helplessness to resist that call. [55]

By presenting her call to ministry as a negation of her will, Kuhlman gained access to the power to lead within charismatic Christianity where, as Wacker notes, an "important credential for leadership status stemmed, ironically, from seeming not to want it."[56] She told stories of her appropriation of religious authority through her own negation many times in her career. One claim she often repeated was that God wanted a man to lead the ministry she was given:

> I'll tell you something very confidentially—the true conviction of my heart. I do not believe I was God's first choice in the ministry he has chosen for these last days. It's my firm conviction. You'll never argue me out of this conviction, never. I'm not quite sure whether I was God's second choice, or even His third choice. Because I really believe the job I am doing is a man's job. I work hard. Few people know how hard I really work—sixteen, seventeen hours a day. I can outwork five men put together, and I'll challenge you on this. But no man was willing to pay the price. I was just naïve enough to say "Take nothing, and use it." And He has been doing that ever since.[57]

The phrase "Take nothing, and use it" summarizes Kuhlman's presentation of her own role in God's selection of her as a leader of a ministry. The strongest assertion of this persona was contained in a message given in the last years of her life: "I surrendered everything. I knew in that moment what that scripture meant, 'If any man would follow me, he must take up his cross.' A cross always means death. That afternoon, Kathryn

Kuhlman died. If you've never had that death of the flesh, you don't understand me. When you are baptized in the Holy Spirit, there will be a crucifying of the flesh. You will die. He doesn't ask for golden vessels. He doesn't ask for silver vessels or he wouldn't have chosen me. All he needs is someone who'll die." Kuhlman then added that by yielding to the Holy Spirit's will for her life to be a minister, "for the first time, I realized what it meant to have power."[58] Through rhetoric such as this, Kuhlman succeeded in gaining authority in the charismatic renewal movement through self-negation. But times were changing, and Kuhlman's self-negating path to authority was no longer the only avenue open to women in ministry. She would come face-to-face with an alternate reality on her own soundstage.

In 1974, Kuhlman invited Ralph Carmichael to appear on her television show. Carmichael was a well-known and respected composer of Christian music.[59] The two chatted amiably about Carmichael's life, and the conversation turned to his mother, Adele. Adele was a powerhouse in her own right, a highly respected minister in the Pentecostal Assemblies of God denomination. Born in 1902 and ordained at the age of sixteen, Adele Carmichael was only five years older than Kuhlman. When she strode on to the stage to join her son, however, her vitality and strength made Kuhlman look frail and small. Carmichael's gown was more elaborate than Kuhlman's, and her hair was coiffed elegantly in a massive twirl on her head, highlighting the dated styling of Kuhlman's self-described "red fuzzy hair." Adele was clearly a force to be reckoned with. The two women sat across from each other in large wicker chairs, and the sheer amount of material in their combined outfits was astounding. Ralph Carmichael, meanwhile, sat quietly between them and for all practical purposes became a part of the scenery as the two women filled the screen with their giant personalities.

Kuhlman began the conversation with a question. "It's not the easiest thing in the world to be a woman preacher. How did you master it?" Carmichael answered in her brisk, matter-of-fact manner, "I had a wonderful husband who was 100 percent for women preachers. As I study the Word, I believe God needs women, has a place for their ministry." Immediately Carmichael presented an image of a woman in a healthy, cooperative marriage in which the husband fully supported the woman's work in ministry. Following this, she argued for women's religious leadership based upon her own exegesis of Scripture. Clearly, the two women based their ministries on very different arguments. Carmichael continued, "Many times I've prayed thanks that God gave you your ministry and not a man." Kuhlman responded to this surprisingly frank statement with a smile and a dismissive wave of her hand, "Really? I always thought I was second or third choice." Kuhlman surely expected this answer to be handily accepted, as always. Not this time. "That's not your worry," Adele said crisply. Kuhlman made another attempt at negation: "I always thought it should have been a man." Adele shot back, "I think you were his [God's] first choice." Carmichael's manner was not unpleasant, but it was clear that she was not going to allow Kuhlman the standard route of self-negation. This female minister was a different type from Kuhlman, one who proudly asserted the right of women to serve as clergy. In a fascinating conclusion to the interview, Kuhlman stated, "I pray that I will have the respect at the end of my ministry that God has given you." Carmichael had the last word. "You will, because God will give it to you."[60] The end credits ran, the music played, and the clear winner was Adele.

Kuhlman's statement "I pray that I will have the respect at the end of my ministry that God has given you" implied that Carmichael's ministry was ending while Kuhlman's was still growing. In actuality, Kuhlman would be dead in a little less than a year and Adele would live to be 101, in ministry until she died.[61] The two women, separated in age by only five years, stared at each other across a conceptual divide, on the one side female religious authority through negation, on the other female religious authority through affirmation. It finally took a woman equal to Kuhlman to dispute her rhetoric of self-negation and offer to the television audience an alternative presentation of liberated female religious leadership in charismatic Christianity.

CHAPTER 5

Producing Change

On September 12, 1973, Kathryn Kuhlman welcomed her guest Arlene Strackbein to her television show *I Believe in Miracles* with these words: "My guest today has never seen one of our telecasts. That seems almost impossible when you consider the millions who have."[1] Kuhlman had a propensity for exaggeration, but by 1973 it was fairly safe to say that millions had been exposed to her syndicated television show. Between 1966 and 1975, during the height of the charismatic renewal movement, Kuhlman recorded over five hundred episodes of *I Believe in Miracles*. Her show was broadcast in syndication throughout the United States and Canada.[2] Kuhlman's use of television to spread the message of Christianity was part of a larger, deeper change in American Christianity that was influenced by the dynamics of television itself. Televising Christianity did more than simply offer a new field for revival and evangelizing; it changed the way the Christian message was presented and received. *I Believe in Miracles* contributed to the changes in American Christianity produced through the medium of television. Never before had a religious leader hosted a television talk show like *Miracles*.[3] Kuhlman's talk show caught the wave of cultural excitement surrounding the new medium of television, and the talk show was a new format in itself, catering to formerly overlooked audiences in daytime and late night.

Charismatic Christianity garnered significant benefits from Kuhlman's talk show. Television viewers could now experiment with new forms of Christianity in the privacy of their homes without the risk of public exposure. This was an important component in the gentrification of charismatic Christianity, since popular culture, the press, and mainstream Christianity still regarded charismatics as freakish. As audiences tuned in to Kuhlman's show, they entered into a world where charismatic Christianity was unexceptional. In each episode they were exposed to testimonies of charismatic experiences of "normal" Americans. The non-threatening space of television combined with the everyday appearance and behavior of the guests made *I Believe in Miracles* a significant contributor to the gentrification of charismatic Christianity.

Television Talk

I Believe in Miracles was a talk show. Although this seems less than striking in the talk-show-inundated society of the present, in 1966 it was a form not seen before. There were radio interview shows and television shows that included discussion, but a show centered exclusively around conversation was new.[4] Kuhlman's earlier television production included testimonials that she guided as an expert interviewer, but these exchanges were more formal and the stage-management apparatus, more visible. On *Your Faith and Mine*, Kuhlman and her "guests" stood around a large, bulky microphone, facing the live audience, and spoke in a more obviously performative manner. In the new format of the talk show, the atmosphere changed from cavernous auditorium to intimate studio. The experience of the audience changed from worship participants to detached onlookers. Kuhlman and her guests conversed with each other as the television audience watched. It was a significantly different means of communicating the charismatic Christian gospel.

Considering the talk show as important to the history of American Christianity requires taking the format seriously as a repository of historical information. Within the world of television itself, talk shows have historically garnered little respect. The recordings of the first shows of late-night talk show pioneers Johnny Carson and Jack Paar were erased so the film could be reused, since the shows were considered to be disposable due to their "intense topicality."[5] Media scholars such as Bernard Timberg note the "dismissive attitude" toward television talk shows found in media scholarship itself. In the beginning, television criticism focused primarily on drama and journalism, with little regard for talk shows. This attitude dominated media studies until the powerful role of talk shows became undeniable during the Clinton presidential campaign. "Bill Clinton was dubbed the first 'talk show president,'" Timberg states. A closer examination of the history of television talk shows reveals that they were gaining social influence long before the Clinton presidency. Television itself changed the way Americans engaged the political process, as evidenced by the audience response to the 1960 Kennedy-Nixon debates. Kennedy's triumph through the airwaves "proved that television had acquired a new level of power in American politics."[6] Talk shows emerged out of this new world of television influence. Over the last half of the twentieth century, the television talk show began to take over the roles traditionally held by television journalism. With a new status in politics and society, talk shows are no longer considered a disposable medium but instead are deemed a depository of historically significant matters.[7]

Televised talk was on the upswing when Kuhlman launched *I Believe in Miracles* in early 1966. While late-night talk was network based, daytime talk shows were increasingly the province of syndicated television. Erickson explains, "Syndicated talk shows flourished during the decade [1960s]. Like game shows, they were inexpensive to tape, had the allure of celebrity glamour, and many were flexible enough to schedule any hour of the day."[8] Kuhlman's production joined several other shows hosted by women and marketed to the daytime audience. Virginia Graham emceed *Girl Talk* from 1962 until 1970, while stripper Gypsy Rose Lee hosted a show perhaps surprisingly devoted to "housewife topics." The editor of *Cosmopolitan* magazine, Helen Gurley Brown, held court for one season in 1967 in a show entitled *Outrageous Opinions*, and Joan Rivers made her entry into television talk shows with *That Show with Joan Rivers* from 1968 to 1969.[9] In 1969 alone, twenty new talk shows went on the air, sixteen of which were produced for syndication.[10]

The talk show format of *Miracles* also drew upon the thriving culture of therapy in the mid-1960s. Psychoanalysis and therapy groups became popular during the show's ten-year run. Kuhlman's background in guiding highly personal revival testimonies served her well in a culture where the revelation of past traumas and issues was seen as the path to wholeness and healing. Communications scholar Mimi White explains, "Therapeutic discourse provides a ready-made and familiar narrative trajectory [for television]: the eruption of a problem leads to confession and diagnosis and then to a solution or cure."[11] The emphasis in *Miracles* on divine healing dovetailed nicely with society's interest in the "talking cure." The "Me Generation," convinced that all healing came from within, delighted in television that reinforced the therapeutic model.

Kuhlman worked comfortably in this confessional environment because of her background in revivals. Old familiar revival forms took on a newness that made them once again interesting and intriguing. On *Miracles*, guests told of their emotional, spiritual, and physical troubles. The guests were testifying and confessing at the same time, and their accounts took the familiar therapeutic trajectory from brokenness to wholeness, with the added interest of the miraculous. On one episode, Kuhlman welcomed a lovely actress named Elaine St. Germaine as her guest. St. Germaine spoke emotionally of her drug addiction and healing. "I was on dope for nine years," St. Germaine confessed. "I turned away from Christianity. I was raised a Southern Baptist. I had fame, but it was empty. I had no values. I began to search in philosophy, eastern religions, I went into psychoanalysis. I got started on LSD. I had sixty-five sessions with LSD." St. Germaine described her loss of interest in life and the sapping of her creativity, due in large part to her use of LSD. She felt empty and in despair. "I tried three times to kill myself with an overdose of sleeping pills. My husband left. I was on a treadmill to hell. I had gone into the occult. I wanted to know all the answers of the universe. I got myself in such forces that only Christ could release me." Over the course of two years, St. Germaine corresponded by mail with Kuhlman, who answered her many letters personally. St. Germaine then decided to attend a Kuhlman service at the Shrine Auditorium in Los Angeles, where she "had a sense of the presence of Christ," and she began to be able to sleep for the first time in years. According to her own account, God delivered St. Germaine through "divine therapy," causing her to enter into deep introspection and then confession, which led to a sense of cleansing and a cure. St. Germaine summed up: "[God is] the greatest psychoanalyst in the world."[12] Inside the world of *I Believe in Miracles*, God as psychoanalyst seemed perfectly logical.

No matter their subject, talk shows such as *Miracles* abided by basic production conventions or rules. No other form of television was like a talk show, not soap operas or game shows or news broadcasts. Talk shows were also distinguished from normal conversation by their guiding principles. Television talk shows were established upon the coordinated foundations of "fresh talk" and television talk. Sociologist Erving Goffman defines "fresh talk" as "talk that appears to be spontaneous, no matter how planned or formatted it actually may be."[13] "Television talk," therefore, was simply "fresh talk" on television. It drew upon the background of talk as experienced on radio, and was "unscripted yet highly planned and invariably anchored by an announcer, host, or team of hosts." Finally, the television talk show was "entirely structured around the act of conversation itself."[14] Within this highly defined space were even more orienting principles. The role of the host was crucial. The host controlled the guests' use of the airtime, guided the talk, and when a "brand name," defined the show itself. Talk shows were also "always experienced in the present tense as 'conversation.' Live, taped, or shown in reruns, talk shows always maintain the illusion of the present tense." Closely linked with this was the sense of intimacy created by the talk show format. "The host speaks to millions as if to each alone."[15] Talk shows were spontaneous yet highly structured, immediate yet virtual, and conversational yet host-controlled.

Even the name "talk show" held within it the tensions created by the new format. Wayne Munson explains, "The name itself epitomizes its promiscuous inclusiveness. The term 'talkshow' combines two communicative paradigms, and like the term itself, the 'talk show' fuses and seems to reconcile two different, even contradictory rhetorics. It links conversation, the interpersonal—the premodern oral tradition—with the mass-mediated spectacle born of modernity." Munson asks, "Is it 'talk' or 'show'? Conversation or spectacle? Both? Neither?"[16] Television talk shows addressed a limited audience within a television studio, yet simultaneously communicated to a larger viewing audience. "They are characterized by a dual consciousness," Timberg notes. "They are a form of rhetoric that is both private and public, personal and mass."[17] Kuhlman entered her television career with a background in "fresh talk" developed in revivals, radio, and early television. *Miracles* took advantage of her experience, and she moved smoothly and successfully into the new world of the television talk show.

Not everyone was as enthusiastic as Kuhlman about television talk shows. Television talk, with its ability to exist in the private and public world simultaneously, disturbed some early critics. Munson explains, "The first significant study [of talk shows] . . . accused television talk-shows of fostering a dangerous 'illusion of intimacy' for lonely spectators."[18] The talk show's first critics pointed with concern to its "'designed informality'; its double game of contrived spontaneity." The simultaneity already present in broadcast media such as radio took on what for some was an eerie amplification through television. Television was "unnervingly immediate."[19] This was due in part to the newness of the experience of "electronic vision," which "brought with it intriguing new ambiguities of space, time and substance: the paradox of visible, seemingly material worlds trapped in a box in the living room and yet conjured out of nothing more than electricity and air."[20] Because of this ambiguity, talk shows seemed dangerously capable of creating the impossibility of "intimacy at a distance," in the critics' own words.

The talk show hosts made use of this immediacy by speaking face-to-face with the audience and communicating in an intimate and seemingly spontaneous way. Some critics were particularly disparaging of these types of programs due to their efforts to mask the corporate reality of all television programming. Talk shows were commodities to be bought and sold, which for some critics made them suspect. Their very breeziness was a product, designed to create a show that was appealing to a market. Munson states, "The genre projects itself as uniquely 'user friendly' and accessible, even as it operates within a media frame that is highly technological, corporate, and residually 'mass' or one-way."[21] This was particularly important in the business of syndication, which by the end of the 1960s was producing the bulk of the talk show market.[22] Syndicated talk shows bore a particular burden of marketability. The shows had to be sold to independent broadcasters, often in competition with network offerings. Such realities led some critics to question the ethics of a show that relied upon creating a sense of relationship between a host and audience when the relationship existed only to sell the show as a product.

As early as 1956, observers noted television's ability to blur the line between reality and fiction. The ability of television to cross the "fourth wall" between audience and show led to concern.[23] This boundary became fluid, allowing the television program to engage audiences in new ways. Was a talk show journalism or entertainment? Disturbingly for some, it was both. Critics pointed to the "hybrid nature" of talk shows, their "textual position somewhere between the theatrical-fictional and the documentary or journalistic."[24] Into this ambiguous space came smiling hosts and hostesses, welcoming the audience into their world of talk. For some critics, this was a dangerous, undefined, corporately controlled and corporately manipulated place to visit. It was deemed particularly dangerous for what was considered the most impressionable segment of the postwar market economy: housewives.

"It's a good thing electric dishwashers and washing machines were invented. The housewives will need them."[25] ABC vice president Alexander Stronach Jr. summarized the concern many male corporate executives had about expanding television programming into daytime: Was it possible for women to watch television during the day and still perform their roles as housewife and mother? Lured irresistibly to market to women in the household, the businessmen wondered if they were distracting the goose that laid the golden egg. Evening news and drama shows were not such a concern for domestic order. In the male television executive's mind, men could enjoy a newscast after returning home from work while dinner was being prepared, and the family could watch evening television together until mother finished the dishes. Late evening dramatic programming was for the adults to enjoy after-hours, when children were in bed and the day's chores completed. Daytime programming was different. Television during the day could potentially interfere with the stay-at-home wife's work. The concerns were almost amusing if they did not reveal such blatant sexism.

The major radio networks hesitated to move into daytime television programming for other pragmatic reasons. The distraction of housewives was not their concern, but just the opposite; women in the home would not watch daytime television because they were "chained to their chores."[26] The hypothesis of the radio executives was this: housewives could listen to radio (and radio advertising) while busily working in the home, but television required much more attention. Therefore, the busy housewife would not want television in her home. Why take money from a sure winner (radio) and put it toward an unproved innovation (television)? Why program for an audience that was not paying attention?[27] But during the 1950s, it became apparent that female daytime viewers *were* paying attention—in droves.[28] In the face of enormous potential profits, it didn't take long for advertisers and television producers to overcome their initial qualms about women viewers. By 1962 advertising revenue topped 225 million for the daytime hours.[29] If a program could capture the attention, and money, of the stay-at-home housewife, it was now a product the television studios wanted.

In their endeavor to engage new viewers, television executives tried to cater to what they saw as the more refined daytime audience. Efforts were made to make television a positive force in the home, albeit a positive force raking in advertising revenue. The *Preamble to the Television Code* of the National Association of Radio and Television Broadcasters reflected the ideal of the genteel television program: "It is the responsibility of television to bear constantly in mind that the audience is primarily a home audience, and consequently that television's relationship to the viewer is that between guest and host."[30] The television was visualized as a guest welcomed into the private world of families. As a guest, certain etiquette should be observed. Only persons of refinement should be presented as visitors to the television viewers' homes. Following this logic, studios hired men who came to be known as "charm boys" to helm daytime programming.[31] Soon, television producers recognized the value of presenting a female personality to the primarily female daytime audience. Women would be more likely to listen to another woman, the reasoning went, especially a woman who was intelligent, charming, and attractive. Local television stations were ahead of the larger networks in understanding the allure of a female show host, and many of the early programs hosted by women were produced for syndication by independent studios.[32] Soon, however, the major studios began to feature women who could charm their way right into the homes and hearts of their female audience.

In 1954, Arlene Francis was the first female host presented by a major studio in a format considered "serious." Her show, *Home*, was the first to offer educational content in a lively and pleasant format.[33] *Home* presented Francis in a way that furthered 1950s cultural ideals of domestic womanhood. Marsha Cassidy explains, "Francis worked hard to come across on *Home* as just one of the girls. 'I'm a homebody,' Francis went on to tell [an interviewer for the July 1954 edition of *Newsweek*, which featured her on its cover]. 'Our show comes right into people's houses. They know me. They like me . . . and I like them.' [*Newsweek* stated] "she further imitated her *Home* audience by 'not wearing a different dress everyday.'"[34] She and other "femcees" like her, including Dinah Shore and Eleanor Roosevelt, hosted shows based upon educating women about the home, fashion, and child rearing. These programs were considered acceptable for a female viewer due to their style and content.[35]

Arlene Francis styled herself as the ideal housewife and hostess while simultaneously presenting a contradictory image: a mature, professional woman engaged in a vital career in television. At the time of her success, Francis was forty-seven years old, although she made it a practice not to reveal her age. As a mature mother of a young child as well as a full-time career woman, Francis was in fact not "one of the girls." These two personas existed at once in her complex role as hostess of *Home*. One feminist scholar explains, "Francis and *Home* regularly offered an ambiguous multivocality that cast doubts on a full withdrawal to homemaking."[36] With her show, a female moved successfully into the male-controlled world of television talk.

By the beginning of the 1960s, Francis's friend Barbara Walters had risen to national recognition in television news broadcasting, a male-dominated arena, replacing Francis as the most well-known female talk figure.[37] Newscaster Walters utilized a different method of interviewing. She asked personal questions and gave guests opportunities to speak for themselves about their lives. Timberg explains, "When [Walters] asked questions like 'What is the biggest misconception about you?' she was providing her interview subjects with a chance to set the record straight and tell the story as they saw it. . . . [A] series of women talk-show hosts brought 'feminine' ways of speaking to news and entertainment."[38] The well-dressed, well-coiffed television "hostess" still had her place in daytime programming, but the presence of "the feminine" on television was expanding beyond daytime talk.

Kathryn Kuhlman: Talk Show Host

By the time *I Believe in Miracles* went on the air in 1966, the women's liberation movement was a new force in American culture and politics. Women were beginning to demand a role in television commensurate with their expanding role in society, and television became a contested arena for women's representation. Daytime television programmers felt the shock waves of the feminist movement as show producers tried to find ways to reach a market no longer seen as monolithic but representing a range of women, from liberal feminist to politically and socially conservative. Programming executives were by and large not active supporters of women's liberation, but advertising revenues were at stake. If women wanted to see women on television and would tune in to see them, then the logical business decision was to feature more women.

When *I Believe in Miracles* began production, the focus of the program was in-depth interviews with a variety of people who had experienced some aspect of charismatic Christianity. Each episode helped establish Kuhlman as a serious talk show host and developed her relationship with her viewing audience. The show began with a time of interaction between Kuhlman and the viewer. At first she sometimes used the opening statement from her daily radio show, "Hello! And have you been waiting for me?" Soon, however, she settled into a standard opening line, "I believe in miracles . . . because I believe in God." In these earlier shows, Kuhlman dressed quite conservatively in attractive but plain suit dresses in demure colors. Kuhlman and her producer Dick Ross seemed to have consciously decided to present her as a professional woman rather than a female evangelist. Her jewelry was restrained, consisting primarily of rings and a gold cuff bracelet. Her "look" was different from that recorded on her program *Your Faith and Mine* from a decade earlier (although her hairstyle was almost exactly the same). She replaced the large corsage, her white suit, and the white high heels with a simple Peter Pan collar and low-heeled pumps. Her image suited a businesswoman of the mid-1960s perfectly.

Using her background in guiding testimonies in worship services, Kuhlman was already adept at the "personalized interviewing" technique used by her contemporary Barbara Walters.[39] When *Miracles* first began, Kuhlman sometimes used a more "hard-hitting" interview style, possibly modeling her approach on television news talk rather than the more relaxed talk show model. During an episode filmed August 14, 1968, Kuhlman grilled David Wilkerson, leader of Teen Challenge Ministries, on the role of parents in the "crisis" the youth were facing on college campuses. Kuhlman and Wilkerson engaged in a stern and sometimes heated debate over what to do about the increased drug use, sexual activity, and general rebelliousness of early sixties' youth. Challenging Wilkerson to posit a response to what Kuhlman perceived as the disintegration of the family and the destruction of the lives of teenagers, she stated, "Is there anything that can be done about it? What is the answer?"[40] Later episodes of *Miracles* do not have this type of vigorous exchange, as Kuhlman set aside the journalistic approach for the more cozy talk show feel.

During the decade *Miracles* was on the air, television talk shows began to reflect the deepening divides in the culture concerning the proper place of women. Bernard Timberg explains, "Within the gender wars and new identifications that were taking place in the mid-1970s, national television audiences were being offered paired role models. If Barbara Walters served as a model for a woman entering the professional news world of men, Dinah Shore represented a woman's traditional role as hostess and homemaker."[41] Southern, blonde, and with the requisite charm, Shore began her talk show career with *Dinah's Place* in August 1970 at age fifty-three. Her telecast presented the image of women preferred by the essentially conservative male programming executives, and she inhabited a talk show world where the domestic ideals of the 1950s were represented in her style and surroundings.

Dinah's Place was taped in a studio made to look like a living room, with comfortable chairs and couches gathered around a central coffee table. Shore ended each show with a wave and a kiss, establishing an amiable intimacy with her audience. Her clothes were beautiful and the height of style, and her hair always perfectly dressed. She presented herself, in word and image, as the quintessential hostess and housewife. For many in her viewing audience who were distressed by the riotous changes in the culture, she was a comforting presence in the home. The often disquieting and disorienting topics of the sixties and seventies were discussed on cushy couches, with light and airy give-and-take amongst host and guests. Dinah made her audience comfortable even as she discussed uncomfortable topics.

By the 1970s, Kuhlman was competing for the same daytime female audience as Shore and chose to present herself along the same nostalgic domestic lines. As *I Believe in Miracles* developed over the first five years, the studio environment and Kuhlman's wardrobe became increasingly elaborate. Columns surrounded by artificial trees, flowers, and various plants gave the impression on camera of a verdant plastic garden.[42] Kuhlman seated her guests in large wicker chairs or white metal patio furniture inside the representation of a garden courtyard. On some episodes the leaves on the false trees fluttered, blown by an offstage fan. Fountains gurgled and occasionally hosted baby ducklings. Kuhlman even shared the stage with a large white cockatoo for one (and only one) opening vignette.[43] Kuhlman replaced her simple business dresses with elaborate gowns. Some of the wardrobe changes can be attributed to the flamboyant styles of seventies' fashion. Other female celebrities of the time dressed in equally colorful and dramatic styles. Viewed in context, her dresses were not anomalous. *Miracles* producer Dick Ross stated, "Kathryn's television wardrobe was always in the best of taste, it is generally agreed."[44] Kuhlman worked to transform her studio into a fashionable television destination and herself into a chic hostess in order to compete with hosts such as the adept Dinah Shore.

Kuhlman's and Shore's welcoming words and the ushering of guests into their studio "homes" were a part of what scholars of talk shows call the "hospitality ritual." In the ritual, the host is portrayed as inviting the guest into her home, the decorated soundstage, for a nice visit together. Timberg explains, "The hospitality rituals are even more consciously enacted when the studio mimes a home, as it did on the Dinah Shore talk show."[45] Unlike Shore, Kuhlman did not offer her guests a cup of tea or usher them on to a communal couch, but she still relied on the hospitality ritual with its powerful domestic imagery. On an episode taped February

14, 1973, Kuhlman told her audience there would be no guests on the show that day. The show would be "just her." "And certainly I'm not a guest—I want you to feel I'm a part of your family," Kuhlman said with a smile.[46] Her style created a comfortable give-and-take with her guests. Kuhlman would often lean in to the guest and make the statement, "Let me ask you confidentially . . . ," as the cameras broadcast the conversation to homes across America. Statements like these, absurd on the surface, were part of creating the illusion of intimacy vital to the effectiveness of the talk show format.

Broadcast into the same living rooms as images of women's liberation demonstrations, the Vietnam War, the Watergate scandal, and the civil rights protests, domestic imagery was anachronistic even as early as 1970. Shore joined Kuhlman and Arlene Francis in the careful manipulation of her public persona in order to offer a "safe" female presence at the helm of a television show. Kuhlman and Shore in particular strove to be ultra-feminine in dress and manner. Both surrounded themselves with the markers of domesticity on their soundstages, and both used these comforting backdrops to distract their more conservative viewers from fully grasping the reality of their independent and professional lives. When Shore began hosting *Dinah's Place* in 1970, she was in the fourth decade of her broadcasting career and already twice divorced. She presented herself as the archetypal white Anglo-Saxon Protestant blonde southern belle, although she was Jewish, brunette, and held a degree in sociology from Vanderbilt.[47] Shore and Kuhlman represented a domestic mythology that never truly existed and, by the 1970s, was becoming infused with a complex mixture of nostalgia and cultural bewilderment. Shore chose to stage her career within the confines of the domestic ideal left over from the 1950s. The decision was good for business. Her show lasted four years, a hit in the highly changeable world of television programming. Kuhlman was even more successful, and played host to her guests for ten years.

For most of its run, *Miracles* emphasized the importance of unpracticed testimony, although not at the very beginning. In the early years, the voice-over announced only "authenticated, firsthand reports," with no mention of the lack of rehearsal.[48] At this early stage, the guests were still being drawn at times from Kuhlman's own congregations. Like *Your Faith and Mine*, some of the first episodes of *I Believe in Miracles* employed testimonies of people who were actively involved in Kuhlman's ministry in Pittsburgh and Youngstown, Ohio. Kuhlman knew the men, women, and children as their pastor, and presented their stories as testimonies familiar to her. As her ministry expanded, people beyond Kuhlman's own congregations began to claim healings they credited to her, especially after she added monthly miracle services at the Shrine Auditorium in Los Angeles in 1965. The increasing number of testimonies by people outside of Kuhlman's own congregations led to the addition of a line to Art Gilmore's voice-over at the beginning of every episode of *Miracles.* Speaking of the guests on the show, Gilmore now stated, "They share their discovery in unrehearsed television interviews."[49]

In her introduction to many episodes of the show Kuhlman said, "We have no script. There's been no rehearsal. It may be only the first time I have seen [my guest on the show]."[50] Kuhlman was speaking the literal truth when she said the interviews were unrehearsed and not prepared ahead of time. However, the principles of fresh talk and the requirements of talk shows made it unlikely the professional interviewer in Kuhlman came into a program completely unprepared. *Miracles* producer Dick Ross described the process for selecting the guests for the television show as he observed it during his days with Kuhlman: "I learned that Kathryn Kuhlman never rehearsed her programs. Many of the people who appeared as her guests she had never met before. Often she learned of their remarkable healing through correspondence. Others might have appeared on the platform at some miracle service, but then only briefly. When letters arrived telling of a remarkable healing, Maggie [Hartner, Kuhlman's close friend and foundation administrator] would research, verify, and do the follow-up. Only after thorough investigation were individuals invited to appear on television programs."[51] As Ross's words demonstrate, Kuhlman's television talk only appeared spontaneous. Its methodical structure was what made its unstructured appearance convincing.

The format of *I Believe in Miracles* combined direct address of the audience with guest interviews, which created an interesting experience for the viewer. At the beginning of every episode, Kuhlman addressed the camera/audience directly and often chatted in a casual way about the subject of the show or her own delight at the healings taking place in her ministry. Following this conversation with the viewers, she would often introduce the musical interlude. Musician Dino Kartsonakis played a piano solo, then soloist Jimmie McDonald sang, accompanied by Kartsonakis. At the end of the music, the cameras switched to Kuhlman seated across from her guest or guests for the day. During the musical segment and guest interview, the viewer retreated into the position of observer, but at the end, sometimes abruptly, Kuhlman would turn and again engage the viewer directly with a call to commitment to Christianity. The experience was similar to watching a play from the front row when suddenly a character turns and addresses the audience firsthand from the stage. At the end of her plea to the viewers, Kuhlman prayed, and at the established words "For Jesus' sake we ask it," the lights dimmed, the music began to play, the camera swept up and back from the scene and continued to look down upon Kuhlman and the guest(s) as the end credits ran.

Interesting dynamics were at work in the shifts in camera angles during Kuhlman's show. According to scholars interested in media literacy, the use of a direct address at the beginning and end of her show had the potential to produce positive responses to Kuhlman from the audience. Art Silverblatt, Jane Ferry, and Barbara Finan explain, "Having cameras at eye level and a straightforward viewing puts the viewer on an equal plane with the subject. Newscasters and commercial actors look straight into the camera. . . . It becomes synonymous with a face-to-face interaction whereby the communicator seems to be addressing the viewer personally. The direct address at eye level creates an intimacy with the performers, inspiring feelings of trust, confidence, and loyalty in the audience." Further, "An eye-level angle also establishes a sense of identification between the media communicator and the subject, as well as feelings of respect and acceptance."[52] The rising sweep of the camera at the end of each episode possibly signaled a "God-like" perspective as the audience could imagine a benevolent God looking down on Kuhlman and her guest as they sat and prayed.

The direct address at the end of *I Believe in Miracles* was also a form of the traditional altar call found in many evangelistic services, and it therefore took on even more significance. At this point in the program the viewer was asked to step out of the position of neutral observer and engage the Christian message advocated on the show. Mimi White notes, "As is so often the case with television, one first has to watch, even with disdain, to be a potential subject for conversion."[53] In the case of *Miracles*, the nonthreatening format made the topic of charismatic Christianity a viewing option for many who would never have watched a more expected presentation. Kuhlman combined the talk show format with her revival past, and through her innovation managed to capture the attention of bemused and detached viewers along with the admiring faithful, right in their very own living rooms.

But not everyone celebrated the expanding presence of television in the home. One 1950s pastor lamented, "The boast of one network is that it 'brings the world right into your home.' Who wants the world as we know it in our homes?"[54] Conservative Christians confronted for the first time by television struggled with its similarities to the theater. According to their worldview, theater was filled with moral ambiguities, deceptions, and illusions. Television often felt like a disturbingly intimate movie house. Advertisements were especially distressing. They were "assaulted with advertisements for alcohol and tobacco, featuring seductive starlets and movie stars."[55] The presence of television in the home blurred the formerly clear lines drawn between the sacred space of home and the profane space of the theater. The world was invading the homes of these Christians through their television sets, and many saw the new medium as a threat to their beliefs.

In contrast, an element of evangelical Christianity believed television's invasive potential could be turned to the use of the gospel. Although the world could broadcast its dangerous images into the Christian living room, the opposite was also true. Christianity could now enter into homes without even having to knock on the door. Some evangelicals connected television's potential power to convert with the established success of radio evangelism. Television was an entrée point into homes, just as radio had been before. By the 1950s, as television came into its own and Americans bought sets at a rapid pace, a significant section of evangelicalism engaged the new media with gusto. Fuller Seminary professor Edward Carnell advised, "TV, while it may threaten to turn every home into a theater, can also turn every parlor into a church." Carnell urged religious broadcasters to "be courageous, remembering that by overtaking man in his solitude TV enjoys an access into hearts which the organized church does not."[56] Television ministries represented in many ways a division within the evangelical movement between "old-fashioned separatists and a more world-affirming neo-evangelical movement led by men such as Billy Graham, himself a pioneer in religious television."[57] Evangelicals such as Graham saw television as a reality of modern life. Its power could be used for good or evil, they reasoned; therefore, every effort should be made to access its potential to evangelize. For this group, the prospect of tremendous returns was worth the risk of televised Christianity.

I Believe in Miracles: A New Kind of Talk Show

Kuhlman agreed with the protelevision evangelicals and recruited the talented and experienced producer Dick Ross to advise her as she developed her own television ministry. Ross had quickly seen the evangelism potential of commercial television, forming Great Commission Films in the early 1950s. Working first for World Vision, he also spent fourteen productive years with Billy Graham, from 1952 to 1966. He then decided to pursue an independent producing career, forming the company Production Associates. Soon after launching his independent business, he began a nine-year partnership with Kuhlman, helping her create the first television program that combined the talk show format with Christian content.[58] Ross and Kuhlman began to work on *I Believe in Miracles* in 1965, following the publication of the best-selling book of testimonies of the same title in 1962. The combination was a success. Who made the decision to pursue the innovative course toward a Christian talk show? Ross claimed the scheme was his idea. In an interview with Kuhlman biographer Helen Hosier, he remembered, "She was thinking of televising her miracle services and I strongly advised against it and, instead, came up with the program format which, for the most part, remained the same all these years."[59] Ross explained, "Television became her medium. It went hand-in-glove with her platform services. The platform services were where the miracles happened; the television series became the means of sharing with millions across the country."[60] The decision to accept Ross's advice and produce a Christian talk show had far-ranging consequences for Kuhlman's ministry and celebrity as well as for charismatic Christianity in America.

The move from radio and print into television was risky for Kuhlman. Television production was notoriously expensive, a reality Kuhlman faced with her first show, and now faced again with her second. Locally produced, *Your Faith and Mine* had been a chancy venture in its own right. Creating *I Believe in Miracles* was even more tricky. *Miracles* was taped on a soundstage at CBS studios, produced by a professional, and distributed nationally through syndication. It was a bold move for the Kuhlman ministry to make. The financial risk was enhanced by Kuhlman's approach to fund-raising for the television venture. As with *Your Faith and Mine*, she did not directly solicit funds from the television audience. Art Gilmore, the show's announcer, reminded the audience at the end of each show that *Miracles* was a production of the Kathryn Kuhlman Foundation, a nonprofit organization dependent upon the freewill offerings of its sup-porters. The foundation's address also appeared at the conclusion of each show. The need for money was not mentioned in any other way.

Although Kuhlman did not present a "hard sell" approach to her view-ing audience, the financial realities presented by the new endeavor did not escape her. The tremendous monetary demands of television minis-try contributed to the choice of the talk show format. A talk show was fi-nancially feasible for the foundation to produce. Erickson explains, "This sort of program could be made on cost-efficient videotape (introduced in syndication as early as 1958), with a whole week's worth of programs taped during one or two marathon sessions, keeping studio costs low, profits high."[61] Dick Ross remembered working with Kuhlman on just such a schedule. "We used to meet every other month for about three hours on Mondays for breakfast preceding the Wednesday and Thursday taping schedule at CBS."[62] Kuhlman's office calendar for 1970 reflects this rigorous taping schedule. May 1970 was a typical month. Kuhlman left Pittsburgh on Monday, May 11, for LA. On Wednesday, May 13, she taped five half-hour episodes, followed by four episodes recorded on Thursday. Sunday, May 17, was the miracle service at the Shrine, then travel back to Pittsburgh or on to other events.[63] Each month followed a similar routine. The relative economy of the format was a major rea-son the talk show appealed to independent producers like Kuhlman and Ross. In comparison to other formats, talk, literally, was cheap.

The cheapness of talk shows could take on other, less positive mean-ings. Production values of talk shows produced for syndication were often significantly poorer than those of the network shows. Erickson explains, "Detractors grumbled that syndication was television's 'poor relation,' lacking the production polish of series financed by the networks and the big sponsors." *Miracles* was no exception to this tendency in syndication. Early episodes were shot on an almost bare soundstage with random, boldly colored lines running along the polished black floor. The setting often contained only a large wooden conference table with Kuhlman's Bible resting on it, a chair for her and her guests, and maybe a plant. If more than two guests were appearing on the show, the cameras would pan to the back area of the stage where cube-shaped chairs and a side table made up a simple conversation area. The set looked like something set up minutes before taping and torn down minutes after, which was likely the case. During one "heart-to-heart" broadcast, Kuhlman sat at her bare conference table and expounded upon a segment of Scripture.

As she spoke, a technician walked behind her in the darkened area in the back of the soundstage. On another episode a loud crashing sound occurred off camera, but the taping continued and Kuhlman soldiered on without breaking stride. Network producers would likely have called for a retake, but retakes took time and cost money. In over four hundred episodes, very few of the opening clapperboards showed "take two." Kuhlman got it in one take, almost every time. Media historian Hal Erickson notes the response of one 1955 syndicated star who disagreed with the prejudices of the network producers. "Who gives a damn about production values on TV? Nobody. The major film studios who went into TV have learned that production values will not sustain any show. What the people want is a story and people they don't resent in their living rooms."[64] It was certainly to Kuhlman's credit that the content of her show and her own personality were apparently engaging enough to overcome a meager production character in the first years.

Miracles worked in concert with Kuhlman's books, radio shows, and miracle services to provide access to charismatic Christianity on a scale not seen before. As Kuhlman noted in a conversation with her guest Edna Wilder, "You had never read *I Believe in Miracles*, never seen a telecast, never heard a radio program?" Wilder said no. Kuhlman then exclaimed, "Where in the world have ya been?"[65] If someone wanted to know about divine healing, Kuhlman's show was there to watch. Occasionally the show would focus on extended teaching by Kuhlman about some topic related to the charismatic movement such as prophecy or the imminent second coming of Christ. It was a nonthreatening format, easily available due to Kuhlman's broad syndication, and it possessed the powerful option for the viewer of *choice*. If you didn't like it, you could switch it off, and no one need ever know you "experimented" with charismatic Christianity.

In its offer of anonymity, televised Christianity shares some characteristics with a tent revival. Like revivals, Christianity on television is offered in a public space where people can hear and see Christian narratives enacted before them. Observers have the choice to engage as a believer or skeptic, or to continue to look on as a simple observer. The difference between TV and the tent is in the duality of the private and public nature of the talk show. The talk show creates what Timberg calls a "talk world," a "point of intersection or a site in which a small group talks to itself while simultaneously addressing an invisible but clearly defined collective audience."[66] The conversations about charismatic Christianity presented on *Miracles* took place between Kuhlman and one or more guests in a small studio in front of a crew of professional technicians. Kuhlman drew out details of charismatic experiences in calm exchanges that were heartfelt without being overcharged with emotion. These conversations were then broadcast around the nation and even the world. This resulted in what Timberg calls the "dual consciousness" of the talk show, "because talk shows address an immediate and public audience at the same time. . . . They are a form of rhetoric that is both private and public, personal and mass."[67] Television enabled a sort of religious voyeurism, where the viewer could watch in privacy. As the viewer encountered the private/public world of conversation as spectacle, there were opportunities privately to observe and even learn about charismatic Christianity, a subject often deemed suspect if engaged in public.

Featuring: Your Average Charismatic

I Believe in Miracles presented charismatic Christianity through a collection of narratives told by those who had experienced it. People curious about charismatic Christianity were able to watch others who looked remarkably average speak about dramatically exceptional manifestations of the Spirit. Over four hundred episodes aired between 1966 and 1975, and most featured very common people telling uncommon stories that contained within them the markers of charismatic Christianity as it developed in the charismatic renewal movement of the mid-1960s to 1970s. Kuhlman and her "normal" guests often spoke about the experiences of divine healing, being slain in the Spirit, and experiencing the gift of a word of knowledge.[68] The viewer of the show was able to relate to the appearance of the guest, to recognize the guest as a person "just like me," except this average Joe or Jane had experienced some aspect of charismatic Christianity.

Kuhlman highlighted hundreds of examples of "average charismatics" on her show. On one episode taped January 16, 1973, Kuhlman welcomed Richard Wolf as her guest. Wolf was a handsome man in his fifties, with stylishly longer gray hair and a fairly rakish appearance. Wolf told of experiencing two strokes that paralyzed 40 percent of his left side. His face bore traces of hard living, with a ruddy complexion and broken veins. But he was well spoken, obviously educated, and quite charming as he recounted his story.

Wolf: I was hospitalized due to excessive use of alcohol. It had caused brain damage. I drank twenty-five years, three years even after I was told of brain damage. I half-heartedly tried to stop. I stopped in 1967, and in 1969 I had an aneurysm. I had violent headaches. In November of 1972 I had a stroke with an aneurysm. I had facial drop. I was in the hospital for a coupla months. I had violent headaches. I took one hundred aspirin a week and codeine. Last September I went to church at the Church of Christ. I believed in God, but I was a skeptic. If things were going well for me, [God] and I were good buddies for a while. A woman from the church suggested you [and] gave us a copy of *God Can Do It Again* [Kuhlman's second best-selling book of healing testimonies]. My wife began to read the book on a trip to Florida. As she prayed, I got worse. She began to pray thanks for my healing. I went to an AA meeting, and I felt the pain—BAM! in my head. I began to throw up blood. I had vowed I would not go back to the hospital. Monday morning October 2, I sat up in bed, and I didn't have a headache. I felt very, very strange.
Kuhlman: Were you amazed?
Wolf: I was scared. I was waiting for the headache to come. I went to work, spent all day waiting for the pain to come, it never did.

Wolf credited his reading of Kuhlman's book *God Can Do It Again* for bringing about a divine healing. As he began to realize he was healed, his wife determined they were going to find a Kuhlman service to attend, "No matter how far we have to go." They found a service in Youngstown, at the Stambaugh Auditorium, only ninety miles from their home.

At the service, Wolf experienced being slain in the Spirit. "I had such a warm glow. You called people up for a spiritual healing. I went up. You said something to me, and next thing I knew I was on the floor. You placed your hand right on my head where I'd had the aneurysm. I was standing upright, trying to hold on. It didn't work, I got zapped again. And then I knew, I knew that my sins had now been forgiven. It's just been so glorious. Now I am doing things like staying in church seven hours, and missing a Browns' game!"[69] Richard Wolf's appearance was strikingly average. He seemed like the sort of man you would see in offices—and bars—in any city in America. His reference to missing football games for church as a sign of his transformation was endearing. He seemed unaffected and natural, even as he spoke of manifestations of the Holy Spirit considered radical by most Christians of his time.

In his testimony, Wolf bore witness to the charismatic marker of being slain in the Spirit. *Miracles* guest Eyona Pargman also discussed with Kuhlman her struggles with osteoporosis and the slaying power of the Spirit that accompanied her healing. "I didn't believe in miracles," Pargman stated. "I am a Lutheran. They call me a Pentecostal Lutheran now." Kuhlman recalled Pargman's healing at the miracle service. "I remember you saying all the time, 'I can't believe it!'" Pargman added, "And you touched me, and the heat went through my body, and I just went down backwards." "Under the power!" Kuhlman exclaimed. "And you, a Lutheran!"[70] Along with Lutherans and all other types of Christians, Catholics also gave their testimony to the slaying power of the Spirit. On April 17, 1975, Kuhlman interviewed Father J. Bertolucci. The young priest and Kuhlman discussed their shared experiences at the World Conference of the Holy Spirit, which occurred in Jerusalem in 1974. "I was at Jerusalem at the same time you were," Father Bertolucci said with a smile. "It was a beautiful experience. You came out, and the power of God was just so real. The Lord started giving you the word of knowledge, I believe we call it. You started calling out healings, people would come up, be [slain]. I wanted you to pray for me. I thought, 'Every Catholic priest and minister in the auditorium should come up so she can pray for you.' You began praying for me, I went down, I went down two times. The second time, you did something. You left the stage and began walking through the people. It was like walking through high grass. People were just falling as you walked."[71] Although Kuhlman herself spent several episodes of *Miracles* carefully explaining the purpose of the slaying power of the Spirit, the number and variety of testimonies about it were invaluable for making this charismatic experience more palatable to the American public.

Father Bertolucci spoke hesitantly of "words of knowledge" in his conversation with Kuhlman. This particular gift became characteristic of charismatic Christianity during the charismatic renewal movement. Kuhlman became a celebrity in the movement due in large part to the manifestation of the word of knowledge in her miracle services. On May 13, 1970, Ruby Haff visited with Kuhlman about her healing from arthritis. Haff was a lovely woman in her late fifties, raised Southern Baptist and a practicing American Baptist. She was invited to a healing service. "I came into the service as an arthritic," Haff stated. "My problem was stupidity. I never thought it could be me. You called out a healing of the spine. I thought, 'Why won't that person say something?' You walked down the aisle, pointed at me and said, 'It's you.' My jaw dropped. I thought people were being rewarded. I thought they had earned these healings. It was as though electricity went through my hands and arms. I looked down expecting to see them sparking!" Kuhlman added, "I had to call you out, or you might still be sitting there."[72] Charming Ruby Haff laughingly told of her own ignorance as divine healing almost passed her by. Kuhlman manifested a word of knowledge, singling out Haff as the one receiving healing. Haff seemed genuinely astonished by her charismatic experience. This type of testimony was effective in presenting the image of charismatic Christians as one of regular people surprised by the miraculous acts of God.

The guest roster of *Miracles* also included very average young people who offered candid testimonies to divine healing. On February 14, 1973, Kuhlman welcomed Lisa Larios with the words, "I want to introduce you to a twelve-year-old girl who believes in miracles." Lisa's testimony was about a healing of cancer in her hip. She was lanky and dressed in a stylish miniskirt jumper. Her long straight hair swung almost to her hips. Kuhlman asked Lisa to show off her "good legs," to which Lisa responded with rolled eyes and a reluctant pose. Isabell Larios, Lisa's mother, joined Kuhlman and her daughter in order to tell the story of Lisa's diagnosis of bone cancer in her hip. "On May 25, they did big surgery on her," Isabell said. "Her hip bone was like Swiss cheese. Cancer had eaten it." Doctors gave Lisa six months to live. "A neighbor told me she wanted me to go [to a Kuhlman service]. It was on Sunday, July 16, 1972. I had never even seen you on TV. I thought, 'Oh, come on.'" Despite her skepticism, Isabell took Lisa to the service. "Lisa didn't know she had cancer," Isabell said. "She didn't know she had six months to live. I didn't know if I should tell her." Kuhlman began to call out a healing of cancer in the wheelchair section (a common way Kuhlman manifested a word of knowledge), where Isabell and Lisa were sitting due to a fall Lisa suffered the week prior. "Lisa felt a warmth in her tummy," Isabell stated. Lisa added, "Like I had a fever in my stomach." Lisa Larios's subsequent doctors' appointments revealed a cancer-free body. Kuhlman asked, "What if you hadn't gotten up? What if you had not put forth the effort?" Lisa replied, "I didn't have to think of that, because I would have done it. I'd never even heard of faith healers." Kuhlman laughed and answered, "I'll tell you a secret. Faith healers don't heal anyone. It takes the power of God."[73]

On *I Believe in Miracles*, Kuhlman obviously enjoyed the working-class guests as much as she had in her *Your Faith and Mine* years. She discussed with Mr. Robles the miraculous healing from leukemia of his daughter and did not censor his admission that he had run a topless bar in San Francisco. She listened attentively as Charles Bokach and his daughter remembered the nights when Bokach came home drunk and beat his wife.[74] She was comfortable with revealing the gritty details of the hard-living people on her show because she recognized the persuasive power of their testimonies of redemption.

As relaxed as Kuhlman was about sometimes coarse details in the testimonies of her guests, she was careful on *Miracles* always to present a gracious visual of charismatic Christianity. Kuhlman did not mind the audience hearing stories about the miracle-working power of God in everyday lives, but she was determined that the people who came on her show would look sophisticated and polished. Kuhlman was aware that charismatic Christianity was negatively associated with the poor and uneducated. In light of this, she consciously manipulated the appearance of her guests in order to promote a new vision of a more middle-class, culturally acceptable charismatic Christianity. Every guest was dressed in attractive clothing. The women always had perfectly styled hair and sported professionally applied makeup. The men wore suits or crisp shirts and slacks. Either the *I Believe in Miracles* staff provided clothing for the guests or clear instructions were given to dress in a smart, conservative style. Either way, even the most humble guests appeared chic and refined in dress and style. Guests might have scarred skin, terrible teeth, or bad grammar, but they always were dressed to impress. Lorna Gall appeared with Kuhlman in June of 1975 to tell about her divine healing. The women sat in the faux garden as Lorna explained that she worked as a custodian at the Butler public schools. Her blue eyeglasses perfectly matched her simple navy dress trimmed in white rickrack. She was the very picture of working-class respectability.[75] Kuhlman's guests such as these demonstrated the normalcy of charismatic Christianity. The casual references to charismatic experiences by average people reinforced the conventionality of these manifestations of the Spirit and the availability of these experiences to the people in the viewing audience. Or, as Harry Stephenson put it, "What God done for me, he can do for anybody."[76]

Appealing to the Elite

Guests who appeared average contributed to the viewers' sense that charismatic Christianity was normal. Meanwhile, another set of guests highlighted the entrée of charismatic Christianity into social and educational circles previously considered beyond its reach. They were notable not for being average, but for being elite. Through their stories, charismatic Christianity was presented as not just normal, but culturally desirable. Colonel Tom Lewis made repeat appearances on the show. Lewis was a television producer intimately involved in the development of the Armed Forces Radio Network during World War II. He was a cultivated, well-known, and respected figure in television production as well as in the Los Angeles community. He told the story of first watching Kuhlman in action:

> Lewis: I was researching you. I was not hostile. I am Roman Catholic, and I found you doctrinally pure. I read about you, watched you on TV. [At the service at the Shrine], I saw people raising their hands, and I thought, "Oh, that's too bad." They were saying, "Praise the Lord." [After some time,] I lost my objectivity. I began to tell God things I didn't know about myself. I thought of myself as gregarious, happy. I started telling God I was lonely and sad. . . . An addict grabbed you—you didn't cringe, you just said, "All right, honey," and held her. . . . I had thought of myself as stylishly sinful. It was all new to me. Soon I raised my hands and I was saying, "Praise the Lord." After Holy Communion [at Mass] the next day, I felt the Real Presence of God in a staggering way. I was shaking.

Lewis concluded, "I felt bewildered when I left the Shrine. I was terribly happy going home in the car." Kuhlman replied, "How has it changed your life?" "I have a greater love for other people, a reverence for their goodness," Lewis stated. "I was not an awful man, but a very incomplete man."[77]

Lewis's story offered an example for the socially elite interested in charismatic Christianity: he came simply to research the phenomenon. His initial experience was one of discomfort and awkwardness, but soon he found himself drawn into the charismatic experience. He also represented a path to charismatic Christianity for Roman Catholics. In his testimony, Lewis did not cease being a Catholic because he accepted charismatic Christianity. In fact, his subsequent experience of the Mass was made more profound. The show featuring Lewis demonstrated in his person and his story the new status of charismatic Christianity in America.

Viewers watching guests like Colonel Tom Lewis saw a refined image of charismatic Christianity that was appealing. Kuhlman spoke once with

Mrs. Penny Rohrer and her son, John. Kuhlman asked, "How did you get to the Shrine?" Penny Rohrer answered, "I began watching your program on TV. I didn't like it at first, but I kept watching. And then I turned on one day and Tom Lewis was on with you . . . and he was telling about his spiritual healing. And I was so impressed with that. I thought, someone so sophisticated and so well known, it would have to be true. It just would have to be. Uh, this would be nationwide TV and he wouldn't be on here [unless it was true]. I kept trying to rationalize it."[78] Rohrer's testimony contained several of the components that made Kuhlman's television show important to the cultural acceptance of charismatic Christianity. The availability of the show allowed a skeptical viewer to watch several episodes over time even though the viewer "didn't like it at first." The experience of watching a respected, "sophisticated" figure like Tom Lewis claim a charismatic experience on what Rohrer considered "nationwide TV" made the difference and led to her conversion to charismatic Christianity. Lewis was willing to substantiate charismatic Christianity on television, and this public witness led Rohrer to accept his story as true.

The testimonies of a variety of culturally elite guests on *Miracles* contributed to the gentrification of charismatic Christianity. Medical doctors were always considered valuable witnesses to the reality of divine healing, and Kuhlman welcomed many to her show. Dr. Kahn Uyeyama visited with Kuhlman about his own baptism in the Holy Spirit. Uyeyama was an associate clinical professor of medicine on staff at the University of California Medical Center in San Francisco. Kuhlman asked Uyeyama to describe what his response would have been to a claim of divine healing prior to his own baptism in the Holy Spirit. Uyeyama answered, "I would have laughed. I was a humanist and an agnostic. I didn't really believe in God. I would have tried to explain away any claims to divine healing." On the basis of his own evaluation of humanity and a study of the works of Karl Marx, Uyeyama had believed that "man was going to raise himself up by his own bootstraps to divinity." After a conviction that Christianity was real, Uyeyama told of being born again and being filled by the Holy Spirit. "The Lord wanted me to speak in tongues," he explained. "I had to give myself completely to [God]. I thought tongues were gibberish. I had to be made a fool for Christ. I was allowed to sing in a strange language. I never sang—I couldn't carry a tune, I would never sing in public." He concluded, "Many of my patients have been divinely healed since I was baptized in the Holy Ghost. I have seen many miracles."[79] The presence of a medical doctor attesting to speaking in tongues and to the reality of

divine healing gave credibility to Kuhlman, to her show, and, by extension, to charismatic Christianity.

Doctors in the academy also appeared on Kuhlman's show. In 1971,
Kuhlman welcomed Dr. J. M. Ford from Notre Dame.[80] "We held a service at the Convocation Center on the campus of Notre Dame," Kuhlman
began as the show opened. "After the service, I was told, a teacher of theology would like to talk to you. I thought Dr. Ford would be a man, and
in came walking this little Dresden doll." Kuhlman had expected a man,
and instead she met Ford, a slight, elegant British woman. In a lilting
accent, Ford recounted her first exposure to prayer for divine healing.
Her mother was diagnosed with inoperable cancer, and in response she
prayed for healing at the blessed sacrament. "Roman Catholicism has
many healings," Ford noted. "We have Lourdes. But the Roman Catholic
Church is very careful to confirm them." Kuhlman then asked Ford when
she "became acquainted with" the Holy Spirit. "I became familiar with
the Catholic Pentecostal movement. [Some Catholic Pentecostals] came
and prayed over me. I was given back the ability to pray. I was given the gift
of tongues [and the gift of prophecy]." Ford added, "The Holy Spirit has
much more of a personality and is much more personal to me." At the end
of the episode, Kuhlman took Ford's hand and said, "I am so glad you are
my sister in Christ." Both women bowed their heads, and Kuhlman began
to pray as the lights dimmed and the ending music swelled.[81]

Reaching Out to Catholics and Mainliners

Ford's presence on the show was notable not just for her status as an
academic, but also for her Roman Catholicism. Featuring Catholics on
Miracles contributed to changing the popular perception of charismatic
Christianity by locating adherents outside of conservative, rural, southern, Protestant circles. Kuhlman welcomed many Catholics to her show
during its ten years, including several priests and nuns.[82] Following Pope
John XXIII's call for a second Pentecost during the Second Vatican Council from 1962 to 1965, the Roman Catholic Church experienced its own
charismatic renewal. Kuhlman's ministry was successful in presenting
stories of Catholics joined with Protestants at Kuhlman meetings, all
claiming the renewal of charismatic gifts in their faith lives. Many of the
Catholic religious Kuhlman interviewed emphasized the ongoing presence of a healing ministry in Catholicism, much as Dr. Ford noted in her

own story. In Kuhlman's discussion with Father Bertolucci, she stated, "You know, our sitting here today could not have happened twenty, fifteen, even ten years ago." Bertolucci agreed and spoke of "the glorious baptism in the Holy Spirit that brings us together. We're not so far apart now." Later in the show, Kuhlman asked Bertolucci, "How is this affecting the Vatican and Roman Catholics around the world?" Bertolucci responded, "I believe this is the answer to Pope John's prayer for a new Pentecost." Bertolucci explained the pope's recognition of the need for the charisms to be renewed in the church. In a final comment, Bertolucci told of a recent moment in the street ministry he had joined. "Get the picture," Bertolucci said, "of an Assemblies of God man praying with this fallen Roman Catholic, an Episcopal priest counseling him, and a Roman priest teaching him about Jesus, in a Baptist coffee house!"[83] In his testimony, the priest happily presented a picture of charismatic Christianity that crossed all denominational lines.

Kuhlman's positive representation of the presence of Catholics in the charismatic renewal movement reflected a disregard for the negative images of Catholicism held by her more conservative followers. Wayne Warner explains, "One of the problems many Evangelicals had with Kuhlman was her view that individuals who attended her meetings from mainline Protestant, Orthodox, and Roman Catholic churches were a part of the Body of Christ. While Pentecostals and Evangelicals were urging bornagain members and clergy to leave these churches, Kuhlman was sending them back in an effort to make a difference in the life of their church."[84]

Kuhlman's definition of the body of Christ was undiscriminating. "I don't think that denominations mean a thing to [God]," she stated in one episode. "Lutheran, Roman Catholic, Eastern Orthodox, Assemblies of God, Four Square . . . he just jumps over all those things we quibble about."[85]

Kuhlman shared with many of her Catholic guests a delight in the charismatic renewal movement's emphasis on a "unity of the Spirit." Post–Vatican II priests involved in the charismatic renewal in the Catholic Church shared with Kuhlman their excitement over Pope John's prayer for a new Pentecost and a renewal of the role of the Holy Spirit in the church.[86] In a conversation with Father Robert Arrowsmith in 1970, Kuhlman stated, "I am amazed at the number of Roman Catholic priests and nuns at the services. There is a great sense of fellowship." Father Arrowsmith agreed, and shared an experience at a Kuhlman miracle service in Sacramento where he attended along with eight Trappist monks. "But there is an even greater miracle taking place," the priest said. "The power of the Holy Spirit is drawing together so many of different backgrounds, Roman Catholic, Baptist, Lutheran . . ." Kuhlman added, "Jesus is getting the body of Christ ready. It doesn't matter our background. He is getting us ready for the second coming."[87] The fellowship of the Holy Spirit that included Catholics was another sign of the end times Kuhlman eagerly anticipated. For her, the body of Christ united in anticipation of the return of Christ included Catholics as well as all forms of Protestants.

Always congenial to Catholics, Kuhlman was even more encouraging of their place in charismatic Christianity after her invitation to a private audience with Pope Paul VI on October 11, 1972. During the visit, the pope "assured [Kuhlman] of his personal blessing on her work and his continual prayers—thus guaranteeing an even larger Roman Catholic following."[88] Kuhlman's attention to the Catholic charismatic renewal increased her audience by adding new viewers from that body of believers as well as situating her ministry firmly within the ecumenical movement taking root in the mainline churches. Episodes featuring eloquent and enthusiastic charismatic priests and joyful charismatic Catholic laypeople contributed to the changing face of charismatic Christianity presented on *I Believe in Miracles.*

Ministers from mainline Protestant churches added to the new image of charismatic Christianity promoted on Kuhlman's show as well. In 1968, Kuhlman spoke with Rev. Donald Shaw about his visit to a miracle service. A small, balding man with heavy glasses, Shaw explained that he had received a copy of *I Believe in Miracles* from a lay preacher during what he described as a "dry period." Intrigued by the book, Shaw attended a miracle service. "I struggled within as I was at the miracle service. What would my colleagues think of me? I thought of the implications of accepting [what I was seeing]. I was fighting pride." Shaw was convinced of the reality of divine healing by what he saw at the service. "I prayed, 'Dear Lord, whatever it is, I want it.' I received new faith, new hope, new life. I went down under the power of God at the miracle service," Shaw remembered. "Did you know it was the power of God?" Kuhlman asked. "It is hard to say. It was so . . . it happened so quickly. But if anybody at that time had told me that I, Donald Shaw, a very proud Presbyterian and an intellectual,[89] would be lying there on my back in Carnegie Hall, before all of those people . . . [Kuhlman began to laugh, and Shaw smiled as he continued] . . . my self-consciousness gone, gloriously happy and for the first time in my life experiencing this kind of joy, I would have said,

'Brother, you're nuts.'" Kuhlman added happily, "A dead Presbyterian minister came alive in Christ!"[90] Shaw's concerns about the effect a charismatic conversion would have upon his status reflected the remains of a cultural charismatic stigma. His willingness to claim his new charismatic status, even in the face of lingering suspicions, signaled the strengthening of charismatic Christianity within the ranks of mainline leadership.

Kuhlman furthered the image of gentrified charismatic Christianity by hosting several times, in 1968, two mainline charismatic "celebrities," Episcopal priest Dennis Bennett and Lutheran minister Harald Bredesen. In 1960, at the age of forty-three, Bennett announced to his Episcopal congregation in Van Nuys, California, that he had been baptized in the Holy Spirit and spoken in tongues. Most historians of the charismatic renewal movement date its beginning to this announcement. *Time* and *Newsweek* magazines featured Bennett's story on their covers. Bennett's 1970 book *Nine O'clock in the Morning* contained a description of the events in the foreword by John Sherrill. Sherrill wrote, "It was shortly after I set out to investigate the whole mysterious subject of a modern Pentecost that I first heard about an Episcopalian Rector in Van Nuys, California who was in trouble. For on April 3, 1960, Dennis Bennett preached a sermon on the underground Pentecostal Movement that was quietly racing through so many churches in America. He told how he, himself, had spoken in tongues. Instantly an explosion went off in his church."[91] Bennett recounted in the book one member of his congregation standing on a chair shouting, "Throw out the damn tongue-speakers!"[92] The subsequent controversy and publicity served as an organizing event for the diffuse and diverse charismatic prayer groups spread throughout mainline churches.

Another charismatic luminary sat next to Bennett at Kuhlman's conference table. Harald Bredesen was ordained as a Lutheran minister in 1944 at the age of twenty-six, and was baptized in the Holy Spirit at a Pentecostal summer camp two years later. He offered to resign from the Lutheran ministry, but the authorities refused his proposal. For several years he held nonpastoral positions and openly spoke of his charismatic experiences. He worked with "Mr. Pentecost," David du Plessis,[93] and also was involved with the Full Gospel Business Men's Fellowship International. In 1957, he became the pastor of Mount Vernon Dutch Reformed Church in New York City. Bredesen was connected to almost every major figure in the charismatic movement, including Pat Boone and also Pat Robertson, who worked as Bredesen's student assistant from 1958 to 1959. Along with Jean Stone, Bredesen coined the term "charismatic" in 1963, in contrast to the designation "neo-Pentecostal."[94] By the time of his appearance on Kuhlman's show five years later, Bredesen was a recognized leader in the movement he had named.

"I have a terrific inferiority complex sitting here next to you two gentlemen," Kuhlman began on December 13, 1969. Bennett and Bredesen sat next to her around a large wooden conference table, each man in black suit and clerical collar. "I know your backgrounds, your degrees, and here I sit here and, uh . . ." Bredesen leaned in toward Kuhlman and broke in with his own finish to her halting statement, ". . . and confer upon us the greatest opportunity we've ever had to reach millions of people!" The three laughed together at the truth of Bredesen's statement. From the beginning, Bredesen and Bennett acknowledged the role Kuhlman's show was playing in spreading the news about the charismatic renewal. Kuhlman was pleased by the comment and the convivial laughter, and continued. "Here I am, I'm not sure what I am," and Bennett interjected this time: "We're not so sure *ourselves* these days." "I heard you were a Christian," Bredesen said to Bennett, and both men laughed again. The gentle manner of the two men, their humility and refined appearance made their bemused attitude about their own charismatic character quite appealing. The various episodes featuring the men covered the gamut of charismatic teaching, as the two mainline ministers conversed easily and comfortably with Kuhlman about the reality of the Holy Spirit and the activity of the Holy Spirit in their churches and in their denominations. Bredesen called the Holy Spirit "the forgotten person of the Godhead," and Bennett added in his soft British accent, "We were taught about him [the Holy Spirit], but I didn't know him as a living being."[95] The image of the two coherent, well-educated, and kindly pastors calmly discussing the importance of charismatic renewal in the mainline churches and in all churches in America was a strikingly new picture of charismatic Christianity presented to the viewing public.

Kuhlman interviewed a wide assortment of guests who contributed to the gentrification of the image of charismatic Christianity in America. An Apollo 15 astronaut; politicians such as Herbert Ellingwood, the legal affairs secretary for California governor Ronald Reagan; current and former senators; professional football players—all sat with Kuhlman on her soundstage. Celebrities like the expected Pat Boone and the unexpected "LuLu" from *Hee Haw* gave their witness to their participation in charismatic Christianity. Revered missionary, Holocaust survivor, and best-selling author Corrie Ten Boom visited with Kuhlman over the course of several episodes, as did Houston police captain John LeVrier. The presence of so many respected, professional people on Kuhlman's show during its ten-year run testified to the growing cultural acceptance of charismatic Christianity in America.

A Testimony Goes Off-Track

Not every episode of *Miracles* provided a neat and tidy presentation of charismatic Christianity. Although guests were certainly "vetted" before appearing, occasionally a guest did not seem amenable to following Kuhlman's lead through the standard narrative arc of the show. On April 10, 1969, Kuhlman sat down to talk with Mr. Mackintosh and Rachel Phillips. Mackintosh was obviously a believer in divine healing and a devotee of Kuhlman. Phillips was neither, a fact that became increasingly apparent during the show. Phillips had gone to Mackintosh, an acquaintance she respected, for advice following the diagnosis of a serious infection in her one kidney. Kuhlman introduced the pair to her viewing audience by declaring, "You'll agree they are the two most unusual guests we've ever had—a Jewess and a businessman."[96] The first words out of Phillips's mouth were "I still can't believe I'm here. This is the last place I ever expected to be." In themselves, Phillips's words were not unusual. Many guests began their stories by expressing a sense of amazement that they were on television, with Kuhlman, testifying to a miracle. The standard narrative of a *Miracles* episode often began with this type of exchange. The beginning salvo would be followed by a story of a skeptic transformed into a believer, or a sick person without hope healed and restored. Not with Rachel Phillips. She meant every word. She truly couldn't believe she was sitting with Kuhlman, and she truly wasn't pleased about it.

Kuhlman and Mackintosh attempted to carry on the interview in the standard fashion. "When the doctors say they can't do anything, it's time to go to Kathryn Kuhlman," Mackintosh said happily. "Of course, going to Kathryn Kuhlman is really going to God," Kuhlman averred. This exchange of pleasantries accomplished, Kuhlman turned to Rachel Phillips for her story. Phillips explained she had not been feeling well when Mr. Mackintosh recommended she attend a Kuhlman meeting. "Mr. Mackintosh knows all the right people, he is a very upstanding citizen," Phillips stated. His position in society made his suggestion to attend a Kuhlman meeting all the more shocking for Phillips. "I thought, he's not one of these! He couldn't be! I just didn't think he was naïve enough to be fooled into believing things like that. But I felt, what do I have to lose?" At this point in the interview, Phillips was still within the preferred narrative arc of *Miracles*. Many guests told of initial skepticism and surprise that educated, well-respected people were charismatic Christians. Phillips's account, so far, was supporting the gentrification narrative quite well. Mackintosh took up the story. "Doctors told her she didn't have more than two years to live. I arranged to meet her after the meeting, so she had to go!" Phillips reluctantly agreed to attend the meeting. It was at this point in the standard narrative structure that Phillips should have begun to speak of her awe and wonder at the miracle service.

The experience of the miracle service was the "pivot point" in most "converted skeptic" testimonies. Not this time. "It was a new experience," Phillips stated coolly. "The people in front of me were very emotional. I was way up in the balcony. I didn't want to be seen. I knew I could get out of there if I needed to. I know an awful lot of sane people. I didn't want them questioning me." Phillips quoted Kuhlman's words at the service, "You said, 'There is a woman with a serious kidney ailment. Whether you know it or not, you are healed.'" Phillips continued, "I was not used to this kind of meeting, so somehow I didn't identify with [Kuhlman's words]. I have a very strong faith in God. If he wants me alive, he will keep me alive. I went to the ladies' room after the meeting and passed a kidney stone the size of a lima bean. I am an RN. The stone had not shown up on an x-ray. It was what was causing the infection." Phillips did not recognize that Kuhlman's word of knowledge was directed at her. Even after passing the kidney stone, she did not make the transition in her story to acknowledging a charismatic-type divine healing. God may have healed her, but if so, it was because he wanted to, not because of Kuhlman. When Phillips returned to the doctor with whom she worked, she did not tell him of her trip to the Kuhlman meeting. The standard reason in a televised testimony for concealing the miracle service visit was so the healed person could tell his or her doctor of the divine origin of the cure in a dramatic moment of revelation. Phillips's reasons were more pedantic. "My doctor thought what happened at Kuhlman meetings was a hypnotic trance. You have to maintain a certain image. I didn't tell him I had been to the meeting at the Shrine because I have to work with this man."

It became apparent that Phillips was not speaking as a converted skeptic and meant every (disbelieving) word she said. The interview became increasingly awkward. Phillips was operating outside of the standard narrative construct of a *Miracles* episode, where the end point was a positive presentation of charismatic Christianity. In a talk show that depended upon tight narrative control, this was dangerous. In response, Kuhlman persisted in asking the same questions as always, determined to overlay the necessary narrative structure on Phillips's problematic story. "How do you account for your healing?" Kuhlman asked after Phillips's dry "testimony." "I feel that God wanted me to be here. . . . I didn't want to come here. I feel that God healed me because he has a purpose for me." Phillips asserted that the reason she passed the kidney stone was that God wanted her to work to bring children out of Vietnam. Kuhlman, in a final effort to lead Phillips back into the charismatic narrative, asked how her experience at the miracle service changed her. "I don't think I've changed any, because I always believed," Phillips said flatly. In perhaps the worst testimony to the effect of charismatic Christianity seen on *Miracles* in its ten-year run, Phillips succeeded in avoiding Kuhlman's determined lead to the very end of the show. It is difficult to imagine Kuhlman ever again inviting Mr. Mackintosh to bring a guest along to her show.

Even in the rare episode where Kuhlman was unable to keep the testimony "on track," the reality of the gentrification of charismatic Christianity peeked through. In her interview, Phillips repeatedly referred to Mr. Mackintosh in terms of respect and admiration. Mr. Mackintosh, then, became the gentrified "foil" for Phillips's disparaging testimony. Phillips said from the start, "Mr. Mackintosh knows all the right people, he is a very upstanding citizen. I thought, he's not one of these!" But Mr. Mackintosh *was* "one of these": a gentrified charismatic Christian.

I Believe in Miracles and the Gentrification of Charismatic Christianity

How important was Kuhlman's television show in the gentrification of the image of charismatic Christianity? This question leads to further speculation about the role of television in producing social change in mid-twentieth-century America. Television broke down boundaries between the public and private spheres of life in America in ways never before experienced. Janet Thumim explains, "The acknowledgment that functional boundaries between the public and the private spheres have been disturbed by the advent of mass broadcasting is now a trope of television studies."[97] Thumim continues, "That television does indeed have a dynamic relation to the processes of daily life—and hence to broad social change—is now widely accepted, and was of course the premise underlying both commercially funded and public service television during the 1950s."[98] The ability of television to change public opinion was noticed and mobilized by proponents of civil rights legislation, opponents of the Vietnam War, and advocates for women's liberation. An entire segment of the advertising economy was predicated upon the belief that television could change opinions and thoughts. As Timberg explains, "[During the 1970s], the nation watched television screens more and more as sets converted to color and the Vietnam War became a living-room war, contested in words and images as well as armaments. Television became increasingly, during this time, the 'talk of the nation.'"[99] By the mid-1960s, access to television airtime was crucial for any group attempting to sway public opinion.

The brutal images associated with the civil rights movement and their motivational power for change impressed upon a generation of politically active men and women the power of television to persuade. The passing of civil rights legislation, the rallying nature of Vietnam protests, and the emergence of second-wave feminism can all partially be attributed to television's interest in each of these "stories."[100] Patricia Bradley carefully underscores the role media played in the presentation of the civil rights movement. Television used its ability to create a narrative through images to paint a sympathetic picture of the activists. While this effort had its humanitarian side, the narrative of the civil rights movement also had the necessary drama and compelling content needed to maintain the large audiences the advertisers liked.[101] From a television programmer's viewpoint, civil rights, Vietnam, and women's lib were all *good stories*.[102] During the days of *Miracles*, so was charismatic Christianity.

At their best, television talk shows like *Miracles* provided a safe space for new ideas. Timberg explains, "Some social critics have seen rays of promise in all this talk. Although there are limits to what can be said and done in all commercial television formats, new constituencies were able to appear on shows like *Donahue* and *Oprah* and speak directly for themselves and their groups without experts or professional broadcasters re-framing their words."[103] *Miracles* provided a place on the dial for gentrified charismatic Christianity, a new concept for most of the American viewing public. The guests on *Miracles* were able to present themselves and their stories in a natural way, through the sharing of stories and seemingly casual conversation. This egalitarianism of the talk show benefited the public image of charismatic Christianity. "Everyday," average charismatics were able to talk about their alternative experiences without the need to defend themselves against cultural predispositions. In the world of *Miracles*, they were normal. In conversations with Kuhlman, divine healing was just another part of ordinary life. In such a welcoming environment, those who had charismatic experiences to share were able to do so without fear of being challenged or marginalized. *Miracles* did not even have a live studio audience to respond to guests. On that soundstage, the charismatic practices that seemed esoteric, fringe, and frightening in the "real world" were transformed into narratives that seemed, after hundreds of repetitions, quite normal. Kuhlman said it often enough; "I have to believe in miracles; I see them every day."

The increasing influence television exerted over cultural opinions was due in part to the success television marketers achieved in weaving television into the fabric of American life. Television produced societal change through its access to the private sphere of the home. Thumim observes, "The domestic site of consumption and the self-conscious simultaneity of audiences' television experience makes it part of everyday life, part of mundane experience in ways that fundamentally alter previously crucial structuring boundaries such as those between past and present, here and there, self and other/s."[104] Television's presence in the home brought new images into the mid-twentieth-century American living room in ways that were mind-altering. New knowledge streamed into American homes through television sets. Hundreds and hundreds of images of charismatic Christians came into the homes of Americans all over the country as Kuhlman's show increased in syndication and the number of television sets owned exploded. The background chatter of divine healing, slayings in the Spirit, and words of knowledge was now welcome in homes where charismatic Christianity was previously unknown. Religion was now mediated through the disorienting means of television, and private devotion melded with public testimony, with denominational boundaries altered by shared charismatic experiences projected on the television screen. The ability to self-identify as a charismatic became based not so much on membership in a church as on membership in a movement largely defined by the media.

Wayne Munson argues that television talk shows were agents of cultural change. "My study of talkshows approaches them as things 'to think with,'" Munson states, "and asks how they construct knowledge, reality, culture, politics, and the self."[105] Rather than destroying community through its privatizing of entertainment and its disruption of live social networks for the sake of virtual communities centered around simulated people, Munson asserts that television talk shows were part of a new social reality based in the media. "It is my view that a medium like the talk-show creates not 'placelessness' but a hyperlocal or cyberspatial 'place.' Old lines are being erased, but new ones are being drawn—new social and political connections, new 'neighborhoods.' The talk show is not so much the last neighborhood in America—however apocalyptic some of the talk about it—as it is the newest and least understood."[106] The new neighborhood created by television talk shows included a freshly gentrified version of charismatic Christianity.

Inside the charismatic neighborhood created by *Miracles*, elite and average mingled comfortably in the imagery projected by the talk show, all sharing the common denominator of charismatic experience. The quietly charismatic Episcopalian comfortably coexisted with the boisterous Vegas showgirl convert, their connectedness existing not in reality but in the fluid, permissive space of television. Father Dennis Bennett didn't have to know the former bar-hopping Richard Wolf personally; they were brothers in Spirit and in television. Charismatics of strikingly different types found on *Miracles* a stage from which to share their stories. As the viewing audience watched and learned, "old lines were erased and new ones drawn," in Munson's words. Television, with its recombinatory ability, took charismatic Christianity in all its diverse forms and helped produce a vision of a charismatic movement.[107] *I Believe in Miracles* helped rewrite and transform the practice of religion in America. The immediacy and flow of television produced in both form and content an adaptable charismatic Christianity that became a more legitimate option for the American public/consumer.

Not Everyone Believes in Miracles: Countering Criticism

I Believe in Miracles helped make charismatic Christianity more respectable by emphasizing its apparent normalcy and appealing to viewers in the privacy of their own homes. The talk show format helped create a casual, welcoming environment that made the often controversial topics associated with charismatic practices seem like just another topic of conversation. *Miracles* invested the culture's image of charismatic

Christianity with a badly needed sense of conventionality. But as the sixties became the seventies, charismatic Christianity took a serious blow to its fragile new respectability in the form of a movie entitled *Marjoe*. The documentary was the intentional self-exposé of former child healing evangelist Marjoe Gortner. The film was released in 1972 and garnered an Academy Award for best documentary. In the movie Gortner, now an adult, returned to the healing evangelism tents of his childhood, where he had been exploited by an unbalanced mother and conniving father. Like a magician revealing the tricks of the trade, Gortner explained the intricacies of Pentecostal meetings to the camera crew in preparation for filming the services where he was going to preach. The crew, made up of men and women with equally long hair, all smoking cigarettes and dressed in tank tops and jeans, were understandably concerned about the Pentecostal church's acceptance of their veracity. Marjoe reassured them that they would be received favorably, because "They accept me as real." The film captured scenes of Gortner in "real life," smoking pot, lounging at loud parties, or happily bobbing on a water bed in skintight jeans. The footage would then cut to extended shots of ecstatic Pentecostal services where Gortner exhorted, healed, sang, and counted the offerings as they poured in. Gortner expertly spoke in tongues and laid hands on people lined up for prayer, leaving them shaking and writhing as they fell to the floor. "You gotta have a gimmick," Gortner explained. "If you are going to go into big-time religion, this is the game you have to play."[108]

Marjoe brought back to center stage the disreputable practices of faith healers that haunted charismatic Christianity throughout its history. Hucksters and charlatans, from Elmer Gantry to Marjoe, represented the reality of fraud and the danger to innocent victims such as the congregations who welcomed Marjoe and followed pastors equally as corrupt. Kuhlman was asked by *Christianity Today*, "How have you overcome the disreputable cloud in which faith healers operate? Has the self-confessed hypocrisy of *Marjoe* affected you or your ministry in any way?" After offering her standard rebuttal of the title "faith healer," Kuhlman continued: "That film has not affected our ministry one bit. I declined to serve on a panel with him. God's Word does not need to be defended. Oh sure, when I was younger I used to fight at the drop of a hat. I started out as a teenager defending my wonderful Jesus. (Remember, I have red hair.) After years of experience, I found out that he needs no defense. He will defend himself. As for the Holy Spirit, all we have to do is be faithful to preaching the Word, and he will defend me." A stern refusal to answer critics was Kuhlman's method of choice. "When it comes to the scoffers, I just leave them to God."[109]

Since the days of the "Battle of the Pulpits" with Dallas Billington, Kuhlman had remained fairly consistent in her refusal to enter into controversy over criticism or questions. She chose instead to work to present a different, more sophisticated image of charismatic Christianity to counter the ministries considered offensive by the American public. She also knew that a soft answer and a lack of defensiveness would make her more appealing to the press as well as the public. She was quick to claim a position of ignorance or innocence when challenged about the failures of her healing services. Eleanor Blau of the *New York Times* documented Kuhlman's standard response: "Acknowledging that many people with severe afflictions leave her services unhealed, Miss Kuhlman said there was much she could not explain or understand. 'I just don't know,' she said, shaking her head. 'I don't know, I don't know.'"[110] Her response was both humble and shrewd. Kuhlman maintained throughout her career that she had no control over the healing taking place in her ministry, and she refused to blame failures on a lack of faith in the sick. She also understood that a self-effacing stance was often a safe haven when confronted with disturbing disappointments. In a caustic article titled "Kathryn Kuhlman Holy Spirit's 'Man'?" Earl Hansen wrote down his observations from a Kuhlman miracle service at a Seattle arena. "Noticing the tear-stained cheeks of a young couple whose tiny daughter had a deformity, a woman, herself widowed at an early age, questioned: 'How do you keep putting yourself back together. How do you keep the hope alive with one let-down after another?'"[111] Kuhlman's answer was consistent and simple: I don't know.

By far the most damning criticism Kuhlman received in her entire career came from medical doctor William Nolen. Nolen wrote an article for *McCall's* magazine that became the basis for a chapter in the best-selling book *Healing: A Doctor in Search of a Miracle*, in which he explored a Kuhlman miracle service. In September 1974, *McCall's* published "In Search of a Miracle," an account of Nolen's experiences as an usher at a Kuhlman miracle service in Minneapolis in June 1973. In 1974, Nolen published a book containing his work on Kuhlman as well as research into "psychic healers" in the Philippines and a practitioner of divine cures who called himself Norbu Chen. According to the back cover of the paperback edition, Nolen's book contained "the startling truth about faith healing and psychic surgery." The promotional blurb continued: "Thousands of

Americans each year flock to Kathryn Kuhlman's faith-healing services, or travel as far as the Philippines to visit psychic surgeons who operate with their bare hands. These healers claim to cure almost anything. Now a surgeon conducts a thorough investigation of this amazing world."[112]

Nolen's investigation did not originate in a study of Kuhlman's ministry. He was initially contacted by Kuhlman supporters Ralph Ryan and wife, identified only as "Mrs. Ryan." The Ryans were acquaintances of Nolen, and Mrs. Ryan inquired if Nolen would be interested in serving as an usher at a Kuhlman miracle service in Minneapolis. The meeting organizer wanted one or two local doctors and nurses available at the service in case anyone was overcome and fainted. Nolen enthusiastically agreed. At this time he was already gathering research on Filipino healers for his forthcoming book, and a further opportunity to study divine healing in an American context was irresistible. Mrs. Ryan's invitation was a coup. Nolen explained:

> Then Mrs. Ryan put the topping on the sundae. "Ralph has another idea, Dr. Nolen. He's wondering if you'd find it useful if he had a couple of legal secretaries take down the names and addresses of people at the service who say they are healed by Miss Kuhlman? He thinks it would be great if someone could check on some of these patients after the service to see if they really have been healed. He's very impressed by Miss Kuhlman, but he's a lawyer, you know, and he likes to be certain that no one is fooling him." "Mrs. Ryan," I said, "you can't imagine how happy I'd be to have all those names and addresses. There are few things I'd like more." (41)

Nolen did not say he made Mrs. Ryan aware of his ulterior motive in agreeing to be an usher. Thanks again to the helpful (and unaware) Mrs. Ryan, Nolen also received access to Kuhlman backstage after the miracle service for a private interview.[113]

Nolen's account of the healing service in Minneapolis was not positive. The Friday before the Monday meeting, Nolen and his wife attended a training event for all three hundred Minneapolis ushers. Duly trained, they arrived the following Monday at the service. Nolen was disturbed by the sight of so many desperately ill people. "Every patient I saw, except of course those who were retarded, had the desperate look of those who have all but given up—who are nearly, but not quite, resigned to their fate" (51–52). Nolen described the healing segment: "Patient and wheelchair delivered to the stage, patient put through running, bending or breathing paces, depending on the nature of the cure. Applause for each performance. Patient and wheelchair returned to the aisle. Asthmatics, arthritics and multiple-sclerosis patients all ran through their new tricks" (60). One young woman's case, Nolen wrote, "shook severely what little hope I had left that Kathryn Kuhlman was, truly, a miracle worker" (61). Nolen was distressed by the young woman's claim of a polio healing when she still manifested all the physical symptoms of the disease. "For Kathryn Kuhlman to really believe that the Holy Spirit had worked a miracle with this girl, it seemed to me that Kathryn Kuhlman would have had to be either blind or incredibly stupid, and she was neither. Was she, then, a hypocrite or a hysteric? I didn't know, but I had begun to seriously question her credibility and that of her organization" (61–62).

Nolen's statement was somewhat disingenuous, since his tone throughout the chapter was that of a person already solidly skeptical of "Kuhlman and her organization." After more descriptions of the service, Nolen stated, "There were still long lines of people waiting to get on the stage and claim their cures, but at five o'clock, with a hymn and a final blessing, the show ended." Nolen watched those who had not been healed leave the auditorium. "I wondered if she really knew what damage she was doing," he wrote. "I couldn't believe that she did" (62–63). His conclusions concerning the miracles of Kuhlman's ministry were clear: "I don't believe Miss Kuhlman is a liar; I don't believe she is a charlatan; I don't believe she is, consciously, dishonest. I think (and this is, of course, only my opinion, based on a rather brief acquaintance with her) that she honestly believes the Holy Spirit works through her to perform miraculous cures. I think that she sincerely believes that the thousands of patients who come to her services every year and claim cures are, through her ministrations, being cured of organic diseases.[114] I also believe, and my investigations confirm this, that she is wrong" (93–94). According to Nolen, no miracles were happening at Kuhlman's services at all; they were only the "show" of a deluded woman convinced she was helping the sick when in fact she was being horrifically harmful.

By characterizing Kuhlman as ignorant and misguided, Nolen's book struck at the core of her ministry and threatened Kuhlman's authority as a religious leader. His criticism left the impression that when Kuhlman gave her stock answer, "I just don't know," she was indeed telling the truth. Kuhlman recognized the danger inherent in Nolen's critique. The gentrified charismatic Christianity she had carefully developed was at risk of becoming once again an object of universal derision. She made the unusual decision to respond to his book. On November 24, 1974, she sat down with Ann Butler of the *Pittsburgh Press* to offer a rebuttal. "I'm taking the attitude that the truth needs no defense," Kuhlman began, her standard rejoinder to criticism. Then she continued. "The Bible needs no defense. The Holy Spirit needs no defense. Therefore it is only with sympathy and pity that I pray for those who lack the spiritual understanding regarding the supernatural spirit of God." With Nolen, however, Kuhlman became personal in her comments. "He was very deceitful. In good faith I gave him the names and addresses of people who had been cured. He ignored the whole thing. . . . Here is a doctor who has had two books published. This is his third. It's pretty hard, most difficult, to make your third book a best seller. He knew he couldn't miss by using me. He chose me so he could get good publicity." In response to Nolen's claims regarding the lack of evidence for actual healings at her meetings, Kuhlman noted the validation of other members of the medical profession and highlighted additional testimonies from those who claimed to be cured. She concluded, "I am definitely sure that Dr. Nolen's personal feelings and analysis will never stop God from performing miracles. Always remember this: You can say something about a person, but you can't touch God."[115] Kuhlman stated she would grant no more interviews about Nolen. "I'm through advertising his book," she said with a laugh. But when offered an interview with the potential for unprecedented exposure for her ministry, Kuhlman could not refuse, Nolen or not.

In late 1974 and into 1975, Kathryn Kuhlman the talk show host became, for a brief moment, Kathryn Kuhlman the talk show guest. Kuhlman's unusual foray into the domain of another television talk show host's turf was motivated by the need to respond to the widespread attention given to Nolen's magazine article and book. In addition to the need for damage control, Kuhlman was also at the peak of her celebrity, and charismatic Christianity was "hot." As the major media figure for this newly chic brand of Christianity, Kuhlman made the guest list of both *The Tonight Show* and *Dinah!*[116] Dinah Shore welcomed Kuhlman to her show on February 3, 1975. Kuhlman joined Lily Tomlin and the actress Esther Rolle from the situation comedy *Good Times*. The women sat on a curved couch around a coffee table, Dinah in the center, Tomlin and Rolle to Dinah's right. By this time Kuhlman was very ill with the symptoms of an enlarged heart, a condition that had troubled her for several years. Despite her sickness, she still managed to project a dynamic persona as she walked on to the stage in a glittery hot pink floor-length gown. She sat to Shore's left, her long legs crossed at the ankles, rings and earrings shimmering.

"I've seen you, you know," Tomlin said as she leaned forward across Rolle almost immediately after Shore's introduction. Kuhlman smiled and responded, "Oh really?" "At the Shrine," Tomlin continued. "I saw so many miracles I got bored." Shore and the audience laughed somewhat uneasily at Tomlin's statement. "I saw at least four hundred miracles," Tomlin continued, then added unexpectedly, "I was very impressed. I got there at 7:00 AM for a 1:00 show. I was totally mesmerized by you." Kuhlman took up the conversation at this point. "What is always so thrilling is to see God at work. I have nothing to do with it." Shore then challenged Kuhlman to take some credit for the healings, which Kuhlman characteristically refused. Pushing Kuhlman on this point, Shore added, "I know Lily couldn't do it!" to which Tomlin replied, "I haven't tried." The audience and the women laughed, relieving the subtle tension in the room. Kuhlman then spoke for a few moments regarding "the simple power of God to heal." Charlton Heston dropped by, in a classic example of talk show planned spontaneity, to promote his new film amid many jokes about welcoming Moses to join Kuhlman. The group discussed whether healing was only available for Christians. Kuhlman stated that she was "convinced God is altogether different than we think. We try to bring God down to our level. He is a merciful, compassionate God. God is bigger than all these things." Throughout the discussion, Tomlin was obviously captivated by Kuhlman. The show went to commercial, and at the return to the broadcast, Tomlin had changed places on the couch. She now sat next to Kuhlman, shoulder to shoulder, affectionately close, with Kuhlman's arm resting gently on Tomlin's leg. In many ways, this collision of images represented the current status of charismatic Christianity as embodied by its primary icon. Still somewhat awkward, charismatic Christianity by 1975 was being gradually accepted by American culture and sought after by American media. Charismatics were still unusual, but now intriguing; still bemusing, but now appealing. By the end of the show, Tomlin was enchanted, and gave Kuhlman an affectionate hug. The world was exposed to the spectacle of the defining leader of charismatic Christianity being embraced by television's elite.

Charismatic Christianity had "made it" culturally by 1975. Due in large part to Kuhlman's groundbreaking talk show, it was now a topic of great interest, especially with the emergence of the media darlings the Jesus

People. Still a target of ridicule for some, charismatic Christianity's role as an object of satire indicated its high level of exposure in American culture. On Tomlin's own show *Laugh-In*, Ruth Buzzi developed "Kathleen Pullman," a character she said was based on Kuhlman. Buzzi told the *Los Angeles Times*, "After the takeoff I received a letter from Kathryn saying, 'No one was more happy with the satire than I.' Now I hear that the director of the Kathryn Kuhlman TV show keeps saying, 'If you don't do it right, we'll get Ruth Buzzi.'"[117] Kuhlman and other leaders excitedly declared the explosion of interest indicative of the renewal of Christianity in America and the imminent second coming of Christ.

Perhaps motivated by the belief that America was at last ready to accept charismatic Christianity completely, Kuhlman decided to record a miracle service in its entirety. Unfortunately, her usually impeccable timing was off.[118] As was the case with other "hot items" picked up by television, charismatic Christianity "was set out on a trajectory that awaits all media products: rise, peak, and compromise."[119] It was the beginning of the end of media interest in charismatic Christianity. But before the end came one final product, a full-length film of a Kuhlman miracle service in Sin City itself: Las Vegas, Nevada.

CHAPTER 6

Filming a Miracle

D espite her enthusiasm for all media, especially television, Kuhlman did not record a miracle service in its entirety until very late in her career. Filmed May 3, 1975, the syndicated special *Dry Land, Living Water* was a rare glimpse into the workings of Kuhlman's trademark meetings. When those who knew Kuhlman only from her talk show tuned in for her special, they saw a markedly different vision of Kathryn Kuhlman and charismatic Christianity. On *I Believe in Miracles*, Kuhlman and her guests shared stories in calm and casual conversation of experiences such as being "slain in the Spirit" and divine healing. In Las Vegas, cameras captured the same events with all their attendant chaos and emotion. Kuhlman also presented a much more melodramatic image of herself inside the convention center in Las Vegas, a persona strikingly similar to that of *Your Faith and Mine*. Kuhlman herself had not changed, and her miracle services were not new; from the days of *Your Faith and Mine*, both remained remarkably consistent. What changed in the Vegas film was Kuhlman's presentation of herself and charismatic Christianity. She removed the mediating presence of testimony and gave audiences access to the complete miracle service experience. In the Vegas film, Kuhlman revealed aspects of her ministry to the public eye that threatened her gentrified image. This last production captured Kuhlman in all her glory, for better or for worse.

Greetings and Introductions

Dry Land, Living Water was a major media production. Guided by producer Dick Ross, it was much more than a glorified home video of a Kuhlman service. The opening scene contained a collage of images of arid scenery, with music underscoring the viewer's first glimpse of the Vegas environment. Cutting to the Las Vegas airport, the film rolled as a jet touched down. Next were scenes of Kuhlman arriving, followed closely by a young female assistant. Kuhlman was professionally attired in a red suit dress, with fashionably large round sunglasses and long swinging earrings. A purse dangled over her arm as she reached out to shake the hand of a man and woman waiting to greet her. Over these images, Kuhlman's own voice narrated the segment. Her first words were a quote from the man in the clip with her: "I want you to know, if it were Elvis Presley arriving, I wouldn't have taken the time to meet him."[1] The voice-over identified the Kuhlman enthusiast as Jerry Gordon, the general manager of Caesars Palace, as he grasped Kuhlman's hand in warm welcome. The narration continued as the film interspersed images of Kuhlman riding in Gordon's limo with footage of the Vegas Strip. Kuhlman nodded, pointed, smiled, and gestured at the scenery going by, determinedly avoiding the camera, which must have been a hulking presence inside the limousine. "Nine million visitors a year, spending billions of dollars on round-the-clock entertainment," Kuhlman's disembodied voice intoned. "Was it sheer presumption to think there might also be a spiritual appetite?" The screen was filled with footage of gamblers playing slot machines, roulette, and blackjack as Kuhlman continued. "What sort of response could one expect here, to the message that the God of miracles wants to satisfy the deepest longings of every human heart?" The scene returned to the limousine, as Kuhlman marveled at the city's wonders.

The limousine segment captured vividly the two images of Kuhlman set to collide in the Vegas film. Although thousands had attended Kuhlman's miracle services over the years and knew of her platform guise, many other viewers of *Dry Land, Living Water* would have been familiar only with Kuhlman's talk show persona. The two were quite different. As background music played, the camera panned through the limousine window, and the frame captured Kuhlman in her chic dress and stylish accessories set against the backdrop of a billboard along the highway. The sign was splashed with the words "Mayor Oron Gregson declares Kathryn Kuhlman Day!" As the limousine passed by the huge advertisement, the image of Kuhlman in full miracle service persona came into view. The towering picture accompanying the text was of a full-length Kuhlman in her white pulpit dress, skirt billowing behind her as she reached forward with long, sinuous arms and hands, wiry red hair encircling her head and eyes opened wide. The image was ghostly, like a spirit floating against the dark backdrop of the billboard. Set against this theatrical backdrop of her alter ego, Kuhlman leaned back against the seat, the very picture of a hip seventies businesswoman.

Kuhlman was involved in all aspects of the Vegas special, and it is almost a certainty that she planned for the limousine to drive by the billboard, to allow the camera to capture what she thought of as an example of her fame and prestige. The opportunity for self-promotion was too tempting. Kuhlman had always been a complex combination of modern businesswoman and revival evangelist. The difference was that now, through the Vegas video, both aspects of her public face could be observed in disconcerting juxtaposition.

Over the billboard picture, Kuhlman's monologue began to crescendo. "Many would say that I, too, was gambling, that the odds were against me as I stated my conviction that the craving of the soul for satisfaction is in reality a spiritual hunger." The footage switched to Kuhlman by a large fountain outside the Las Vegas Convention Center. She stood looking past the camera, purse in hand, sunglasses glinting, as her voice declared, "Then within me I felt an overwhelming surge of confidence. Yes, the world's most glittering resort city would indeed respond." Dramatic running chords of a harp surged into an explosion of voices singing the hymn "Nothing Is Impossible" to exuberant piano and organ as film clips flashed on the screen of charter buses, automobiles, and hundreds of people crowding into the convention center parking lot. Video of the crowd flowing into the center was interwoven with pictures of license plates from various parts of the country. The camera recorded people in wheelchairs and resting on canes, men and women, predominantly but not exclusively white, middle-aged or older, gathering in Vegas to see a miracle service live and in person.

Background to the Vegas Service

As earlier chapters demonstrate, the miracle service became the foundation of Kuhlman's ministry after her move to Pennsylvania in the 1950s. She may have held miracle services earlier than this, but it wasn't until she began holding services in Pittsburgh and Youngstown, Ohio, on a regular basis that her ministry became known for healing.[2] After her divorce, Kuhlman began the chapter of her career that lasted until her death, a ministry focused on services of miraculous healing. Her first television show, *Your Faith and Mine*, was simply an excerpt from a Kuhlman miracle service. Each episode included the opening segment of music and prayer, as well as testimonies to miraculous healings from various guests. The people who testified on *Your Faith and Mine* told about receiving divine healing in Kuhlman services. These miracle services were not captured on film but in the stories of those who had experienced them. The services included a healing segment, but this healing segment was not filmed. As Kuhlman's career developed, she expanded her miracle services to include larger meetings around the country and the world. In 1965, she began to hold monthly meetings at the appropriately named Shrine Auditorium in Los Angeles. The Shrine services provided the bulk of testimonies for her best-selling books and her popular talk show. Hundreds of her talk show guests spoke of their experiences at the Shrine and in miracle services in Tulsa's Mabee Center and convention centers in Chicago and St. Louis, among other cities. Even so, the stories gave only snippits of the total service, interpreted through the experience of the testifier. Likewise, none of her books contained a complete account of a miracle service.

Kuhlman moved incrementally toward filming a miracle service in the last decade of her life. According to producer Dick Ross, Kuhlman pitched the idea of filming her miracle services sometime after she began to work with him in 1965. Ross was against the idea. Oral Roberts and A. A. Allen, Kuhlman's colleagues in divine healing and television ministry, had not been successful with such a format. Ross advised Kuhlman against filming her miracle services and led her toward the talk show format of *I Believe in Miracles*. Ross stated plainly, "The Las Vegas Special—the ninety-minute film of the meeting in Las Vegas—was really Kathryn's idea."[3] Kuhlman biographer Jamie Buckingham had a different account. He said Ralph Wilkerson, pastor of Melodyland Christian Center, had the idea: "[Kuhlman] had never allowed cameras in her services. Ralph, however, convinced her to make just one tape, which could be kept so those of future generations (in case there were future generations) could see something of her ministry."[4]

Buckingham's version of the story is incorrect in several details. Kuhlman allowed cameras into her services from the mid-1950s forward, beginning with *Your Faith and Mine*. In the years just prior to the Vegas film, Kuhlman's segment of a charismatic conference held at Melodyland Christian Center was filmed as well as her service at the Second World Conference on the Holy Spirit in Jerusalem in 1974. Parts of the Jerusalem film were featured on episodes of *I Believe in Miracles*. The issue for Kuhlman did not seem to be the presence of cameras in her services. Not filming the miracle service was more a business issue. Ross advised her not to make the miracle service the focus of her television ministry. Ross was a savvy and successful producer who had been involved in the world of Christian film for many years. Other healing evangelists such as Oral Roberts were criticized for the very type of show Kuhlman was proposing. Audiences were distressed by the riotous images of healing meetings. A smart businesswoman herself, Kuhlman took Ross's advice and sat at the wicker chair helm of her very successful talk show that lasted for ten years. But it seems Kuhlman never let go of the idea of filming a miracle service for television. By 1975, Ross had agreed to the filming and later stated that the service "was the best thing I've ever done with her."[5]

Las Vegas and the End Times

Despite his inaccuracies, Buckingham's account offers helpful insight into Kuhlman's decision to make the Vegas film. In the quote from Ralph Wilkerson above, the parenthetical aside is possibly more valuable than the quote itself: "Ralph, however, convinced her to make just one tape, which could be kept so those of future generations (in case there were future generations) could see something of her ministry."[6] "In case there were future generations" points toward a foundational component of Kuhlman's miracle services. Throughout her ministry Kuhlman presented her miracle services as harbingers of the end times and the second coming of Jesus. On one episode of *I Believe in Miracles*, she shared clips of the Vegas special with her television audience. She stated, "We have never filmed any part of a miracle service, except clips from the Jerusalem service. The service was so electric, I thought, is this the service when everyone is going to be healed? There will be a service before the rapture when everyone will be healed."[7] She also discussed her confidence in the likelihood of a mass miracle healing service with David du Plessis on her television show. "I believe in a short time all the gifts will be restored," Kuhlman said to du Plessis. He responded, "If we will do whatsoever

[God] says, miracles will happen all the time." Kuhlman concluded, "I believe there will be miracle services where everyone is healed."[8]

Kuhlman declared that the advent of miraculous healing in her ministry was a signal of the entrance of the church into its final dispensation. The framework for understanding the miracles claimed in her services was provided by this end-times emphasis, a premillennial dispensationalism she had carried with her since her first days of ministry. "You and I are living in the last days," she declared. "This great spiritual awakening we're having among the youth is prophecy fulfilled."[9] The miracle services did not exist unto themselves, Kuhlman explained. They were pointers toward the return of Jesus. "When the Bride goes out to meet the Bridegroom, it goes out in glory," Kuhlman stated, in reference to the church's impending experience of the second coming. "That's exactly what we're seeing today. There's a great spiritual movement on. We're seeing great manifestations of the Holy Spirit, great miracles in the entire world. The Bride is being perfected. It's about time, you know, for the Bridegroom to come. 'The last stitches are being put in my wedding garment.' That's what I think when I see the great miracles at the services."[10] In an interview with Catholic charismatic leader Ralph Martin, Kuhlman stated, "this is the closing moment of this dispensation, really."[11] She often spoke of her excitement about living and ministering in the "last days" and her belief that the charismatic movement was part and parcel of the consummation of history occurring in her lifetime:

> We're living in the most glorious hours the church has ever known since its beginning. Do you want to know why the great "coming out"? Things are happening now that could not have happened twenty-five, ten, five years ago. This great coming out in Catholicism . . . I have been preaching the gospel for a long, long time—there is never a service that there aren't Catholic priests, nuns, a rabbi there. The gifts of the Spirit are being restored. Again we're seeing gifts of wisdom, knowledge, healing. Around the world, believers are being baptized in the Holy Spirit.[12]

"We're living in the closing hours, the closing seconds," Kuhlman taught in a 1968 television episode.[13]

Kuhlman expressed her desire many times to continue being a part of what she understood to be the momentous march toward the second coming of Jesus. "I'm glad I'm alive," she stated in 1971. "I want to be a part of this great spiritual awakening."[14] She was very animated in her many interviews with end-times author Hal Lindsey as they spoke about his calculations in his best-selling books *Late, Great Planet Earth* and *Satan Is Alive and Well on Planet Earth.* "It's thrilling to see these things come to pass before our very eyes!" Kuhlman said excitedly on one broadcast featuring Lindsey. Lindsey added, "I am so sure [Jesus] is coming again, and he is coming in this generation." Kuhlman replied, "I believe there are people now who are living who will see this prophecy fulfilled."[15] In 1975, she cried out to David du Plessis, "I am so excited! I want to live! I have never wanted to live so much as I want to live today. This is the church's finest hour!"[16]

By 1975 Kuhlman was very ill with serious heart problems. Her awareness of her failing health may have strengthened her desire to record a miracle service as she began to consider the disturbing fact that she might die before Jesus came back. Dick Ross believed her increasing frailty contributed to the decision to allow the Vegas film. "In all the years we worked together we had an agreement that cameras would not be used during a miracle service. The first time it was done, it was almost without her full consent in Jerusalem. Perhaps God in His wisdom knew Kathryn had less than a year to live and burdened her to preserve one miracle service as a testimony for posterity."[17]

There was a precedent for Kuhlman to make recordings for future generations. In a discussion with Lindsey concerning the second coming of Jesus, Lindsey advised Kuhlman, "Our voices on this show are giving a prophetic warning, then God will take his people, then judgment will follow." The television show offered Lindsey and Kuhlman the opportunity to warn the viewers of the imminent return of Jesus and the attendant judgment for those who did not believe in him. Believers in Jesus would be taken first, and then the world would be judged. Known as the "rapture" and the "tribulation," these concepts were familiar to Kuhlman and a familiar part of her theology. "I have made two thousand [audio] tapes, so that when I am gone, they can be played on the radio to get the word out," Kuhlman told Lindsey. "I'm preparing for it [the second coming]."[18] The statement "When I am gone" refers to Kuhlman's belief that she would be "raptured," or taken to heaven before the time of judgment on the earth. During the "tribulation" period following the rapture, people on earth would still have the opportunity to accept Jesus as the Christ and escape the final judgment to come. She wanted her audiotapes to be used to teach unbelievers during the tribulation so they could also be saved from judgment. Always open to the latest media innovations and a devotee of videotape, Kuhlman may have filmed her Las Vegas miracle service partly for the same reasons. Perhaps she intended the video to be used alongside her audiotapes to convince those "left behind" of the "reality of God's wonder-working power," as the introduction to her television show stated. Kuhlman believed she was living in the last days of earth before the judgment of Christ. Because of this belief, she became even more committed to the use of television to communicate what she saw as God's final warning to humanity, the truth of which was evidenced by signs and wonders such as her own miracle services.

Dry Land, Living Water was the grandest media event the Kuhlman ministry ever produced. All other rationale aside, it would be easy to attribute its existence purely to the vanity of Kuhlman. She did enjoy the attention she received from her media productions. Jamie Buckingham states, "Videotaping—through the television industry—became the most dominant fact in Kathryn's life during her last eight years. She loved it. She loved the glamour, the excitement, and the challenge."[19] But the Vegas film was more than a monumental ego trip, although self-gratification certainly played its part. The motivations for the film were a mixture of self-aggrandizement, a strong commitment to end-times evangelism, and a fear of death and obscurity.

Dry Land, Living Water

"I haven't come today to convert Las Vegas, know that," Kuhlman stated at the beginning of her miracle service. "We'll have the same sort of service here today that we have in St. Louis; Providence, Rhode Island; Ottawa, Canada; in Sweden, in London, because remember, all cities are made up of humanity and human nature is the same everywhere." Kuhlman's assertion about the format of the service was partially true. The segments of the miracle service captured on film in Las Vegas were consistent with descriptions of miracle services found in her books, seen on her television show, and recorded on *Your Faith and Mine.* This consistency was due in part to Kuhlman's exacting control over every aspect of the events. Biographer Helen Kooiman Hosier records one conversation with a pastor concerning Kuhlman's management:

> "She had a sharp eye for detail," said John Wilkerson, pastor of an Assembly of God church in Pacific Grove, California, in a conversation we had following her death. The Wilkersons had been active in some of

Kathryn's meetings in Minneapolis a number of years ago. "There wasn't a thing going on in the auditorium, both before, during, and after the meetings, that she wasn't aware of. Oh, she was pernsickety," he laughingly explained. "I don't mean this in an uncomplimentary way," he emphasized, "but everything had to go just right at the meetings. That was Kathryn. . . . Before a meeting she'd be back there, behind the platform, controlling and giving orders. She'd look out over the auditorium and if there was a box or a bag, or something in the aisle, she'd spot it. [She would tell someone to go and move it out of the aisle.]"[20]

Biographer Wayne Warner also notes Kuhlman's style of leadership. "[Kuhlman] preferred having complete control rather than just being a speaker for a convention or sharing a platform with others. Asking her to come out on a platform and sit with others who were on the program until it was time for her to speak was like asking the President of the United States to sit through other speeches until it was his turn. It might happen but not often. It was a matter of protocol."[21]

Kuhlman defended her need for control over the miracle services by explaining that she never knew when the Holy Spirit would begin working in a service. Therefore, she needed to be able to speak for as much or as little time as she felt necessary. A convention or a multispeaker gathering required keeping to a schedule, moving through a service in a certain way in order not to go beyond the designated time and cause difficulties for the speakers or events that followed. Eventually Kuhlman's fame and drawing power made her valuable enough to persuade conference planners to acquiesce to her demands. The Full Gospel Business Men's Fellowship International featured Kuhlman at many conferences, but as Warner notes, "It was a matter of FGBMFI and other groups adjusting their program to fit Kathryn's. She had one way to conduct a miracle service—the way she felt the Holy Spirit had instructed her—and there would be no changes."[22]

In the opening segment of the first film ever made of a Kuhlman miracle service, the scene of the bustling parking lot filled with charter buses faded to a panoramic vision of a huge choir in full voice, standing rank upon rank around the back seats of the large convention center. The men wore seventies-style tuxedos and the women full-length pastel gowns, some in pink, some in yellow, others in baby blue, with a smattering of nuns in black-and-white habits. On the platform a small ensemble of instrumentalists was arranged center stage, accompanying the thunderous voices along with an offstage organ. As the chorus sang the triumphant hymn "Nothing Is Impossible," an image of hands playing the piano was momentarily superimposed over the scene and then faded away as the camera again focused on the choir. These were the hands of pianist Jimmie Miller. For her entire ministry, Kuhlman gathered around her a staff of highly trained vocalists and musicians. From her early years with pianist Helen Gulliford, she continued to tap into the power of music, following the standard style of the deliverance evangelist. Some of the artists whose music was captured on the Vegas sound track had been with Kuhlman for decades. The ever-present organ music underscoring every moment was still played by Charles Beebe, the same organist who followed her every move and emotion on *Your Faith and Mine*, and Miller was still on the piano, as he had been since the beginning of her Pittsburgh ministry.[23]

Others on the stage reflected the changes in the Kuhlman ministry, dramatic changes that challenged her statement that this was "the same sort of service." The choir was directed by a tall, middle-aged, gray-haired gentleman named Paul Ferrin. Ferrin was an innocent bystander in two severe shocks to Kuhlman's ministry during 1975. The first involved a protracted and bitter fight with Kuhlman's solo pianist Dino Kartsonakis and his brother-in-law Paul Bartholomew. Bartholomew was Kuhlman's assistant and distributor of the Kuhlman Foundation's television programs. Warner stated, "Of all the people she hired and fired, she would take two names to her grave as traitors to her ministry." The two names were Kartsonakis and Bartholomew. Ferrin, who had known Kartsonakis since high school, stated, "She was heartbroken over Dino."[24] The disagreement between Kuhlman and the two men was complex and nasty. In 1974, Bartholomew had already sued Kuhlman over a battle for media representation. Kuhlman became dissatisfied with Bartholomew and turned what the *Los Angeles Times* dubbed "a multi-million Kuhlman Foundation media account" over to the Hollywood firm of Rullman and Munger. Because it was shown that Bartholomew was still under contract with Kuhlman at the time she changed representatives, Kuhlman eventually left Rullman and Munger and settled out of court with them for $52,000. Kuhlman, for her part, threatened Dino with dismissal if he married a woman she did not consider suitable. Ferrin explained that Dino had "a controversial girlfriend," who had been living with singer/actor Ed Ames before dating Dino. Kartsonakis persisted in his relationship and demanded higher pay for his appearances with Kuhlman. In February of 1975, Kuhlman fired Dino.

Scrambling for a replacement pianist for her television show, she contacted Ferrin, director of music at Bethel Church in San Jose, California. Ferrin recalled, "One evening, I got a phone call: 'Can you be in LA tomorrow morning at CBS Studios with a tux on?'" Ferrin said yes, and flew to the studio. When he arrived, it was business as usual. "Dino wasn't even mentioned," Ferrin remembered. "If Kathryn Kuhlman wanted you gone, you were *gone*." Replacing Dino was difficult for him, Ferrin remembered, and he is still to this day hesitant to "run Dino down," in his words. Still, Ferrin noted that "Dino was nobody until [Kuhlman] found him. He had no notoriety. She provided a beautiful office for him, paid for all the records he did. He sold them, and she never expected to be repaid. She went on his arm to every meeting."[25] Kuhlman then fired Bartholomew as her assistant, although a contract prevented her from terminating him as her television syndicator for another year. Upping the ante, Bartholomew threatened her with an exposé if she did not raise his pay. The *Los Angeles Times* carried the story of the fight, which brought embarrassment to the Kuhlman ministry. *People* magazine caught the story, and published Bartholomew's version of the tale:

> The cause of Kuhlman's falling-out with him, Bartholomew suspects, may be his sleek, dark-haired brother-in-law—and her former pianist-companion—Dino Kartsonakis. The 33-year-old Kartsonakis, who performed with Kuhlman for five years, broke with her last February after she refused to give him a $20,000-a-year contract and, he claims, vigorously objected to his steady girl—now his wife—Debby. At first, says Kartsonakis, a former Juilliard School of Music student with a dozen record albums to his credit, he had been attracted to Kuhlman as a performer and fellow believer. Later, he says, she began to "feel relaxed around me and could let her red locks down." A devotee of expensive restaurants and first-class travel, Kuhlman frequently took Kartsonakis along as an escort, and reportedly paid for his tailor-made suits. In return, he maintains, she possessively demanded all his attention and criticized anyone he dated. "As long as I had a whip and a chair, everything was all right," he jokes, "but every once in a while I had to escape the cage."[26]

Finally, months later, in September, Bartholomew agreed to a settlement in order to release Kuhlman from her contractual obligation to him as television distributor. In Vegas, therefore, there was no Dino.[27]

No grand piano, and no handsome young Greek man in elaborate tuxedo and pinkie ring. A mainstay of the Kuhlman ministry was gone.

Kuhlman called on Ferrin to stand in for another absent artist in the Vegas service as well. As Ferrin directed the Kathryn Kuhlman Chorus, he stood in the place of a pillar of the Kuhlman miracle services. Kuhlman's beloved choir director, Dr. Arthur Metcalf, died of a heart attack on February 20, 1974. Metcalf was with Kuhlman from 1955 until his death. He was the former director of the Pittsburgh Civic Chorus and the leader of Kuhlman's well-known choirs, which recorded several popular albums under Metcalf's leadership. He was also a longtime friend of Kuhlman. She was shaken and deeply saddened by his death. As the cameras swept the Vegas platform as the opening segment continued, things in the service may have been "the same sort" in form, but not in content.

The Opening

As much as things had changed, however, things also stayed the same. In an abrupt edit, the film cut from the chorus singers to the arrival of Kuhlman on the platform. Almost to a gesture, almost to a tippy-toed mincing step, her actions were identical to the beginning of the episodes of *Your Faith and Mine*. Like the billboard image captured earlier in the film, she was dressed in her floor-length pulpit dress, with long flowing sleeves and a high neck. A microphone dangled from a lanyard around her neck—high-tech media for 1975. As the music shifted to her theme song, "He Touched Me," she swept across the platform, turned and backed away from the exultant choir, directing as she tipped her head back to look at the rows of singers above her. Applause began to mount as the audience became aware of her presence. Kuhlman then took center stage, and the crowd came to its feet in a standing ovation. She continued to direct, to sing over the hymns, calling out the next lines, in a carbon copy of her much younger self guiding and conducting the gathered people in the Carnegie Auditorium in Pittsburgh twenty years before.

But Kuhlman's worsening health was apparent. As she called out over the singing, her speech was less crisp, affected in ways consistent with a person who has troublesome dentures. Her hair was wiry and still defiantly red, styled in a frantically teased attempt to look full and healthy. She was always tall and thin, but by 1975 she had become slightly bowed and brittle in appearance, more so than her sixty-eight years would imply.

Similar in many ways to an aging but still vibrant stage actress, Kuhlman's weakness was visible only in flashes, often overcome in bursts of movement and strength. The best word for her appearance in the last few years of her life is fragile. Even when she became energized and characteristically "big" in her presence on the platform, it was not with the verve she projected even one or two years prior on her television broadcasts.

Kuhlman's visual presentation of herself on the Vegas platform was also "the same but different." She chose to stand alone on the stage except for the musicians and Ferrin, who was clearly a supporting figure. In 1975, Kuhlman's gender was not as central an issue for her authority as a religious leader, although it was still an ever-present threat she could not overlook. She did not fill the stage with men who offered her a "covering" for her leadership as a female minister. She no longer needed the visual substantiation of men in suits and ties lined up behind her on the platform, as she had in the 1950s. Although photographs and descriptions of other miracle services indicate that Kuhlman did not completely abandon the practice of lining up dignitaries on the platform behind her, the fact that she chose not to do so in the one miracle service filmed "for posterity" is intriguing. In the miracle service of 1975, Kuhlman's authority was validated by the sheer number of people in her entourage and in the convention center. Although she featured her soloist Jimmie McDonald during the opening portion of the service and was joined by male associate Gene Martin during the healing segment, the men were in patently subordinate roles. Kuhlman alone was at the physical and conceptual center of the service.

Kuhlman didn't fail, however, to point out dignitaries in her audience, powerful and influential people who came to see her and thereby gave her cachet and authority. As she moved from the opening segment to the official time of welcome, Kuhlman used the presence of powerful people in her services to undergird her own authority. She stated, "We are making history today in Las Vegas!" Applause erupted. "Literally!" she added. Kuhlman spoke coyly of the mayor and city council of Las Vegas voting to declare the date "a certain day," a reference to the proclamation of the day of the service as Kathryn Kuhlman Day. As she spoke, the camera focused on a couple in the audience, and the title "Mayor Oron Gregson" flashed on the screen. After emphasizing the presence of the mayor, Kuhlman turned to the right side of the audience and walked over to address the rows of people seated on the convention center floor. "I see here in the front row some of the most distinguished men in the medical profession." Kuhlman crossed her arms and sat back on her heels, eyebrows raised, chin down, and said in a deep voice, "What are *you* doing here?" The audience laughed, but Kuhlman was only partially joking. In 1975, medical doctors were a sore subject.

The attendance of prominent physicians and the prestige they conveyed were deemed crucial by Kuhlman following the denunciation of her ministry by Dr. William Nolen. She took her time emphasizing the presence of the sympathetic physicians at the Vegas service. Continuing the casual give-and-take time with her audience, she strode to the side of the stage and looked down upon the row of doctors obediently seated at her right hand. She stood, tall and somewhat angry, literally "looking down on" the medical professionals. Kuhlman in this way visually presented herself as dominant over the defeated physicians, the triumphant healer and her converted physician followers. Without a smile, Kuhlman said sternly to the doctors, "I'm glad you're sitting on the front seat so you won't miss anything." The "tough girl" attitude was somewhat for show, since these were doctors familiar to Kuhlman and enthusiastically supportive of her ministry. "I see a couple of you who first came to the services as skeptics." She shook her head and curled her lip in apparent disdain. "Dr. Casdorph, you were one of the greatest skeptics I ever had. There were times I could have killed ya." She paused for the laughter, and the camera cut to Casdorph, a handsome gray-haired younger man who nodded in agreement as his name flashed under him, "H. Richard Casdorph, M.D." The row also included Dr. Claire King, who appeared on several episodes of *I Believe in Miracles* to testify to his conversion to belief in divine healing due to Kuhlman's ministry. Since these on-screen titles had to be added in the editing process following filming, it was clear Kuhlman wanted to make absolutely sure the Vegas video captured the doctors' confirmation of the healing service. "The greatest surgeon in the world has to wait for a supernatural power to do the healing," Kuhlman asserted in the summary of this segment, a familiar statement to her followers. "And it's just like that." The audience applauded.

The Message

"I'm going to speak to you for a very, a very short time, not more than ten minutes. But I'm going to talk to you about something vitally important." With this, Kuhlman began the transition to the preaching segment. Kuhlman often held to the traditional evangelistic service format of music, message, and altar call, inserting miracles after the message and before the altar call. Some references to miracle services indicated testimonies played a part, similar to the format used in *Your Faith and Mine*.[28] Other observers characterized the message segment as simply a "warm-up" for the big show of miracles to follow. In explanation for the varied lengths of her messages, Kuhlman maintained she did not cause the miracles in her services to begin. She had to wait until the Holy Spirit began to heal. At that point she was able to discern the healings already taking place through the spiritual gift of a word of knowledge. In the processes of a miracle service, the beginning of the healing miracles was dependent upon the Holy Spirit's timing. Kuhlman had to wait. While she waited, she preached. Sometimes this meant a message of only a few minutes, sometimes she would speak for much longer periods of time. She would speak until miracles began.

"This is not a sermon," Kuhlman continued in typical fashion. "I'm just talking to you, because I feel that I owe it to you." Kuhlman wanted her messages in miracle services to be perceived by her live audience as spontaneous and unplanned in order to validate her right as a woman to speak. According to Kuhlman's rhetoric, what God told her to say was so momentous that she was obliged to overcome her natural reticence and speak. Otherwise, she wouldn't have spoken at all (even though thousands were gathered to hear her). She was simply sharing what had been told to her. In other words, she had no choice but to say what she said; she "owed it to them."

Kuhlman's miracle service messages were descended from services of healing evangelism played against a Pentecostal backdrop and were influenced by the Pentecostal understanding of the role of sermons. Grant Wacker explains the importance of the unprepared sermon for Pentecostal preaching: "The issue here was not whether it was permissible to write the sermon out and read it (obviously not), nor whether it was all right to rely on an outline (generally not). Rather the question was whether God sanctioned humanly constructed sermons at all." Wacker describes healer Maria-Woodworth Etter's preaching, which could easily be a description of Kuhlman as well. "No one insisted more strenuously that until the moment she started to speak, she had no idea what she would say. Invariably 'the power came,' [Woodworth-Etter] avowed. 'All I had to do was open my mouth.'"[29] In a sentence not notable for its logic but clear in its import, Kuhlman once declared, "So if you've come here today to hear me preach a sermon, forget all about homiletics. . . . I don't even know what it means. I'm just talking to you about the Lord and my own personal experiences."[30]

Disclaimers aside, preaching was Kuhlman's first love. "I might as well confess that I'd rather preach than do anything in the whole wide world," she stated on one television episode. "I just love it."[31] Until the decade of the Shrine services and her talk show, Kuhlman led weekly Monday night Bible studies in Pittsburgh and Sunday services at Stambaugh Auditorium in Youngstown, Ohio. But as the miracle services grew in popularity, people came to see miracles and lined up to be healed, not to hear Kuhlman preach and teach. Kuhlman understood that this was her role in a miracle service based on many years as a deliverance evangelist. Preaching by necessity took a back seat to healing. Historian David Edwin Harrell explains, "Salvation from sin was preached, but whatever the intention of the evangelists, it was never the central theme of their meetings. The common heartbeat of every service was the miracle—the hypnotic moment when the Spirit moved to heal the sick."[32] Faced with the demands of her international miracles ministry, Kuhlman turned over her Sunday services to her associate David Verzilli.

In an interview in 1980, Steve Zelenko, Kuhlman's radio engineer and longtime adviser during her Pittsburgh ministry, expressed regret at the dominance the miracle services attained in the Kuhlman ministry. "The healing services got larger and larger, out of hand. The responsibility was awesome and she would have liked to quit them, but she couldn't. She often said she'd rather preach and teach, but the services had become too big, her schedule was too much, and it was a vicious circle. She couldn't stop them. The people wanted more and she felt a tremendous responsibility to them."[33] The television show also began to demand more financial resources. The costs of *I Believe in Miracles* were tremendous. Kuhlman kept a grueling schedule of miracle service appearances in order to fund the broadcasts. This is not to say that Kuhlman was a helpless victim of the miracle services. As the head of her foundation, the director of her media ministry, and the primary decision-maker, she lived the life she chose. As Charles Loesch, thirty-year employee of Kuhlman, said, "For all the years I knew her, she was the boss. She made all the decisions."[34] But success had its costs, and Kuhlman chose to set aside her first loves, teaching and preaching, to attend to the demands of the miracle services.

Making fine use of the speaker's method of "starting soft so you have some place to go," Kuhlman began her Vegas talk with quiet intensity and began to build. "This is a time of uncertainty," she said softly. "There is uncertainty in the very atmosphere. People are asking, 'What's happening?'" During this segment, the cameras were trained tightly on Kuhlman as she stood still in the center of the platform, speaking quickly, hushed but passionate. "If I had come to Convention Center six months ago, five years ago, and would have told you that the hour would come when the United States of America would have a president and a vice president who was not elected by the American people, you would have called me a fake, you would call me a fanatic." The auditorium, filled with thousands, was completely silent as Kuhlman spoke. "And yet do you realize that we as a nation, the greatest nation—and don't minimize the United States of America. This very hour I stand before ya, first of all I'm proud that I belong to the King of kings and Lord of lords, that I am a Christian, that God is my heavenly father. Secondly, I am proud that I am an American." The audience applauded at this first of several tangents. Kuhlman drew her head up and to the side, staring out of the side of her eyes as the image of her dramatic countenance was superimposed over simultaneous footage filmed from the back of the convention center of her standing on the platform, a small figure bathed in white light.

Visitors to miracle services such as comedienne Lily Tomlin described Kuhlman as "mesmerizing." Biographer Jamie Buckingham emphasizes Kuhlman's importance to the miracle services:

> The greatest secret was Kathryn herself. She insisted on being the focus. She never sat down during those four and five-hour meetings. . . . In fact, she was always doing just a little something to keep the audience's attention on herself. To the critical eye it seemed she was "upstaging"— raising her hand when Jimmie hit a high note, or turning to the choir and making some grand gesture when Dino finished his playing. It seemed like the epitome of ego, always demanding the spotlight. But the more discerning ones saw it as wisdom. Kathryn knew about the necessity of spiritual focus. . . . She knew better than to permit a dozen little healing services going on in the congregation while she was conducting the service from the platform. Kathryn knew there could be but one leader— and she was it. She never relinquished that position of authority. It was one of the secrets of the miracle service.[35]

In a miracle service, the power and vitality of Kuhlman's presence on the stage were more important than the content of her message.[36]

Grant Wacker observes the same concerning Kuhlman's predecessor, Aimee Semple McPherson. He writes of Aimee's "platform charisma," then adds, "Apostolic preachers cultivated an almost legendary ability to capture an audience's interest and move it to action. . . . Almost no one, except the most ardent partisan, ever thought to attribute [McPherson's] success to the conceptual weight of her sermons. Yet virtually all acknowledged her platform prowess."[37]

From the platform, Kuhlman suddenly cried out, "Watch something!" She dramatically declared, "For thirty-nine centuries the Seed of Abraham have been scattered!" The Vegas message consisted primarily of teaching about the end times and the role of Israel in that process. It reflected Kuhlman's intense interest in these topics, topics she spoke about her entire ministry but that came to the forefront at the end of her life. She spoke of the covenant made between Israel and God as she stalked from side to side on the platform. She stopped at one point, lifted her head and squeezed one eye closed in a face that can only be described as "pirate-like," as she stated, "War is inevitable. There will be war in the Middle East." She slapped one outstretched hand into the other in a gesture usually reserved by evangelists for punctuating a sentence with a slap of an open Bible. "The word of God says Israel will be absolutely indestructible!" she yelled, as the applause began and grew. "And that's the word of God!" she stated over the crescendo of clapping, freezing with one hand pointed skyward in a grand gesture. The camera cut from Kuhlman to an image of a woman in the audience, a huge bouffant hairdo framing a face covered in black-rimmed glasses, hands against her mouth, eyes opened wide in fascination. The camera returned to Kuhlman in a choppy edit, obvious due to the abrupt silence of the applause. She continued to preach about the role of Russia in the coming wars, as well as the whole house of Israel acknowledging Jesus the Christ as the Messiah. As she spoke of these things, she arched her back and threw her chin into the air, eyes wide open as if she was seeing a vision of what was to come.

Kuhlman's message concerning the approaching judgment was grim. She moved to the edge of the platform and pointed at the audience. "And remember something," she said in a whisper. "There'll be suffering in the world. Suffering such as the world has never known." She lowered her head and cocked her left shoulder with a wry smile. "I would like to stand before you this Saturday afternoon and tell you, whatever you want to call it, a recession, call it whatever you want to, but beloved, the future is dark. And it's getting darker. And it's getting darker." Kuhlman then outlined the reasons for the miracle services themselves; she said they were a part of the prophetic outpouring occurring all over the world through the charismatic renewal movement. Miracles such as those occurring in her service pointed to the return of Jesus Christ. The Vegas service was not just one individual event. The service and Kuhlman's ministry as a whole were connected to the bigger picture of the second coming of Christ. "Watch something for just a split second now!" she yelled, as she shuffled backward, sweeping her right arm upward and putting a growl on the word "watch." "You want to know the 'why' of these miracles? You want to know the why of it? It's not Kathryn Kuhlman. It's not some personality." She snapped her finger and pointed at the audience. "I've given you the picture, the world picture, but remember something . . ." She lowered her voice into its deepest register and stared at the audience with blazing, unblinking eyes.[38] "There is the spiritual side." Kuhlman asserted again her belief in a coming miracle service "where literally every single person in that place will be healed by the power of God." The sick and dying in the audience must have also hoped for such a service that day. "I believe that with every atom of my being," Kuhlman said, bowing her head as the audience applauded.

"And that's exactly what's happening." In a whisper, with expert timing, Kuhlman took up the message again just as the applause began to diminish. She explained her role in the consummation of history signaled by her miracle services. "These great crowds come, not because of Kathryn Kuhlman." Kuhlman's voice broke as she characteristically shifted into the third person in her standard narrative of self-negation. "I wouldn't walk across the street to see her. I've news for you. She's the most ordinary person you've ever seen in your life. I want you to know that. And the only reason I am standing before you, the only reason that God is using the one that you see in the way that he is using her is because . . . ," she shook her head slowly as she continued, "I was born without talent." Kuhlman delivered this segment in a voice choked with emotion, and just as she reached the crescendo of sentiment in the story of her own lack of worth, she nimbly shifted into first-person self-deprecating humor. With a demure tilt of the head, she continued. "I've always had an inferiority complex about my looks. Born with just fuzz on my head. I was the kind of baby, they'd say to Mrs. Kuhlman, 'What a *healthy* child.'" Laughter rippled through the audience, relieving the tension produced by the emotional declarations of Kuhlman's insignificance. Kuhlman let the laughter play out as she rocked her head side to side, rolling her eyes at her own story. "Freckled! I bought so much freckle cream when I was a kid in Concordia that the first layer of skin peeled off. And one day, I just looked up and said, 'Wonderful Jesus, I don't have a thing. Not a thing. But if you can take nothing and use it, I offer you that nothing.'

"You and I are dependent upon the power of the Holy Spirit," she stated, beginning the closing segment of the message. "Remember this moment!" she yelled. She stared unblinking upward, her voice moving into a monotonic, almost chanting rhythm as she seemed to be describing a vision above her. "God in position, the great creator, I like to think of him as being the Big Boss. At his right hand in the position of high priest, the very Son of the living God, and everything that you and I receive must come through Jesus." Kuhlman's statements outlined her understanding of the relationship of the miracle service to her picture of the triune God. Kuhlman's pneumatological priority in her understanding of the Godhead shaped her presentation of God's role in the miracles in her service. In her theology, God was in charge and Jesus must be glorified by whatever took place in the service, but it was the Holy Spirit who was present in that auditorium in Vegas. It was the Holy Spirit who healed.

Kuhlman began to pace across the platform as she continued to speak, generating energy through her movements and building anticipation. "The Holy Ghost, the mighty third person, is here, and as he moves upon this audience, it's a moment like this that I feel like being seated, because you don't need me." Stopping center stage, she leaned forward to give some basic directions to the waiting people. "You may have never been in a service like this in your life before. I do not lay hands on you and pray on you. You come after you have been healed." Kuhlman stretched out her arms to her side and began to nod her head. "You slip up the steps over here or the steps over here," she explained, pointing. "Eyes closed for just a minute," she said, in a statement closely associated in revivals with an altar call. In Kuhlman's service, however, the call was for those who had been healed during her message to come forward to testify to their miracles. Following her own direction, Kuhlman closed her eyes and leaned her head back, arms still open. "Every eye closed in this great place of worship today." She paused, and then turned sideways, thrusting her head back even farther, throwing back her shoulders and extending her long arms even farther. She opened her eyes, and cried, "MOVE upon this people!" In this moment, Kuhlman belied all her self-negating talk. She invoked the healing power of the Holy Spirit with all the authority of any priest. She followed with a quick summary, "And we vow before the

Father, we vow before the Son, and we vow in the presence of the Holy Spirit to give you the glory. We vow." Then she said again, "Move upon this people! Forget about Kathryn Kuhlman. Forget about anyone else in this place today. Just close your eyes for just a moment." She paused. The room waited. Kuhlman stood with her side to the audience, her arms dropped to her sides, then she tensed, with hands in a fist.

Skills crafted through long years of weekly preaching and teaching guided Kuhlman as she built and then released tension, as she used the full range of her voice, all of her body, and her finely tuned sense of timing and humor to guide her audience inexorably to the first manifestation of words of knowledge. In the hushed Vegas auditorium, Kuhlman lowered her head and began to speak. "I rebuke that emphysema in the mighty name of Jesus. While I was speaking just now somebody received a healing for emphysema." She looked out into the audience as she held her body rigid. "Just breathe very deeply. You'll find that you're breathing perfectly. . . . Just breathe very deeply as the power of the Holy Ghost has gone through that body of yours. It happened while I was speaking." The miracles had begun.

The Healings

By the time healings broke out in the Las Vegas Convention Center, an elaborate and precise organizational structure had brought the audience carefully up to that moment. One worker in Kuhlman's services explained, "Kathryn was a born organizer. She was like a spiritual general in the Lord's Army. Her ushers were trained, one by one, to handle problems and emergencies. The choir had a special director to prepare them for ministry. Lady Advisors were taught to be led by the Holy Spirit. Workers were assigned to a special area, so all the audience could be ministered to."[39] Ushers, sometimes as many as three hundred men, were trained in how to handle any disruptions, how to respond to those claiming healings, and in basic crowd control techniques such as directing people to the bathroom. The "Lady Advisors" played their part as well. Buckingham explains, "Perhaps most important, yet least recognized, were those few hand-picked women . . . who roamed the vast audience when the actual miracle part of the service got underway. They were charged with discerning, looking, listening, and encouraging those who had been healed to come forward and testify."[40] For special miracle services that occurred on the road, choirs were gathered from local churches and rehearsed in the days before the services. The Pittsburgh, Youngstown, and Los Angeles services had permanent choirs. These choirs rehearsed regularly and contained members who sang in Kuhlman miracle services for many years.[41]

The well-oiled machine of a Kuhlman miracle service was subject to the same criticisms as all carefully constructed revival services. Earl Hansen of the *Seattle Post-Intelligencer* noted with some cynicism the Kuhlman ministry's early preparations for a miracle service in his city: "Kathryn Kuhlman had pushed for months throughout her Sunday television program for a big turnout Thursday. Whether solicited response aided her managers and the Holy Spirit in knowing, in advance, that she could now fill the 6,600 seat Arena is only an outsider's guess. Her newspaper ads included a telephone number for seating on chartered buses, and among those who came on stage claiming to have been healed while Kathryn preached were some from Wenatchee and Vancouver—the same places a number of last year's winners were from."[42] What some saw as careful preparation and planning appropriate to a professional ministry others saw as manipulation and "showbiz."

Early advertising helped fill the auditoriums where Kuhlman appeared, often beyond capacity. Admirers and detractors alike commented on Kuhlman's pleasure at an overflow crowd. "Kathryn was obsessed by crowd size," Buckingham writes.[43] This desire for large numbers in her audiences, in her choirs, and in her ministry was not unusual in a minister with a background in healing evangelism. Jack Coe, an Assemblies of God minister and healing evangelist in the post–World War II healing revival, engaged in a competition with his rival Oral Roberts over the size of their meeting tents. Evangelists compared crowd size, numbers of those healed, and width and breadth of tents in an effort to establish dominance in the revival field.[44] Kuhlman pointed to overflow crowds as a sign of her success and effectiveness in ministry. Trained in part by Pentecostals, Kuhlman was subject to what Wacker calls "Pentecostals' perennial fondness for bigness."[45]

Kuhlman took pride in the fact that her services drew not just large but overflowing crowds. Buckingham states, "Although it was good psychology to have her meeting halls filled, there was something in her that craved the satisfaction of knowing that 'thousands were turned away, unable to get in.'"[46] This was a complex delight for a healer to have. Kuhlman often expressed sadness at the plight of those who were not healed in her services. She even declared that one of the first questions she wanted to ask Jesus Christ in heaven was why everyone was not healed. Her dismay seemed genuine, but inconsistent. She did not seem to connect her grief for those who were not healed with an equivalent sorrow for the people who were turned away at the doors of the various auditoriums where she appeared. The press picked up on this. In 1972, Ron Yates of the *Chicago Tribune* wrote an article highlighting the experiences of those who did *not* make it through the doors of Chicago's Arie Crown Theater for a Kuhlman service:

> A collective groan went up from the throng as ushers strung blue velvet rope across the lobby in front of the glass doors. "Looks like I'm too late again," sighed the old man [suffering from arthritic hands] as I eased my way through the crowd near him. "How long have you been waiting to get in?" I asked, noting his pallor. "About three hours. This makes the second time I've missed her this year. The other time was back in Ohio." With that he turned and made his way slowly through the crowd toward an exit. I climbed over the rope along which at least a dozen ushers were stationed. "Press," I said, showing my press card to an usher who stood resolutely in my way. "Sorry," he said, shaking his head. "I can't let you in here. If these people see me open the theater door for you they might not understand, especially those who have been waiting since this morning. They could get nasty." [Yates looked back over the crowd.] All wore the same look of despair on their faces—like they had missed the last train home and now would have to wait for another one which might never come.[47]

Thousands packed the Vegas meeting hall, and if the service was true to form, hundreds were also turned away.

The moment Kuhlman began to pronounce words of knowledge about healings taking place in the Las Vegas Convention Center, people began to move toward both sides of the platform, eager to testify. In rapid succession she identified healings for emphysema, cancer, a release of "great pain," and the opening of an ear. She stated, "Something, I don't know what it is, but something is happening in the wheelchair section. That's the only thing I know. Something's happening back there." Kuhlman continued to speak as Gene Martin and Jimmie McDonald along with other ushers lined the people up on each side of the platform to wait their chance to speak into the microphone at center stage. Kuhlman turned to the choir, lifted her hands to direct, and said, "Just softly, choir, 'Alleluia,' softly, as the power of God goes through this body." The choir began to sing the de facto anthem of the charismatic renewal movement as Gene Martin brought forward the first person to testify.

As Kuhlman spoke, ushers and Lady Advisors patrolled the audience, acting as gatekeepers for the platform and allowing only those they determined were healed to come forward. This "culling" practice was criticized by detractors as exemplifying the "stage management" that occurred in Kuhlman services. Hansen's scathing article in the *Seattle Post-Intelligencer* noted the fate of one "unauthorized" platform visitor at a Seattle miracle service. "Among the evening's early arrivals was the youthful spastic who two-caned his way onto the Opera House stage last year before the ushers got him out of there. This time the best he could do was a seat up front."[48] The careful control of access to the platform in a Kuhlman service was not all show business. The reporter's account of the ushers hustling the struggling young man off the platform seemed damning, but the rules at Kuhlman services were clear. One did not go to the platform to be healed. One went to the platform because one had already been healed. It was not the case, therefore, that Kuhlman employees "weeded out" tough cases such as the handicapped young man.

The hundreds of testimonies recorded in Kuhlman's books and on her television show, the great majority of which occurred at miracle services, included every disease imaginable. The range of healings at the miracle services was so inclusive it prompted another reporter's dismay:

> There is something confusing, maddening about the crazy-quilt roster of healings and testimonials. It is sprawling, hectic, healings raffled off like bogus antiques at an auction. Cosmic diseases are linked with those merely comic. Cancers and carbuncles, blood clots and bunions. Welts and warts. There are no patterns, no pauses . . . nobody knows where to look next or who has been cured of which disease. Like kids at the circus, they are torn between the elephants, clowns and tumblers in the three rings, caught in a frustrating dilemma of riches. Only on the platform is there order, and there it is consummate. Everything about Kathryn is studied, professional.[49]

As one observer wrote, "it's either the Greatest Story Ever Told, or The Greatest Show on Earth."[50]

Dry Land, Living Water featured multiple testimonies to healing. The first testimony was characteristic. "What's this, Gene?" Kuhlman asked

Gene Martin as he brought forward an awkward little woman to speak at the center microphone. Martin replied but was away from the microphone and could not be heard. "The power of God is on her?" Kuhlman said, repeating Martin's statement. The little woman carried a cane, and Kuhlman asked her, "Is there no pain?" "No," the woman answered. "Give her a great big 'God bless ya!'" Kuhlman said, gesturing broadly toward the audience. Applause built as Kuhlman told the woman to "stomp down on the floor." Kuhlman stepped forward and placed her hands on the woman's face. She rested her thumbs underneath the woman's chin and laid her long fingers along her cheeks. Kuhlman prayed aloud as she grasped the woman's head. A male usher stepped up behind the woman as Kuhlman prayed. Anticipating the woman's next movement, the usher deftly caught her as she fell backward into his arms, "slain in the Spirit." He lowered her gently to the floor where she lay quietly, her head draped to the side, eyes closed. "That's power!" Kuhlman said, turning to the audience and pointing to the woman on the floor. "I don't understand it," she continued. "I only know I have nothing to do with it!"

The healing segment of the Las Vegas service included multiple examples of people being "slain in the Spirit." Viewed within the flow of the service overall, the collapsing bodies added to the constant movement and energy on the platform, as well as to the sense of being right on the edge of chaos, chaos held back only by Kuhlman's assertive presence. Many had spoken on Kuhlman's talk show of the experience of being slain in the Spirit, but the mediated versions did not fully communicate the strangeness of the experience as viewed in the film. The anticipation of a slaying could add awkwardness to the service, as exemplified by the second woman who came forward to testify. The emotional woman was crying because she had been healed and "was not a believer." Kuhlman asked her where she went to church, and the woman mumbled an answer. Kuhlman discovered the woman was Jewish, which delighted her. Kuhlman put her arm around the woman and kissed her on the cheek. After the woman testified to her healing, Kuhlman grasped her head in her "prayer grip" and prayed for her, but the Jewish woman did not fall backward. She simply looked confused. Kuhlman declared, "I'm so glad for ya!" then turned to another couple coming across the platform. The Jewish woman wandered off screen, unslain. Kuhlman offered no explanation as she continued.

In two instances the slaying phenomenon resulted in wigs going awry. One woman fell backward after Kuhlman's prayer over her, and as she hit the floor in the usher's arms her wig slid forward. Eyes still closed, she reached up and pulled her wig back in place as the cameras quickly cut from her to Kuhlman. In the most dramatic slaying moment in the film, a young man brought forward his mother to testify to her healing from facial paralysis due to a stroke in 1972. The mother was an attractive, petite woman with a bouffant auburn wig and a red and white polka-dot pantsuit. The son was in tears as he spoke to Kuhlman. As the son and Kuhlman discussed the woman's illness and healing, the woman's left knee buckled visibly, but she recovered. Soon after, she moved slightly toward Kuhlman, then fell backward to the stage without being touched. The son was visibly shocked, but as he realized what had happened, he smiled, raised his hands quickly up and down, said, "Praise the Lord!" and knelt by his mother and took her head in his arms.

Shouts and squeals of surprise and excitement could be heard from the spectators as Kuhlman laughed and clapped her hands together in delight as she turned to the audience. She pointed toward the woman on the floor, now attended by her son and an usher, and shouted, "That's power!" The camera caught Paul Ferrin also grinning, arms crossed as he watched the incident, then turning to look back at the choir to share the moment. "That, my friends, is the power of God!" Kuhlman stated. The son helped his smiling mother sit up and worked with her to straighten her bouffant wig. Kuhlman continued to speak. "That's proof to the old skeptic that I didn't push her down!" The audience laughed and applauded. The mother and son made their way to the microphone, the woman still beaming happily as she continued to adjust the wig sitting drunkenly on her head. "Oh, honey, forget about the wig," Kuhlman said with a smile, smoothing the woman's hairdo into place. "That's all right, honey, that's all right. Honey, that's beautiful, that's beautiful," Kuhlman said soothingly as she took the woman's arm and led her to the microphone. "In a minute I'll take it off and see how it looks on me."

The most challenging moment in the Las Vegas healing segment was the arrival on the platform of a wobbly woman with a testimony of healing from multiple sclerosis. Her presence on the stage indicated that she must have been "cleared" by the ushers and Lady Advisors to come and tell Kuhlman about her healing. The woman was very frail, with pale blonde hair pulled back in a ponytail and large round glasses on an angular face. Dressed in an orange pantsuit, she stood staring at Kuhlman, the characteristic rocking of multiple sclerosis making her unsteady. "I have multiple sclerosis!" she declared in a high squeak, with spittle caught in the sides of her mouth as she smiled in wide-eyed wonder. Kuhlman stood looking at her, then said, "Well, you stand there as if you are scared stiff." "Well, I am so excited!" the woman replied, still smiling, still rocking gently on her rickety legs. Kuhlman watched as the woman walked shakily back and forth on the platform, then called one of the doctors from the front row onto the platform. "Come here, Johns Hopkins, I knew I'd need you," she said as she waved Dr. Richard O'Wellen to the stage. The physician told of the woman's state when she arrived. She was in a wheelchair and unable to walk. The woman told Kuhlman about the wheelchair she just bought, "a fancy new one." "Take it back and get a refund!" Kuhlman declared. "I guess I'll have to!" the woman answered, and the audience applauded. "This is the first time I have lifted my knees in five years," the woman said excitedly. She lifted her knees in jerky motions as Kuhlman cautioned the audience to remember "she's using muscles and ligaments that she has not used for five years. Give her a week to exercise those legs!" Kuhlman did not pray for the fragile woman, who would seemingly shatter if "slain in the Spirit." Instead the woman was helped carefully down the stairs by an usher, and filmed as she pushed her wheelchair toward the seats, stopping to lift her knees one last time for the camera. Although the woman was indeed walking, something she testified she could not do when she came to the convention center that day, the marks of MS were still present even as she declared herself healed by God.

The assertion of "progressive healing," where the healing required time to take full effect, was also used by Kuhlman in reference to the next person presented to her on the platform. A small boy walked jerkily across the stage as his grandmother testified to his healing from rheumatoid arthritis. After praising the boy and watching him walk back and forth, Kuhlman sent him down the main aisle pushing his own small wheelchair. Kuhlman again reassured the people that the boy would continue to improve over time. The camera followed, catching images of a woman covering her mouth in emotion as he passed and a man snapping a picture of the boy. "He'll put the old wheelchair away and be riding his bicycle tomorrow!" Kuhlman cried from the stage.

Dramatic segments such as these were interspersed with other, more lighthearted moments. In one amusing exchange, Kuhlman welcomed an older man in shirtsleeves who came to the platform to testify to a healing of his hearing after Kuhlman spoke a word of knowledge about an ear being opened. Kuhlman covered the microphone around her neck and walked around behind him, asking, "Do you hear me now?" "I hear you," he replied, in a monotone voice indicative of loss of hearing. Of course he could hear her; everyone could hear her. Kuhlman's voice was amplified throughout the convention center by the microphone in front of the man. These types of stage antics were not on the talk show or spoken of in her books, and they threatened to link Kuhlman with the type of theatrical, emotional charismatic Christianity from which she endeavored to distance herself her entire career.

As the Vegas service came to an end, Kuhlman told the audience to look up and "take anything you want from the Master. Just look up right now and worship him." She directed the choir to reprise the chorus "Alleluia," and walked from side to side on the platform, praying over the retreating lines of people, as Jimmie McDonald and the ushers escorted them off the stage. The people jumbled together as they waited to descend the stairs, but finally Kuhlman was again alone on the platform except for the backdrop of the musicians. In accord with her assertion that miracles were an evangelistic tool, she gave a traditional altar call to the crowd. She spoke of spiritual healing, which she called "the greatest miracle, because even a miraculous healing will end." Kuhlman would not pray for people's healing, which was the Holy Spirit's responsibility, but she was glad to pray for their salvation.

"Come from all over the auditorium and I will pray for you," she offered. She told the choir to begin to sing "There's Something about That Name." As they sang, she said, "That miracle that is for all eternity, that's what I want. Jesus says come, and the Holy Spirit says come. And still they come. Come from the balconies! He'll give you that greatest of all miracles. That wonderful new birth experience." People spilled into the aisles and made their way toward the floor in front of the platform while Kuhlman continued to call to them. "If you can't get out into the aisles, just stand where you are. Put up both hands—come on!" The choir sang. "And still they come," Kuhlman sighed. With the image of people gathered around the platform, the film ended, cutting to footage of a fountain outside the convention center, dancing in multicolored lights as the credits rolled. No ending monologue to match the opening scenes. No summary statement or wrap-up at the end. Like the miracle service itself, once it was over, it was over. Cut. Wrap. Print.

More Than Miracles

Throughout her career, Kuhlman worked ceaselessly to hone an image of her ministry as refined, professional, and most especially, not fanatical. The carefully crafted media image of Kuhlman as the grand dame of gentrified charismatic Christianity predominated on her television show and in her books. Kuhlman the best-selling author held her own on the bookshelves alongside Betty Friedan and Norman Vincent Peale. Kuhlman the talk show host shared cultural space with genteel colleagues such as Dinah Shore and Barbara Walters. Kuhlman the miracle lady did not share such gentrified associates. The Kuhlman of the miracle service platform was heir to the theatrical Sister Aimee McPherson, "holy roller services,"[51] esoteric healers of the post–World War II era, and old-fashioned tent revivalists. For those outside the historic Pentecostal churches and other Christian groups with a revivalist past, the service itself had little cultural or historic context. Viewed with no knowledge of its predecessors in Pentecostalism, or the services of McPherson, Charles Price, or even the healing evangelists of the post–World War II revival, segments of the Kuhlman film presented a charismatic otherworld untouched by gentrification. The Las Vegas miracle service offered a vision of charismatic Christianity that was genuine but also disconcerting for the viewer who resided outside of charismatic circles.

Although the Las Vegas service was carefully controlled by Kuhlman and Dick Ross, the film removed the softening filter of the talk show and revealed Kuhlman and charismatic Christianity with all their strengths and weaknesses. In a risky move, Kuhlman chose to feature in the Vegas film some of the most marginalizing attributes of charismatic Christianity such as the slaying power of the Holy Spirit and end-times prophecy. The meeting was characterized by flying wigs, people falling to the floor, and lines of eager audience members waiting to take the microphone to testify to divine healing. And then there was Kuhlman, the extraordinary deliverance evangelist finally captured on film. She died less than a year later, and the gentrified Kuhlman of the talk show and best seller faded from the cultural memory, leaving only the wild-eyed platform personality for posterity.

History has been unfair to Kuhlman due in part to the availability of *Dry Land, Living Water.* Despite the significant contributions she made to the gentrification of charismatic Christianity in America, *Dry Land, Living Water* in many ways obscured her longer history and froze her ministry in one day and one service. The impression left by the Vegas film was accurate, but incomplete. The exuberance and strangeness revealed in the film were a part of charismatic Christianity, but not indicative of its character overall. Kuhlman was every bit as flamboyant and over-the-top as she sometimes appeared in the Vegas special, but the miracle service persona represented only one aspect of a complex and multifaceted woman. Although she was known throughout her career as "the Miracle Lady," Kathryn Kuhlman was always more than just the miracles.

Death of a Healer

I t's always news when a miracle healer falls ill, which is why Kathryn Kuhlman was determined not to let it be known how sick she truly was in 1975. The heart condition Kuhlman battled the latter part of her life dramatically worsened over the course of the year. Her refusal to change her pace likely contributed to the deterioration of her health. Paul Ferrin recalls, "She struggled with her own illness. She saw it as a thorn in her flesh."[1] Between the Las Vegas film in May of 1975 and her admittance to a Los Angeles hospital on November 22, she maintained her grueling schedule. A typical Kuhlman month included miracle services in Pittsburgh and the Shrine service in Los Angeles, various appearances around the country, and four days of taping up to sixteen programs for the television broadcast. Kuhlman was maintaining her television and platform ministry while still operating in the crosshairs of criticism generated by William Nolen's book. Due to the stress, she experienced a frightening heart flare-up in July, but after treatment at a Tulsa hospital she returned to her travels. She attended a series of meetings in the southern United States in October, followed by a return to Israel for the Second World Conference on the Holy Spirit in November.[2] Upon her return to the States, Kuhlman held her Shrine service Sunday, November 16, packing the house once again. The taping sessions for *I Believe in Miracles* began just days afterward. On one episode taped November 20, Kuhlman was visibly exasperated by the current state of affairs in her ministry. "I don't believe I've ever said this on television, but I feel compelled," she stated in the opening segment. "If you do not understand these miracles, then simply say you don't understand it. But don't criticize these miracles. Be humanitarian enough to look up and say, 'I don't understand it, but I praise God for it.'"[3] Kuhlman was sick and tired, and it showed.

Looking back at that November taping session, producer Dick Ross remembers the moment he realized how ill Kuhlman truly was. He and Kuhlman always spot-checked all the shows together after a taping, a process consisting of a careful review of each and every episode before it was allowed to be aired. Kuhlman wanted to review her own work and also regularly allowed the show's guests to view a few minutes as an act of appreciation. Kuhlman would not miss this time under any circumstances, Ross recalls. She saw it as vital to maintaining the quality of the broadcast. Then, one day, she could not finish the work. "She looked up at me and for the first time in ten years she said, 'Dick, will you scrub the screening of the shows,' and she meant by that, 'Will you cancel my screening them this time?'" Ross continues, "It was not only her habit to see them, but she enjoyed it. So we knew she was really ill."[4] Ferrin also remembers this last series of recordings. "The last time I saw her," he recalls, "it was the second day of the last eight episodes. She was taping four episodes, and she had to go lie down between each episode."[5] Kuhlman was indeed very sick; in fact, unknown to her, she had wrapped her last broadcast and led her final miracle service.

Kuhlman's dramatic last year was marked not only by health crises but also by the painful legal controversies with Dino Kartsonakis and Paul Bartholomew, and the emotional devastation caused by the death of Arthur Metcalf. Into this emotional and physical morass came Dana Barton "Tink" Wilkerson and his wife Sue. Tink Wilkerson was a car dealer in Tulsa, Oklahoma, and a regent at Oral Roberts University. In May of 1975, Kuhlman was without a business manager after firing Bartholomew. Wilkerson stepped in to advise Kuhlman, and his wife Sue befriended her. The two had struck up a casual acquaintance with Kuhlman a few years before the Bartholomew lawsuit, and Kuhlman became increasingly dependent upon the couple after the controversy was settled out of court. In many ways Kuhlman was repeating the mistakes of her early years: in a time of crisis and deep insecurity, she looked for support from a man who in many ways was an unknown, rather than from established friends and trusted advisers. At the end of her life, weakened and vulnerable, she seemed desperately to want a strong male figure in her life to comfort her and care for her. Kuhlman often admitted how she missed the comforting role her father played in her life before his death. Maggie Hartner was a dear friend, but she was disqualified as a candidate for a paternal role.

That position was taken by Tink, who, at forty-three, was not the right age to be "Papa," but, more to the point, was the right gender.

Unfortunately, much like "Mister" Burroughs Waltrip, Tink was less reliable than Papa Joe Kuhlman. As her new business adviser, Wilkerson guided Kuhlman toward foolish decisions, such as purchasing a yellow two-door Mercedes-Benz for $18,000. He also persuaded Kuhlman of the need to own a personal $750,000 Lear jet, just like Oral Roberts.[6] Kuhlman's accountant Walter Adamack objected strongly to the purchase. Adamack had been with Kuhlman since the first days of the Kuhlman Foundation, which he helped create.[7] Kuhlman rejected the advice of her long-trusted counselor and agreed to lease the airplane from Wilkerson for $12,000 a month. Kuhlman's willingness to acquiesce to the Wilkersons' leadership in matters such as the plane was strikingly out of character for a woman notorious for a dogmatic opposition to change and an even more radical commitment to control. After Kuhlman's death, Wilkerson told a reporter that he and his wife functioned as "a buffer between Kathryn and the media. I was trying to shield her as much as possible. . . . She was under a terrible strain." He added, "Kathryn didn't really have a lot of friends. Her own people (in the Foundation) were, by and large, very busy." He continued, "She was a lonely woman. Most people wanted something from her, other than just to be a friend. They wanted to be near her for a healing, or for spiritual reasons, or to exploit her. Ours was a genuine friendship."[8] Wilkerson's statement was a manipulative justification for his efforts to isolate Kuhlman from her friends and foundation colleagues in her last year of life. Most poignant was the separation from Marguerite Hartner, whom Kuhlman often called "my Maggie."[9] Hartner had been at Kuhlman's side since she came to the Pittsburgh area in 1946, and was in many ways the motivating force behind Kuhlman's decision to move her ministry in the first place. When Kuhlman relocated, Hartner left her job at a telephone company and committed her life to Kuhlman's ministry. For close to three decades following, "few people . . . were as close and devoted to Kathryn as was Maggie."[10] But during Kuhlman's last year, she allowed the Wilkersons to supplant Maggie as her confidante and closest adviser.

As Kuhlman's health continued to deteriorate, she was drawn further and further from Hartner, both geographically and emotionally. Despite the Wilkersons' claims to be her guardians and caregivers, Kuhlman maintained an exhausting pace with their assistance. Three days after returning from the second World Conference on the Holy Spirit in Israel in November, she preached at the Shrine. Kuhlman sent Hartner to Pittsburgh to handle the business of the foundation as she taped the television broadcasts, culminating in a complete physical collapse. Kuhlman's condition became critical, and she was admitted by the Wilkersons to St. John's Hospital in Los Angeles, where she came close to death from heart failure. The doctors were able to stabilize her condition, and the Wilkersons were at her bedside constantly.[11] Hartner visited, but Jamie Buckingham states that the visit was "an unhappy experience. They hardly spoke."[12] Buckingham does not offer details about the rift between the two women. He uses the story as another example of the dramatic change in Kuhlman's relationships during her illness. Maggie returned to Pittsburgh on Thanksgiving Day.

If the story of Kuhlman's association with the Wilkersons consisted only of accounts such as those during her health crisis in Los Angeles, their claims to be "good friends" would be tenable. But on December 17, Kuhlman made dramatic changes to her will under the legal guidance of Tink Wilkerson's own Tulsa lawyer, Irvine Ungerman. In the new will, made from her hospital bed in Los Angeles, Kuhlman left the bulk of her estate to the Wilkersons. Tink Wilkerson claimed not to have any knowledge of a new will, even though he summoned Ungerman to Kuhlman's side.[13] With this exploit, all of Tink Wilkerson's previous actions become dubious, from his insinuation of himself as Kuhlman's business manager to the sweeping control he assumed over her personal life. The secret new will, with Ungerman as its sole executor, was filed on December 17, 1975. No one in Pittsburgh was told, and preparations were made to transport Kuhlman back to her home for Christmas.

Kuhlman rode in her private jet only two times. The Lear carried her to Pittsburgh from Los Angeles for her final Christmas at home. Maggie Hartner and Steve Zelenko, her longtime radio sound engineer, took Kuhlman to her house, where she was attended by two nurses. After dropping Kuhlman off, Tink turned Kuhlman's plane around, touched down in Tulsa to pick up Sue, and traveled on to Vail for a lovely Christmas holiday at their ski cottage. Eight days after the new will was made in his favor, Wilkerson seemed much more comfortable leaving Kuhlman unsupervised. The day after Christmas, Kuhlman's condition became so severe that heart surgery was required to save her life. Although she was in Pittsburgh, with excellent hospitals and surrounded by friends and foundation colleagues, Wilkerson chose to fly her to Tulsa on the private jet for the heart surgery. Wayne Warner notes that there was confusion as to why her surgery was scheduled in Tulsa, "a thousand miles from those closest to her," and not Pittsburgh. "Pittsburgh had better-known hospitals and doctors, but friends in Pittsburgh were not making these kinds of decisions. Tink Wilkerson was."[14] According to Buckingham, Wilkerson once again began to restrict Maggie Hartner's access to Kuhlman, telling her to stay in Pittsburgh until he called her for the surgery. The jet left Pittsburgh on Saturday, December 26, and Wilkerson told Hartner the operation would be on Wednesday. He would send the plane in time for her to be present. Instead, Kuhlman's condition deteriorated dramatically, and she underwent open-heart surgery at Hillcrest Medical Center the next day, Sunday, December 27. No one from Pittsburgh was at the surgery. The Wilkersons requested their friend Oral Roberts to stand by at the procedure, and Roberts did so. Kuhlman survived the operation, but was very weak.[15]

The December 29, 1975, edition of the *Los Angeles Times* carried the story "Kathryn Kuhlman OK after Heart Surgery." The copy began, "Kathryn Kuhlman, the internationally known 'miracle healer,' was reported in satisfactory condition in a hospital [in Tulsa, Oklahoma] today after open-heart surgery." The source of the report was Wilkerson, whom the *Times* referred to as "a long-time friend of Miss Kuhlman" and her spokesperson: "Tink Wilkerson said physicians had replaced a mitral valve in Miss Kuhlman's heart on Sunday. She was hospitalized [in Tulsa] in July for what her physician described as a 'minor heart flare up.' Wilkerson said Kuhlman had been in a Los Angeles hospital since late November but 'was not responding to treatment as rapidly' as she did last summer in Tulsa."[16]

Despite the positive headline, Kuhlman was not "OK." Although she lived through the initial operation, she developed an abdominal obstruction the following Friday that required emergency surgery. The following two weeks were marked by further complications and medical procedures to aid drainage from Kuhlman's left lung, which was impeded by the size of her heart.[17] Meanwhile, Wilkerson persisted in reassuring the press that Kuhlman was recovering well. The December 30 *Pittsburgh Press* relayed typically optimistic news of Kuhlman's recovery: "[Miss Kuhlman] is expected to be hospitalized for two-and-half weeks and will then require an additional month of recuperation, said her long-time friend and Tulsa auto dealer Tink Wilkerson. 'She should be able to resume her regular schedule when it starts in March,' he said."[18] According to Buckingham, Wilkerson also called Hartner every day, reassuring her of

Kuhlman's improvement and instructing her to continue plans for the Shrine services and a planned miracle service in Oakland in April. Maggie Hartner did as she was told.[19]

In the meantime, Oral Roberts returned to pray for Kuhlman, and Kuhlman's sister Myrtle arrived from California. Roberts and his wife came to Kuhlman's hospital room. He recalled, "When Kathryn recognized us and that we were there to pray for her recovery, she put up her hands like a barrier and then pointed toward heaven." The couple retreated, and Roberts's wife said, "She doesn't want our prayers. She wants to go home."[20] Kuhlman died February 20, 1976, at the age of sixty-nine, attended by her sister Myrtle, Oral and Evelyn Roberts, and Tink and Sue Wilkerson. Told to stay in Pittsburgh, Maggie was not present at Kuhlman's death. Perhaps she honored her old friend by managing her appointment calendar one final time.[21] On the foundation office calendar for February 20 someone wrote, "KK went home."[22]

If it is news when a miracle healer falls ill, it is even bigger news when a miracle healer dies. The February 21 *Pittsburgh Post Gazette* carried the story "Kathryn Kuhlman Is Dead." The article stated, "Evangelist Kathryn Kuhlman, who recently underwent open-heart surgery, died at 9 o'clock last night in a hospital in Tulsa, Oklahoma." The cause of death was listed as pulmonary hypertension. In an article Kuhlman would have treasured, the *Post-Gazette* reporter listed her as "in her mid-50s," and attached a lovely picture of Kuhlman from at least ten years earlier. The next day, the *New York Times* carried the story "Kathryn Kuhlman, Evangelist and Faith Healer, Dies in Tulsa." She was deemed "one of America's most popular evangelists and faith healers," a designation shared "by devotees and doubters alike." The article called Kuhlman "almost glamorous." The *Pittsburgh Press* splashed the boldfaced headline "Kathryn Kuhlman, Faith Healer, Dies," and placed a caption under a current picture that read "Kathryn Kuhlman, Best Known Faith Healer." Despite their use of her most despised title, the article did call Kuhlman "the most famous woman evangelist in the world."[23]

The foundation immediately publicized memorial services. On February 22, Kuhlman's associate pastor David Verzilli, forty-three, led services at Stambaugh Auditorium in Youngstown, Ohio, at 10:30 a.m.[24] The following evening, Verzilli welcomed mourners to the First Presbyterian Church in downtown Pittsburgh. The press reported that over three thousand people attended the ceremony.[25]

Verzilli began the service by proclaiming it Kuhlman's "coronation service." "She fought valiantly to the end," he said. Kuhlman's body was already in transit to her place of burial in California, and Verzilli explained why she was not lying in state. "She always was at her best for her Lord, she always looked her best. Her weary, worn body was not to be given to the world to look at. She wanted to be remembered at her best—alive." Verzilli struggled with his own emotions as he remembered Kuhlman. "We have lost our best friend. . . . No words can adequately describe our preacher lady. . . . [She was] an inspiration to millions of believers, of all denominations, a household name of all America." He paused, then continued, "I told Marguerite [Maggie Hartner] before the service that we both need healing. Our hearts are broken. What are we going to do without our preacher lady?" In a free-form style, Verzilli moved from topic to topic as he spoke. He remembered Kuhlman's hands. "Hands that are strong, that have socked many a man into the Kingdom." He spoke honestly about Kuhlman's personality. "She was so dominant. Her personality was so all-powerful. She would just wrap us in her grip. . . . Marguerite said, 'If I could only have her back and holler at me one more time.'"

In a revealing moment, as Verzilli struggled with words to say, he declared, "It's time I grow up anyhow and get away from Momma's apron strings." With Kuhlman gone, Verzilli was a possible successor to her ministry. Verzilli repeated, almost in a dazed manner, "A powerful personality—very powerful."[26] Possibly too powerful to replace. He announced that the Friday morning miracle services at First Presbyterian would be canceled but the ministry would continue with Sunday services at Youngstown and Monday evening services at First Presbyterian. Verzilli had been officiating at Youngstown for several years following Kuhlman's addition of the Shrine services in Los Angeles, so this was not a dramatic change. He chose to retain the Monday evening Bible studies at First Presbyterian and stopped the Friday miracle services. Verzilli was not a miracle worker. He was a Bible teacher. Although his preferred designation for Kuhlman was "preacher lady," most of Kuhlman's followers were seeking a miracle healer. Verzilli could not fill that vacancy.

Kuhlman was buried the next day, February 24, at Wee Kirk O' the Heather in Forest Lawn Memorial Park in Glendale, California. She had purchased a plot in the fashionable graveyard in 1969.[27] Still directing Kuhlman's business affairs, Tink Wilkerson arranged the service, invited 150 private guests, and asked Paul Ferrin to play the piano and Oral Roberts to speak. Roberts agreed, under the impression that he was one of several speakers for the special occasion, considering the brevity of his friendship with Kuhlman. In fact, he was the only speaker, which he learned to his surprise (and discomfort) upon arrival at the service.[28] Verzilli was not asked to speak, despite his administration of both of Kuhlman's memorial services in Pittsburgh, nor was Maggie Hartner. All of Kuhlman's Pittsburgh friends were left out of the service. Even more so than before her death, Wilkerson had little reason to pay any notice to the desires of Pittsburgh colleagues concerning Kuhlman.

Among words of tribute and affection, Roberts's eulogy also contained a segment that captured the importance of Kuhlman and her ministry to the gentrification of charismatic Christianity:

> In 1971, when she first came to Tulsa, a young woman came to town in advance. She came to the Oral Roberts University and wanted to know if our students would help form a choir. And of course we were thrilled to do that. When the meeting started the audience was like a list from "Who's Who." I've lived in Tulsa nearly thirty years and have never seen anybody come to Tulsa who could break through such a wide range of society and bring together people from virtually every walk of life—the pastor of the First Methodist Church, the pastor of the First Baptist Church, various Catholic priests and nuns. There were heads of industry—I know because I knew the people. And then the meeting started. The miracles of our Lord began to come upon the people. Catholic nuns fell under the Spirit. I'd never seen a nun do that. Then later that day I saw the pastor of one of our largest churches fall in the Spirit. Then I saw the owner of one of the largest companies in the oil industry fall under the power of the Spirit, and I began to realize there was something beyond what I'd ever seen in a public service in Tulsa or anywhere else.[29]

Roberts was simply remembering an important moment in his history with Kathryn Kuhlman, but he was also memorializing the marked changes her ministry had produced on charismatic Christianity overall.

After the eulogy, the service drew to a close. Honorary pallbearers, almost certainly selected by Tink Wilkerson, included the Reverend Rex Humbard, well-known evangelist and pastor of the eight-thousand-seat Cathedral of Tomorrow in Akron, Ohio; the Reverend Ralph Wilkerson, pastor of Melodyland Christian Center in Anaheim, California; and the Reverend Leroy Sanders, pastor of North Hollywood Assembly of God.[30] Following Tink Wilkerson's pattern, none of Kuhlman's closest coworkers were selected. Kuhlman knew Humbard well from shared ministry with his family in Ohio in the 1950s, although there is no indication she was in a close relationship with him at the time of her death. She had begun her Shrine services in Los Angeles at the invitation of Ralph Wilkerson. Sanders was not a figure of note in her life.

Kuhlman's grave was marked with an unembellished bronze plaque that memorialized her opening words from the *I Believe in Miracles* television show:

Kathryn Kuhlman
I Believe in Miracles
Because I Believe in God
February 20, 1976

Tink Wilkerson may not have done much right at Kuhlman's funeral, but he knew her well enough to know that she would be pleased to have a tombstone that marked for posterity only the date of her death, and not the date of her birth.[31]

Settling the Estate

Ceremonies and services complete, on February 25 Kuhlman Foundation representatives turned to the sad but necessary business of Kuhlman's will. The foundation held copies of the will made in January of 1974. In it, the bulk of her estate was designated as a trust. Five people were listed as recipients of an annual 5 percent return on the trust, including Kuhlman's sister Myrtle and Marguerite Hartner. When all five died, the balance of the trust estate would go to the Kuhlman Foundation. One week later, the foundation was notified that the 1974 will was declared void by the register of wills office in Pittsburgh. Of greatest import in the new will was the absence of any bequest to the foundation, and the gift of the residue of the estate, after taxes and fees, to Dana Barton "Tink" Wilkerson.

Suddenly Tink Wilkerson was front-page news. The *Pittsburgh Press* declared, "Church Gets Nothing from Kuhlman Estate." The March 26 article contained details of the controversy: "Kathryn Kuhlman, the evangelist who solicited thousands of dollars in contributions from her followers, has left none of her cash estate of $257,500 to her foundation or the church. Although she doled out money to two sisters, a sister-in-law and twenty employees, the bulk of her estate was left to an Oklahoma car dealer and his wife. D. B. Wilkerson, Jr., and his wife Susan of Tulsa will receive Miss Kuhlman's stock holdings, her Fox Chapel home and all her antiques, art objects, and paintings."[32] Wilkerson maintained the claim he had no knowledge of the contents of the new will, although he knew the will existed. The Kuhlman Foundation employees were shocked by the new will, but had no legal ground for an appeal. The *Pittsburgh Press* took up the story with the April 6 article "Heirs Suspect Kuhlman Will, Do Nothing." Various long-standing employees shared their concerns about the effect contestation of the will would have on Kuhlman's legacy, and for the sake of the ministry's reputation chose not to oppose the will. Reluctantly committed to honoring Kuhlman's last wishes, many were still angry and suspicious of the dramatic changes to the will. Thirty-year employee Charles Loesch stated, "I feel she was taken advantage of in all ways."[33] Wilkerson took every opportunity to defend himself in the press, stating that he believed "a bit of animosity" was created with the foundation by virtue of the change in the will.[34] A master of understatement, as evidenced by his cheery reports concerning Kuhlman's dire condition up until her last breath, Wilkerson must have understood that the foundation was grappling with its almost sure demise due to his inheritance. Asked by *Pittsburgh Press* reporter Ann Butler if the foundation would continue, he declined at first to answer. "Finally, he shook his head, saying, 'In my opinion, Miss Kuhlman was the Foundation.'"[35] With this rationalization, Wilkerson took the money from Kuhlman and signed the death warrant for the foundation that bore her name.[36]

With no financial resources provided from the Kuhlman estate, the days of the Kathryn Kuhlman Foundation as it existed in 1976 were numbered. The television show and miracle services were over. The radio ministry continued. The audiotapes of her radio show that Kuhlman had preserved in preparation for the end-times rapture provided material for several years of broadcasts. The end was inevitable, however. The *Pittsburgh Post-Gazette* for Saturday, April 24, 1982, declared, "Kuhlman's Radio Voice Falls Silent."

> Kathryn Kuhlman is going off the air. The final re-broadcast of her radio programs nationally will be Friday. The Kathryn Kuhlman Foundation will close May 29. This will end the ministry of the world-famous evangelist who died in 1976. "We ran out of money. It cost us $66,000 a month to keep going," said Marguerite Hartner, executive director of the foundation, which has headquarters in the Park Building, Downtown. Hartner said she refuses to add pleas for money to Kuhlman's broadcasts. "I will not beg. Miss Kuhlman did not believe in begging. That's the way she

wanted us to do it." According to Steve Zelenko, a broadcast engineer
with the foundation for nearly twenty-five years, Wheaton College near
Chicago will get the original tapes and television programs. It has a Billy
Graham collection and has agreed to accept the Kuhlman material. . . .
Hartner, more than thirty years with the foundation, said she felt terrible
about the closing. "It's such a blow. It hurts so deeply. We just didn't
get the support," she said. But she added, "Some people have been so
wonderful. They helped us so much. . . . This was our very life. We did
our best," Hartner said.[37]

Announcer Hal Botham hosted the final broadcast from the Canadian
studio. "We will no longer be coming in to your home, your business, or
your automobile on a daily basis," Botham said quietly, and signed off
with "Good bye, God bless, and we'll meet again"; and then came Kuhlman's voice as the closing coda: "There can be no defeat in Christ Jesus.
You were not made for defeat. Give that one victory, for Jesus' sake."[38]

A Complex Legacy: Kathryn Kuhlman and Gentrified Charismatic Christianity

Years after her death, charismatic Christians still remember Kathryn
Kuhlman. Many revere her ministry and career. *The New International
Dictionary of Pentecostal and Charismatic Movements* declares Kuhlman
"The world's most widely known female evangelist," and ends its entry
for her with "she was a star even until her death just short of her 70th
birthday."[39] *Charisma* magazine, the masthead of choice for contemporary charismatic Christianity, featured Kuhlman in an online article in
2014 under the heading "Passing the Baton." "These Christian leaders
appeared on the cover of *Charisma* before they died," the article stated.
"We still celebrate their legacy." Kuhlman's entry identified her as "Still
the world's most widely known female evangelist."[40] Her books are still
in print, a testimony to their continuing appeal, and are published by
Bridge-Logos Publishers of Gainesville, Florida, a press closely associated
with current charismatic Christianity.

Kuhlman is the topic of several YouTube videos, with enthusiastic
posts on the supporting message boards. "This is the power we are seeking, the power of the Holy spirit. I Love being in his presence. Teach us
Katherine, your voice is still heard," Mary Morrone wrote. "Blessed Har-

riet" posted, "Wow this woman of God was really anointed, I just feel the Presence of the Lord around me just listening to her."[41] She also has a Facebook page and lives on as #kathrynkuhlman on Instagram.

Kuhlman is also fondly remembered by many charismatic female evangelists who list her as influential in their call to ministry. Historian Scott Billingsley credits Kuhlman as a role model for the generation of female charismatic leaders who followed her and who "began challenging the patriarchal social order of the charismatic movement." Leaders such as Marilyn Hickey, Juanita Bynum, and Joyce Meyer benefited from Kuhlman's pioneering leadership within the charismatic renewal.[42]

Despite continuing attention among charismatic Christians, outside of that community Kathryn Kuhlman is largely forgotten. Several factors contributed to her relatively quick movement from popular celebrity to cultural insignificance. On a basic level, Kuhlman did not put in place simple mechanisms for perpetuating her ministry. She did not designate a successor. She did not build any buildings or establish a church. The only tangible institutional representation of her ministry, the Kathryn Kuhlman Foundation, contracted almost to incapacity after her death due to lack of funds from her estate. These actions were consistent with Kuhlman's assertion that the ministry was to be focused not upon her person, but upon the Holy Spirit. Kuhlman in fact became the irreplaceable center of the ministry, and the loyalty of her followers was tightly bound up in personal affinity for her. As a result, her capricious behavior at the end of her life disenfranchised many of the very people who would have worked hardest to preserve her legacy and promote her ministry to new generations.

Kuhlman also faded from cultural memory because she functioned in American culture more as a broadcast media figure than as a religious leader. The world of media does not assume successors; it is religious traditions that have succession. No one expected that somehow Kuhlman's ministry as a media product would be sustained by the heroic advance of a new scion. The search for the "heir" to Johnny Carson on *The Tonight Show* was exceptional. The much more common reality shared by countless talk show hosts before and after Carson, including Kuhlman, is this: television shows end.

In the vacuum created by Kuhlman's failure (or refusal) to craft a legacy, other figures began to create inheritance narratives. After Kuhlman's death, Oral Roberts became the uncontested center of the divine healing movement and a logical choice for a leader gentrified charismatics would find appealing. By 1976 Roberts was an established minister of the Methodist church after leaving the Holiness Pentecostal Church eight years before. Oral Roberts University (ORU) welcomed Billy Graham to its service of dedication in 1967 and received full accreditation in 1971. Dick Ross produced a series of well-received television specials for Roberts beginning in 1969.[43] At age fifty-eight in 1976, Roberts was at the peak of his career and, with Kuhlman's death, carried more influence in the charismatic community than any other leader. In the message he gave at Kuhlman's memorial service, Roberts shared what he claimed was a communication from God regarding Kuhlman's legacy. The vision followed the news of Kuhlman's death. "My first thought was, 'Oh dear God, another one is gone.' That was my first human reaction," Roberts stated. "Then I said, 'What about your healing ministry, Lord? Another one is gone.'" Roberts continued: "Then I remembered. Her words hit me like a thunderclap. 'It is not Kathryn Kuhlman. She cannot heal anybody. It is the work of the Holy Spirit.' And the Lord revealed some special things to me about her homegoing. I saw that a very special healing light will shine across the land, and in her death her ministry will be greater than in her life. I saw that the Lord will raise up many others for a very special ministry of His precious healing power. It's going to be greater than ever for the healing of the people."[44] Roberts declared that Kuhlman's ministry would continue, but not as a succession from one healer to an heir. The healing power of the Holy Spirit would be released into many ministries of healing. Roberts certainly intended to include his own ministry in the many that would inherit Kuhlman's "healing light." With her death, Kuhlman's followers would be seeking a new leader. Roberts was more than happy to welcome her admirers into his own fold. With a cover featuring a smiling Kuhlman in her white pulpit dress, Roberts published his words in his association's magazine *Abundant Life* in May 1976. His eulogy, spoken over a woman he had only come to know in her last years and presented at a funeral tainted by the questionable actions of ORU regent Wilkerson, became a valuable marketing piece for Roberts. Roberts's self-serving "vision" in many ways defined Kuhlman's legacy and guaranteed that her ministry would fade from view, dispersed into the manifold inheritors of the same Holy Spirit she had served, with Roberts taking his place as the first and foremost heir.

Others who claimed Kuhlman's "very special ministry of [God's] precious healing power" were the succeeding generations of charismatic female evangelists. These women stepped into the arena prepared by

Kuhlman's influence but espoused beliefs and teachings associated with a prosperity gospel theology Kuhlman would have found anathema. Scholar Kate Bowler says this theological strain in modern American religion, also called word/faith or name it/claim it theology, is centered on four themes: faith, wealth, health, and victory.[45] Like their forebears in positive thinking and New Thought, adherents believe that through the power of their positive minds they can control their lives, including attaining wealth and avoiding illness. Kuhlman grappled with the definition of faith throughout her ministry; she was unwilling to base a healing or a blessing on a person's faith or lack thereof. Kuhlman believed in gumption and the material blessings of a life submitted to God, but she didn't emphasize financial rewards or offer blessings in return for donations. Kuhlman believed in miracles, but she also believed, "If you're a part of humanity, there will be sickness, there will be heartache, tears, sorrow, and death." Kuhlman was educated by Higher Life Victory proponents, but she also recognized the persistence of sin in the life of a Christian.[46] Leaders such as Hickey, Meyer, and Bynum place intense emphasis on the faith of the believer and the compulsion the believer's faith places on God to act. For positive confession adherents, all that is necessary to achieve success, health, and wealth is to "name it and claim it." Kuhlman spent her career firmly upholding the absolute sovereignty of God and would not have supported a theology of positive confession. Put even more simply, Kuhlman stated, "You and I have no right to command God to do anything."[47] Kuhlman's legacy among female charismatic evangelists, therefore, is found in the increased opportunity she provided for these women to lead, not the unorthodox and harmful theology they embrace.[48]

One person, however, was not content to be only one of "many others," as Roberts prophesied. Benedictus "Benny" Hinn made a career out of claiming Kuhlman's legacy as his own, despite his espousal of theology she would have found heretical and practices she would have judged abhorrent. Hinn attended a Kuhlman meeting in Pittsburgh in December of 1973 at the urging of a friend. During the service, Hinn experienced shaking sensations and felt that Kuhlman was speaking directly to him as she explained the role and person of the Holy Spirit. This was the beginning of his fixation on Kuhlman's ministry. He attended many Kuhlman meetings over the next two years, and listened each night to Kuhlman on WWVA, a radio station in Wheeling, West Virginia. Hinn claimed to be invited by a Kuhlman representative to attend a Pittsburgh service in November 1975 in order to meet Kuhlman afterward. The meeting was canceled due to Kuhlman's illness, and Hinn returned to Canada without meeting her. Kuhlman died in February. Hinn later wrote and spoke about Kuhlman in terms so easy and familiar that an uninformed observer would assume the two had known each other for years. The truth is, Hinn never met Kathryn Kuhlman at all.

Hinn began his professional association with Kuhlman's ministry in 1977, after her death. At the invitation of the Kuhlman Foundation, Hinn and Kuhlman soloist Jimmie McDonald spent the next three years traveling across Canada and the United States, leading what Hinn called "film rallies." "Jimmie McDonald sang, the Vegas film was shown, and I spoke," Hinn recalled.[49] Hinn took his engagement to preach at the Kuhlman rallies as a sign of a deep, if fabricated, connection to the person of Kuhlman and her ministry.[50] Over the next two decades, Hinn established a lucrative career based upon the assertion that he had "caught" Kuhlman's mantle, just as Elisha had caught Elijah's mantle as it fell.[51] Unable to provide any proof of Kuhlman's actual designation of him as her successor, he made his claims based upon self-aggrandizing visions and interpretation of Scripture. Hinn established monthly "Miracle Crusades" in which he traveled around the United States and the world, producing miracle services that were copies in form of Kuhlman's services.[52] The connection between Hinn and Kuhlman was a myth, however, carefully crafted by Hinn to leverage Kuhlman's popularity within charismatic Christianity and to access the respect her ministry had achieved. Hinn needed a springboard for his own career, and Kuhlman's foundation provided it for him. He needed legitimation within charismatic circles, and his claims of connection with Kuhlman's carefully gentrified ministry offered a direct path to influence within the leadership of the movement. Hinn used the dead Kuhlman's hard-fought respectability to undergird his own disreputable practices.

Benny Hinn is not Kathryn Kuhlman's successor. His promotion of prosperity gospel teaching, his emphasis on the most extreme forms of spiritual manifestations in his services, his solicitation of large sums of money from followers, and his unorthodox theological statements disqualify him. Yet, Hinn's dogged determination to connect his ministry with Kuhlman produced a false association between the two in popular culture. This concocted bond has done significant damage to the legacy of Kuhlman. Throughout her career she worked to present herself carefully as a representative of a gentrified charismatic Christianity. Ironically, Hinn has succeeded in connecting her with his ministry, which is known for scandal. He has co-opted Kuhlman's legacy. She has become a citation linked with Hinn rather than a historical figure in her own right, a cipher emptied of her own character and story, reinterpreted by Hinn to serve his own purposes of promoting his career.

Because of this incorrect association with Hinn, Kuhlman was and is linked with charismatic leaders connected to the audacious prosperity gospel, the "new face of popular religion."[53] Beginning in the years following Kuhlman's death, Hinn, along with others such as Jerry Falwell, Pat Robertson, and in particular Jim and Tammy Faye Bakker, undid much of the work Kuhlman and the charismatic renewal accomplished in gentrifying charismatic Christianity.[54] Gentrified charismatic Christianity was always a fragile proposition. The sex scandals, prison terms, and blatant corruption of the televangelists of the eighties and beyond, combined with the turn toward the health and wealth gospel of many charismatic leaders, transformed much of charismatic Christianity into a form Kuhlman did not support. For her, the Holy Spirit was always a gentleman; the vulgarity of the prosperity gospel would not fool her, no matter how gentrified it might try to look.

Although not as prevalent as the prosperity gospel form, versions of the gentrified charismatic Christianity of Kuhlman's ministry have lived beyond her, such as the Vineyard Christian Fellowship. Vineyard churches, founded by John Wimber in Anaheim, California, were particularly well suited for gentrified charismatics. Dubbed "neo-charismatics," independent, nondenominational charismatic churches such as the Vineyard experienced significant growth in the latter part of the twentieth century. Wimber, a former professional musician, became a Quaker pastor before joining Calvary Chapel under Charles "Chuck" Smith. Wimber's congregations soon split from Calvary Chapel to form a new fellowship of churches focused on healing. Wimber's use of words of knowledge in his healing services rather than healing lines or "point of contact" healing was in direct line with Kuhlman's approach. Wimber admits Kuhlman's influence, although at first he did not care for her "affected speech, flamboyant dress, theatrical presentation and mystical demeanor." Even when he was uncomfortable with Kuhlman's style, Wimber admits to being "moved and puzzled when I heard her clear preaching of the gospel." He adds, "This is not to belittle Kathryn Kuhlman's ministry. Since that time I have come to appreciate and learn from her."[55] Wimber owes a significant debt to Kuhlman for preparing the way for his type of charismatic church. He states, "I never saw anyone practice healing in a way that I would want to do it. I wanted to be socially acceptable, highly regarded in the community, sophisticated."[56] Without Kuhlman's efforts at gentrification, Wimber might not have found a place within charismatic Christianity for the practice of healing he wanted. As it was, the Vineyard Fellowship became a movement that grew to include over five hundred congregations and a prodigiously successful worship music division.

Due in part to the transformation Kuhlman helped effect, charismatic Christianity is now a dominant form of Christianity in America. Scott Billingsley acknowledges Kuhlman for influencing "an entire generation of charismatic ministers—both male and female—who used her style and techniques to build their own successful careers in the late twentieth century."[57] Since Kuhlman's era of leadership in the 1960s and 1970s, charismatic Christianity has continued to increase in numbers and influence in America. A 2008 report by the Barna Group titled "Is American Christianity Turning Charismatic?" indicated that 80 million Americans accepted the designation "charismatic" or "Pentecostal" Christian. Although the renewal in the mainline churches and Roman Catholicism waned, charismatic Christianity spread through evangelical churches by means of music and worship style, creating evangelical congregations with overtly charismatic worship.[58] As evangelicalism grew in numbers and dominance in American religion in the latter part of the twentieth century, gentrified charismatic Christianity settled into a new environment, and thrived. Since that time, charismatic Christianity has become the brand of choice for most Protestant Christians.[59] Kathryn Kuhlman was a leader in this charismatic coup.

In July of 1976, the Kathryn Kuhlman Foundation produced an hour-long program entitled "Kathryn Kuhlman: A Legacy." In the opening scene, a camera pans slowly over an empty soundstage as Kuhlman's disembodied voice once again says, "Take nothing and use it." In some ways, the image of an empty stage was apt. As a media figure, Kuhlman effectively disappeared at her death. But her legacy was not restricted to her soundstage, and she left behind much more than "nothing" for future generations to use. The transformation of charismatic Christianity in the twentieth century owes a great deal to its former superstar. It is time to bring back to the stage of American religious history the compelling, sometimes difficult, and always intriguing figure of Kathryn Johanna Kuhlman, the "miracle lady."[60]

Notes

Notes to the Introduction

1. "Johnny Carson Show–Tonight Show, Kathryn Kuhlman Segment," *I Believe in Miracles*, October 15, 1974, VHS, V125, Collection 212, the Kathryn Kuhlman Collection, Archives of the Billy Graham Center, Wheaton, Illinois.

2. Vinson Synan, *The Holiness-Pentecostal Tradition: Charismatic Movements in the Twentieth Century* (Grand Rapids: Eerdmans, 1997), 187.

3. Alma Whitaker, "Tell of Cures by Miracles," *Los Angeles Times*, June 18, 1923.

4. "Straton Defends Healing Services," *New York Times*, June 24, 1927.

5. David Edwin Harrell Jr., *All Things Are Possible: The Healing and Charismatic Revivals in Modern America* (Bloomington: Indiana University Press, 1975), 99, 100.

6. Lawrence E. Davies, "Bishop Pike Warns Clergymen about 'Speaking with Tongues,'" *New York Times*, May 7, 1963.

7. For more information about the origins of American Pentecostalism, please see chapter 1, "Pentecostalism's Roots in the Premillennial, Healing and Holiness Movements, 1880–1901," in Edith Blumhofer, *Restoring the Faith: The Assemblies of God, Pentecostalism, and American Culture* (Urbana: University of Illinois Press, 1993), and the introduction to Grant Wacker, *Heaven Below: Early Pentecostals and American Culture* (Cambridge, MA: Harvard University Press, 2001).

8. Blumhofer, *Restoring the Faith*, 50–51.

9. Blumhofer, *Restoring the Faith*, 54–56.

10. Wacker, *Heaven Below*, 1.

11. Blumhofer, *Restoring the Faith*, 101; Vinson Synan, *The Century of the Holy Spirit: 100 Years of Pentecostal and Charismatic Renewal* (Nashville: Nelson, 2001), 149; Synan, *The Holiness-Pentecostal Tradition*, 146; Wacker, *Heaven Below*, 1.

12. "News of Southern Counties: Local Correspondence," *Los Angeles Times*, July 2, 1924.

13. Historian Grant Wacker stated that the majority of early twentieth-century

Pentecostals "resembled most Americans, both demographically and biographically." Wacker, *Heaven Below*, 216.

14. Blumhofer, *Restoring the Faith*, 104, 106; Synan, *The Holiness-Pentecostal Tradition*, 146.

15. Wacker, *Heaven Below*, 199.

16. Stanley Burgess and Eduard M. Van Der Maas, eds., *The New International Dictionary of Pentecostal and Charismatic Movements* (Grand Rapids: Zondervan, 2002), s.v. "charismatic movement."

17. "Neo-charismatics" was the term used for the third generation of Christians to develop under the overall heading of charismatic. Emerging in the late 1970s, they are defined as "participants in independent, postdenominational, nondenominational, or indigenous groups or organizations, such as the Vineyard Christian Fellowship." Burgess and Van Der Maas, *New International Dictionary*, xix–xxi.

18. "Pope John XXIII Convokes the Second Vatican Council," December 25, 1961, https://jakomonchak.files.wordpress.com/2011/12/humanae-salutis.pdf.

19. Richard Quebedeaux, *The New Charismatics II: How a Christian Renewal Movement Became Part of the American Religious Mainstream* (San Francisco: Harper and Row, 1983), 60.

20. Quebedeaux, *The New Charismatics II*, 99.

21. Burgess and Van Der Maas, *New International Dictionary*, s.v. "charismatic movement."

22. Burgess and Van Der Maas, *New International Dictionary*, s.v. "charismatic movement."

23. Burgess and Van Der Maas, *New International Dictionary*, s.v. "Catholic charismatic renewal."

24. Burgess and Van Der Maas, *New International Dictionary*, s.v. "charismatic movement."

25. By the time of Kuhlman's death in 1976, the fragile bonds that produced the subset of gentrified charismatic Christianity had begun to fray. Many frustrated charismatics left their mainline and evangelical churches after what they saw as the failure of their congregations to pursue spiritual renewal. By the early eighties, some proponents of charismatic Christianity (re)joined forces with Pentecostalism, as both fell under the sway of the prosperity gospel/health and wealth teaching. This theological shift for charismatic Christianity had negative consequences, and the 1980s saw scandal after scandal for people in charismatic Christianity's wider circles. I address this more fully in the epilogue.

26. Only two dissertations have been written about Kuhlman, both of which focus mainly on her rhetoric and speaking style, not her position in American Christianity. The dissertations are: Katherine Jane Leisering, "An Historical and Critical Study of the Pittsburgh Preaching Career of Kathryn Kuhlman" (PhD diss., Ohio University, 1981), and Todd Vernon Lewis, "Charismatic Communication and Faith Healers: A Critical Study of Rhetorical Behavior" (PhD diss., Louisiana State University and Agricultural and Mechanical College, 1980). Leisering offered an overview of Kuhlman's career, but it was based primarily on secondary sources, and her argument mainly concerned Kuhlman's sermons and homiletical style. Neither dissertation adequately explored Kuhlman's role in the larger transformation occurring in American Christianity.

27. Sydney Ahlstrom, *A Religious History of the American People* (New Haven: Yale University Press, 1972), 1086n6. Ahlstrom first discusses Pentecostalism in the section titled "The Ordeals of Transition." Under the further subheading "Dissent and Reaction in Protestantism," Ahlstrom describes "a disintegrative tendency" in the Holiness movement. "Gradually an ordering process began to dissipate into the chaos of competing evangelists, independent congregations, and loosely organized nondenominational associations." Two groupings emerged from the "chaos," a "moderate" form that retained the name "Holiness" and "a more extreme alternative, which adopted the name 'Pentecostal.'" Earlier, Ahlstrom described charismatic doctrines such as faith healing and premillennialism as "radical conceptions" that were causing theological "alarm." "Ordeal," "dissent," "disintegrative," "chaos," "extreme," "radical," "alarming": these are terms that reveal unease with charismatic Christianity in American religious history. Ahlstrom, 806.

28. Elaine Lawless's work on Pentecostal woman preachers highlights the complexity of achieving and maintaining authority in conservative Christian groups. "The girl who wishes to be a pastor must also be a wife and mother, and she must extol the virtues of those capacities at every opportunity. She must declare her 'motherly' nature, exclaim her delight in being a wife and mother, her joy in her children, her home. And she must deny her sexuality as a possible temptress while at the same time she must acknowledge her inferior status as woman and submit herself to all men. The role is a complex one, full of pitfalls and possible infractions. The woman pastor clearly has to balance her life on a tenuous pivot—any move too far in any direction could cause her to lose her hard-earned position of spiritual power and religious authority." Elaine Lawless, *Handmaidens of the Lord* (Philadelphia: University of Pennsylvania Press, 1988), 164.

29. Kristin Kobes Du Mez, *A New Gospel for Women: Katharine Bushnell and the Challenge of Christian Feminism* (New York: Oxford University Press, 2015), 187.

30. Donald T. Critchlow, *Phyllis Schlafly and Grassroots Conservatism: A Woman's Crusade* (Princeton: Princeton University Press, 2005), 13.

31. "Johnny Carson Show–Tonight Show, Kathryn Kuhlman Segment."

Notes to Chapter 1

1. *Healing in the Spirit: A Wide-Ranging Exclusive Interview with Kathryn Kuhlman*, pamphlet published by *Christianity Today*, July 20, 1973, in Box 1, Collection 212, the Kathryn Kuhlman Collection, Archives of the Billy Graham Center, Wheaton, Illinois; hereafter cited as KKC.

2. Kathryn Kuhlman, *A Glimpse into Glory* (Gainesville, FL: Bridge-Logos Publishers, 1983), 28. It would be easy to explain Kuhlman's denial of formal training as characteristic of an anti-intellectualism assumed to be prevalent in charismatic Christianity, especially Pentecostalism. Grant Wacker undercut this error, stating, "If some pentecostals disparaged formal education, most rushed to defend it, at least education of the right kind." The "right kind" of education was that "conducted under Christian auspices with Christian purposes." Kuhlman did not criticize formal education in others, and even accepted the first honorary doctorate presented by Oral Roberts Uni-

versity in 1972. For Kuhlman, denial of formal training was a device she employed to protect her role as a female leader, not a criticism of education in itself. Grant Wacker, *Heaven Below: Early Pentecostals and American Culture* (Cambridge, MA: Harvard University Press, 2001), 152.

3. Helen Kooiman Hosier, *Kathryn Kuhlman: The Life She Led, the Legacy She Left* (Old Tappan, NJ: Revell, 1976), 50–53.

4. "Dr. Robert Hoyt, MD, and Dr. Claire King, MD," *I Believe in Miracles*, September 19, 1967, VHS, V271, in KKC.

5. In contrast, the early life of Kuhlman's closest contemporary on the divine healing platform represented in many ways the standard narrative of a leader of a faith healing ministry. Oral Roberts pointed to an early sickness as a source of his focus on healing. He was born in 1918, eleven years after Kuhlman. His parents were involved in ministry in the Pentecostal Holiness church in Oklahoma. At the age of seventeen, Roberts's life took a dramatic turn when he collapsed in a high school basketball game due to an attack of tuberculosis. Roberts claimed he was healed soon after in a tent revival service conducted by a traveling evangelist in Ada, Oklahoma. He was also cured of stuttering at this time. Soon after this dual miracle of healing, he began his career as a teenage preacher. See David Edwin Harrell Jr., *All Things Are Possible: The Healing and Charismatic Revivals in Modern America* (Bloomington: Indiana University Press, 1975), especially chap. 3.

6. Kuhlman, *A Glimpse into Glory,* 56.

7. Heather Curtis, *Faith in the Great Physician: Suffering and Divine Healing in American Culture, 1860–1900* (Baltimore: Johns Hopkins University Press, 2007), 6.

8. Many historians list the post–World War I period as a time of great interest in the miraculous ability of God to heal human bodies. Jonathan Baer argues that this increasing emphasis was likely influenced by the twin traumas of World War I and the influenza epidemic that affected 25 percent of the American population in 1918. Others see the massive expansion of scientific approaches to medicine producing nonscientific responses. See Jonathan Baer, "Perfectly Empowered Bodies: Divine Healing in Modernizing America" (PhD diss., Yale University, 2002); E. Brooks Holifield, *Health and Medicine in the Methodist Tradition: Journey toward Wholeness* (New York: Crossroad, 1986); Amanda Porterfield, *Healing in the History of Christianity* (New York: Oxford University Press, 2005); Paul Starr, *The Social Transformation of American Medicine* (New York: Basic Books, 1982).

9. Wayne E. Warner, *Kathryn Kuhlman: The Woman behind the Miracles* (Ann Arbor, MI: Servant, 1993), 24.

10. "Interview with Myrtle Parrott and Kathryn Kuhlman by Jamie Buckingham," December 1974, T2111 (audiocassette), Collection 212, in KKC.

11. *Heart to Heart with Kathryn Kuhlman* (Gainesville, FL: Bridge-Logos Publishers, 1998), chap. 1, "The Beginning of Miracles," 2–3.

12. "Worshipers Too Noisy, Haled to Night Court," *Chicago Daily Tribune*, August 11, 1924.

13. "30 Quit Straton Church; Oppose Healing Service," *Chicago Daily Tribune*, November 1, 1927.

14. Baer, "Perfectly Empowered Bodies," 55.

15. Baer, "Perfectly Empowered Bodies," 55.

16. Baer, "Perfectly Empowered Bodies," 289.

17. "Interview with Myrtle Parrott and Kathryn Kuhlman by Jamie Buckingham."

18. Stanley Burgess and Eduard M. Van Der Maas, eds., *The New International Dictionary of Pentecostal and Charismatic Movements* (Grand Rapids: Zondervan, 2002), s.v. "Price, Charles Sydney"; Baer, "Perfectly Empowered Bodies," 301–2; Harrell, *All Things Are Possible*, 17; Warner, *Kathryn Kuhlman*, 24–25.

19. Burgess and Van Der Maas, *New International Dictionary*, s.v. "Price, Charles Sydney."

20. Edith Blumhofer, *Aimee Semple McPherson: Everybody's Sister* (Grand Rapids: Eerdmans, 1996), 176.

21. Burgess and Van Der Maas, *New International Dictionary*, s.v. "Price, Charles Sydney."

22. Harrell, *All Things Are Possible*, 17.

23. Burgess and Van Der Maas, *New International Dictionary*, s.v. "healing in the Christian church."

24. "Rolf and Roberta McPherson," *I Believe in Miracles*, February 15, 1973, VHS, V236, in KKC.

25. *Healing in the Spirit.*

26. Rolf did not challenge Kuhlman's statements on the television show but allowed them to stand. Warner argues that Kuhlman sat in on classes at the LIFE Bible College on the basis of several interviews, including the above-mentioned conversation with McPherson's son Rolf. No official documentation exists proving that Kuhlman attended the school. Warner, chapter entitled "Training in the West: A Well-Kept Secret," in *Kathryn Kuhlman*, 34–35.

27. By 1922, McPherson had developed her "Four Square Gospel" message. In 1923, she built the Angelus Temple in Los Angeles, and soon after began publishing her monthly periodical entitled the *Bridal Call*. She then authored three books and opened her LIFE Bible College. During the 1920s Sister Aimee itinerated widely, holding meetings in, among other cities, St. Louis, Denver, and several cities in California as well as in her native country, Canada. Matthew Avery Sutton, *Aimee Semple McPherson and the Resurrection of Christian America* (Cambridge, MA: Harvard University Press, 2007); Blumhofer, *Aimee Semple McPherson*; Burgess and Van Der Maas, *New International Dictionary*, s.v. "McPherson, Aimee Semple."

28. Blumhofer, *Aimee Semple McPherson*, 169.

29. Blumhofer, *Aimee Semple McPherson*, 174.

30. Baer, "Perfectly Empowered Bodies," 294.

31. The words of the hymn are: "Be of sin the double cure, save from wrath and make me pure."

32. Blumhofer, *Aimee Semple McPherson*, 215.

33. This concept of the atonement made McPherson unpopular with the fundamentalist Christians of her day. Responding to reports of her teaching in the San Diego revivals in 1921, the editor of the *Moody Monthly* from Moody Bible College in Chicago offered cautionary words. Teaching healing as a part of Christ's atoning work on the cross "proved especially troublesome, since it seemed to obligate God to heal and failed to explain satisfactorily the cases in which healing did not occur. . . . Sister's healing seemed to demand invalids to exercise personal faith; her teachings seemed

to imply that strong faith effects a cure, and the permanence of the cure depends on persistence in faith." In Blumhofer, *Aimee Semple McPherson*, 223.

34. Timothy Gloege, *Guaranteed Pure: The Moody Bible Institute, Business, and the Making of Modern Evangelicalism* (Chapel Hill: University of North Carolina Press, 2015), 29, 103–4.

35. Burgess and Van Der Maas, *New International Dictionary*, s.v. "dispensationalism."

36. Blumhofer, *Aimee Semple McPherson*, 205. See Blumhofer's chapter entitled "Content" for more information about McPherson's thought.

37. Blumhofer, *Aimee Semple McPherson*, 215.

38. Blumhofer, *Aimee Semple McPherson*, 206–7.

39. Pictures and recordings of McPherson show Sister in a white pulpit dress, modeled after a Salvation Army uniform. Kuhlman's dress on her first television show in the 1950s bears a greater resemblance to Sister than her later, more flowing pulpit gown. McPherson spoke with a stylized inflection similar to the fashion of movie stars of her time. It is difficult to determine if Kuhlman imitated Sister Aimee or simply incorporated the standard manner of public speaking popular at the time, but she retained the idiosyncratic style throughout her career. Aimee's dramatic manner, her striking white dresses, and her distinctive style of speaking seem to have made a lasting impression on the young Kuhlman.

40. Blumhofer, *Aimee Semple McPherson*, 231.

41. Kathryn Kuhlman, permanent record, Simpson Bible Institute, 1924–1927. Simpson Bible Institute is now Simpson College, Redding, California. The transcript was provided to Wayne Warner in the early 1990s. Warner, email message to author, November 16, 2007.

42. *Heart to Heart with Kathryn Kuhlman*, 5.

43. *An Hour with Kathryn Kuhlman*, n.d., T2113 (audiocassette), Collection 212, in KKC.

44. O children of Zion, be glad
  and rejoice in the Lord your God;
 for he has given the early rain for your vindication,
  he has poured down for you abundant rain,
  the early and the later [latter] rain, as before. (Joel 2:23, NRSV)

45. Baer, "Perfectly Empowered Bodies," 81; Burgess and Van Der Maas, *New International Dictionary*, s.v. "Simpson, Albert Benjamin."

46. Baer, "Perfectly Empowered Bodies," 86–87.

47. Burgess and Van Der Maas, *New International Dictionary*, s.v. "Simpson, Albert Benjamin."

48. Gloege, *Guaranteed Pure*, 145.

49. Baer, "Perfectly Empowered Bodies," 78.

50. Gloege, *Guaranteed Pure*, 146.

51. Burgess and Van Der Maas, *New International Dictionary*, s.v. "Simpson, Albert Benjamin."

52. George M. Marsden, *Fundamentalism and American Culture* (New York: Oxford University Press, 1980), 78.

53. Biographer Wayne Warner records that an unnamed former classmate of Kuhl-

man's "reluctantly stated" that Kuhlman was expelled from Simpson in 1926 after being caught after hours with a male student. *Kathryn Kuhlman*, 34.

54. "Interview with Myrtle Parrott and Kathryn Kuhlman by Jamie Buckingham."

55. "Interview with Myrtle Parrott and Kathryn Kuhlman by Jamie Buckingham."

56. Elaine Lawless, *Handmaidens of the Lord* (Philadelphia: University of Pennsylvania Press, 1988), 76.

57. Kuhlman, *A Glimpse into Glory*, 8–9.

58. Ann Braude, *Sisters and Saints: Women and American Religion* (Oxford: Oxford University Press, 2008), 29.

59. Braude, *Sisters and Saints*, 28–29.

60. "Interview with Myrtle Parrott and Kathryn Kuhlman by Jamie Buckingham."

61. "Interview with Myrtle Parrott and Kathryn Kuhlman by Jamie Buckingham."

62. The story of Kuhlman's beginning in ministry is in both of her major biographies ("Tents and Turkey Houses," in Jamie Buckingham, *Daughter of Destiny* [Gainesville, FL: Bridge-Logos Press, 1999]; "Kathryn in the Pulpit," in Warner, *Kathryn Kuhlman*), as well as in the biographical summary that accompanies the KKC. Additional details are included in "Interview with Myrtle Parrott and Kathryn Kuhlman by Jamie Buckingham."

63. *Heart to Heart with Kathryn Kuhlman*, 4.

64. Warner, *Kathryn Kuhlman*, 57.

65. Hosier, *Kathryn Kuhlman*, 50–53.

66. Wacker, *Heaven Below*, 164.

67. Nancy Cott, *The Grounding of Modern Feminism* (New Haven: Yale University Press, 1987), 215.

68. Cott, *Grounding of Modern Feminism*, 180.

69. Wacker, *Heaven Below*, 160.

70. Warner, *Kathryn Kuhlman*, 49.

71. The Kuhlman collection does not contain any scrapbooks from the rest of Kuhlman's life. It seems she kept a photographic record only of these certain years, a fact I find revealing in itself. This was probably the happiest time in Kuhlman's life.

72. Hosier, *Kathryn Kuhlman*, 51.

73. Hosier, *Kathryn Kuhlman*, 51.

74. Lee Canipe, "The Unlikely Argument of a Baptist Fundamentalist: John Roach Straton's Defense of Women in the Pulpit," *Baptist History and Heritage*, Spring 2005, 24–26.

75. Fundamentalist Baptist minister John Roach Straton, pastor of Calvary Baptist in New York City, invited Utley to preach at Calvary, stirring up criticism from his fundamentalist colleagues. Straton's interactions with Utley led him to make a case for women in ministry based upon the distinction between "pastor" and "preacher." This was very similar to the argument Kuhlman used to defend her own ministry. "If God inspired the prophet Joel to envision women preaching under the power of the Holy Spirit, and if God guided the apostle Peter to declare that the coming of the Holy Spirit had fulfilled Joel's prophecy, then, Straton reasoned, Bible-believing Christians must not dare to silence a woman called by God to preach. . . . Straton deliberately distinguished between the roles of pastor and preacher: in accordance with scripture, he believed, only men could serve God as pastor, but anyone whom

God calls could serve Him as a preacher of the gospel." Canipe, "The Unlikely Argument," 27–33.

76. Canipe, "The Unlikely Argument," 26.

77. Thank you to Thomas Robinson for correcting the unfair portrait of Utley as a washed-up child star, offering instead a story of a child and woman struggling with the pressures of her evangelistic career. I also am working to correct an unfair and false legacy for Kuhlman, and I am glad the stories of both Utley and Kuhlman are receiving the rehabilitation they deserve. Thomas Robinson, *Preacher Girl: Uldine Utley and the Industry of Revival* (Waco: Baylor University Press, 2016), 204.

78. Hosier, *Kathryn Kuhlman*, 53.

79. Kuhlman, *A Glimpse into Glory*, 27.

80. "Considered whole, the primary evidence suggests that something like half of the travelling evangelists, divine healers, and overseas missionaries were women." Wacker, *Heaven Below*, 160.

81. Wacker, *Heaven Below*, 171.

82. Burgess and Van Der Maas, *New International Dictionary*, s.v. "role of women."

83. Joel 2:28 NIV.

84. Burgess and Van Der Maas, *New International Dictionary*, s.v. "role of women."

85. Wacker, *Heaven Below*, 171.

86. "Interview with Myrtle Parrott and Kathryn Kuhlman by Jamie Buckingham."

87. Paul Ferrin, phone interview with author, March 19, 2013, Harrison, Arkansas.

88. Ferrin, phone interview with author. Ferrin's wife, Marjorie Daniels, is related to the Anderson sisters; her mother and two aunts made up the trio.

89. Ferrin, phone interview with author. Ferrin is quoting his father-in-law.

90. "Biography of Kathryn Kuhlman," Collection 212, in KKC.

91. Buckingham, *Daughter of Destiny*, 62.

92. Tona J. Hangen, *Redeeming the Dial: Radio, Religion, and Popular Culture in America* (Chapel Hill: University of North Carolina Press, 2002), 5.

93. Hangen, *Redeeming the Dial*, 11.

94. Hangen, *Redeeming the Dial*, 6.

95. Hangen, *Redeeming the Dial*, 64–65, 69.

96. Bernard M. Timberg, *Television Talk: A History of the TV Talk Show* (Austin: University of Texas Press, 2002), 3–4.

97. Hangen, *Redeeming the Dial*, 6.

98. Hangen, *Redeeming the Dial*, 5.

99. Hangen explains, "Radio opened the possibility that words spoken in one place could affect listeners located far away, replicating and reinforcing with technology what McPherson previously believed only God, operating through the Holy Spirit, had been able to do." Hangen, *Redeeming the Dial*, 74.

100. "Evangelicals generally did not obtain an equal share of the free time offered by local stations. A Federal Council of Churches study published in 1938 revealed that while evangelical groups broadcast more programs over a larger number of stations for a higher number of hours than Roman Catholic and mainline Protestant groups, they were twice as likely to be charged for access to the air." Quentin J. Schultze, ed., *American Evangelicals and the Mass Media* (Grand Rapids: Zondervan, 1990), 76.

101. Hangen, *Redeeming the Dial*, 17.

102. Schultze, *American Evangelicals*, 76.

103. See chap. 36, "My First Healing," in Kuhlman, *A Glimpse into Glory*, 153–58.

104. "Papa's Funeral," *I Believe in Miracles*, February 10, 1971, VHS, V389, in KKC. Paul Ferrin noted that the meetings in Denver were not based on healing. Ferrin, phone interview with author.

105. Reprinted in Kuhlman, *A Glimpse into Glory*, 153–58. Most of Kuhlman's published articles were edited and some were ghostwritten. This article shows signs of an editorial voice, but in its basic facts it follows essentially the same story she told on her television show.

106. Scrapbook belonging to Kathryn Kuhlman, Collection 212, in KKC.

107. Warner, chapter entitled "Way Off Course with Mr. Waltrip," in *Kathryn Kuhlman*, 81–89; Buckingham, chapter entitled "The Slaying of the Egyptian," in *Daughter of Destiny*, 69–78 .

108. Warner, *Kathryn Kuhlman*, 102–3.

109. According to friends of Kuhlman from the Denver Revival Tabernacle, she simply "disappeared." Close friends did not know where she had gone. Helen Gulliford stayed in Denver and continued to be involved in the ministry at the Tabernacle, but Kuhlman "just left." Ferrin, phone interview with author.

110. Stephanie Coontz, "Divorce, No-Fault Style," *New York Times*, June 16, 2010, http://www.nytimes.com/2010/06/17/opinion/17coontz.html.

111. B. A. Waltrip v. Jessie Annabelle Waltrip, Decree No. 13868, District Court, State of Iowa, Marion County, June 29, 1937; quoted in Warner, *Kathryn Kuhlman*, 86.

112. Burroughs Allen Waltrip v. Kathryn Johanna Waltrip, Case No. 34784, Clark County (Las Vegas), Nevada, filed February 18, 1947.

113. This was one of the handful of times Kuhlman claimed to have spoken in tongues.

114. *An Hour with Kathryn Kuhlman*.

115. Paul Ferrin, Kuhlman's choir director and pianist in her last years, is married to Marjorie Daniels. Daniels and her family were close friends with Kuhlman during her ministry in Denver. Ferrin stated that Kuhlman enjoyed talking over old times with him. Once Kuhlman asked Ferrin, "Did the Daniels [Marjorie's family] ever hear from Dr. Waltrip?" Ferrin answered no. Kuhlman never mentioned Waltrip to Ferrin again. Ferrin, phone interview with author.

116. For years Kuhlman deliberately obscured her marriage and divorce and refused to speak about Waltrip. At one point she stated that she had not been married at all, since she passed out before the vows were made. Even as late as 1974 she was reluctant to answer a reporter about the match. "Question: Ever married? Answer: Yes, but it was so long ago, nobody ever bothers to mention it." Ann Butler, "She Believes in Miracles," *Pittsburgh Press Roto*, February 3, 1974. The fact that she married a divorced father of two only to leave him, prompting divorce proceedings against her, was understandably not something she chose to dwell upon in her writing and speaking.

Notes to Chapter 2

1. The cassette recording of Kuhlman's message entitled "The Beginning of Miracles" was one of the most requested by her followers. It was also the title of the first essay in a posthumous collection of transcribed radio messages entitled *Heart to Heart with Kathryn Kuhlman*. The story was also printed in a booklet entitled *What Is the Key?*, which was published in the early 1960s. This pamphlet was offered during broadcasts of *I Believe in Miracles* free of charge by self-addressed stamped envelope to anyone who requested it. The standard narrative Kuhlman recounted regarding the beginning of miracles in her ministry is contained in these three records. Kathryn Kuhlman, *What Is the Key?*, Box 1, Collection 212, in the Kathryn Kuhlman Collection, Archives of the Billy Graham Center, Wheaton, Illinois; hereafter cited as KKC.

2. *Healing in the Spirit: A Wide-Ranging Exclusive Interview with Kathryn Kuhlman*, pamphlet published by *Christianity Today*, July 20, 1973, in Box 1, Collection 212, in KKC.

3. Jamie Buckingham, *Daughter of Destiny* (Gainesville, FL: Bridge-Logos Press, 1999), 88–89; Wayne E. Warner, *Kathryn Kuhlman: The Woman behind the Miracles* (Ann Arbor, MI: Servant, 1993), 122.

4. Warner, *Kathryn Kuhlman*, 124, 118–19.

5. Buckingham, *Daughter of Destiny*, 91.

6. Pittsburgh had a long history of religious broadcasting prior to the advent of Kuhlman's radio ministry. Schultze explains, "The first non-experimental regular radio broadcast began when Westinghouse established Pittsburgh station KDKA, which went on the air on November 1, 1920. Only two months later KDKA carried the first radio broadcast of a church service from Calvary Episcopal Church. It was the birth of broadcast ministry." Hangen adds, "Radio and radio evangelism were born together." Quentin J. Schultze, ed., *American Evangelicals and the Mass Media* (Grand Rapids: Zondervan, 1990), 71; Tona J. Hangen, *Redeeming the Dial: Radio, Religion, and Popular Culture in America* (Chapel Hill: University of North Carolina Press, 2002), 21.

7. Warner, *Kathryn Kuhlman*, 126.

8. Warner, *Kathryn Kuhlman*, 126.

9. Many guests on her shows over the years noted their initial dislike of her voice and her dramatic speech, but then revealed a sort of fascination that accompanied listening to her highly stylized deliverance.

10. Warner, *Kathryn Kuhlman*, 125.

11. Warner, *Kathryn Kuhlman*, 126.

12. Warner, *Kathryn Kuhlman*, 138.

13. Kuhlman, *What Is the Key?*

14. Perhaps Kuhlman's discomfort with healing lines, prayer cards, and the concept of faith and healing that surrounded them was also a part of her rejection of McPherson's influence. At Sister Aimee's services, Kuhlman would have seen the type of healing methods she disliked. This paragraph is taken from the pamphlet *What Is the Key?* Kuhlman's voice is clearly shaped by the editor or ghostwriter of this piece, but the basic narrative is repeated in various forms in other, less editorially constructed forms and is therefore reliable.

15. Kuhlman, *What Is the Key?*

16. *Heart to Heart with Kathryn Kuhlman*, 1.

17. *Heart to Heart with Kathryn Kuhlman*, 6.

18. *Heart to Heart with Kathryn Kuhlman*, 6–7.

19. *Heart to Heart with Kathryn Kuhlman*, 8–9; Kuhlman, *What Is the Key?* Interestingly, the woman is not named in either of the accounts, or in any of the many other references to this story.

20. *Heart to Heart with Kathryn Kuhlman*, 8–9.

21. Kuhlman, *What Is the Key?*

22. *Heart to Heart with Kathryn Kuhlman*, 1–17.

23. U.S. Department of Veterans Affairs, "America's Wars," May 2017, https://www.va.gov/opa/publications/factsheets/fs_americas_wars.pdf.

24. Stanley Burgess and Eduard M. Van Der Maas, eds., *The New International Dictionary of Pentecostal and Charismatic Movements* (Grand Rapids: Zondervan, 2002), s.v. "Assemblies of God."

25. Ronald Numbers and Darryl Amundsen, eds., *Caring and Curing: Health and Medicine in the Western Religious Traditions* (New York: Macmillan, 1986), 526.

26. David Edwin Harrell Jr., *All Things Are Possible: The Healing and Charismatic Revivals in Modern America* (Bloomington: Indiana University Press, 1975), 49–50.

27. *Heart to Heart with Kathryn Kuhlman*, 10.

28. "Evangelist Barred in Fund Dispute," *Pittsburgh Press*, June 19, 1948.

29. Warner, *Kathryn Kuhlman*, 123.

30. Kathryn Kuhlman, *Faith and Gumption*, c. 1950s, T5 (audiocassette), Collection 212, in KKC.

31. Kathryn Kuhlman, *A Glimpse into Glory* (Gainesville, FL: Bridge-Logos Publishers, 1983), 88.

32. Kathryn Kuhlman, *In Search of Blessings* (Gainesville, FL: Bridge-Logos Publishers, 1989), 99.

33. Kuhlman, *Faith and Gumption*.

34. Kate Bowler, *Blessed: A History of the American Prosperity Gospel* (New York: Oxford University Press, 2013), 13–14.

35. Historian Beryl Satter links the origins of Peale's "positive thinking" to New Thought in American Christianity. "The continued draw of New Thought principles [is] attributable to the fact that its central concepts—that God is Mind and that human thought, the manifestation of Creative Power, can affect circumstances—are fundamentally ambiguous and can be interpreted to fit almost any personal or political goal. New Thought's intrinsic ambiguity explains why it outlived its turn-of-the-century origins and remained a force in American culture." Beryl Satter, *Each Mind a Kingdom: American Women, Sexual Purity, and the New thought Movement, 1875–1920* (Los Angeles: University of California Press, 2001), 251.

36. Kuhlman's own story "The Beginning of Miracles" was first published in *Guideposts* in 1971.

37. Craig R. Prentiss, "The Power of Positive Thinking" in Colleen McDannell, ed., *Religions of the United States in Practice*, 2 vols. (Princeton: Princeton University Press, 2001), 2:251.

38. Prentiss, "Positive Thinking" in McDannell, *Religions of the United States*, 2:251.

39. Roy M. Anker, *Self-Help and Popular Religion in Early American Culture* (Westport, CT: Greenwood Press, 1999), 117.

40. Prentiss, "Positive Thinking" in McDannell, *Religions of the United States*, 2:253.

41. R. Laurence Moore, *Selling God: American Religion in the Marketplace of Culture* (New York: Oxford University Press, 1994), 241.

42. Prentiss, "Positive Thinking" in McDannell, *Religions of the United States*, 2:255.

43. Prentiss, "Positive Thinking" in McDannell, *Religions of the United States*, 2:255.

44. "Carey Reams," *Your Faith and Mine*, c. 1950s, VHS, V495, Collection 212, in KKC.

45. Kuhlman, *Faith and Gumption*.

46. Kuhlman, *A Glimpse into Glory*, 53–54.

47. "Tabernacle Gift of Evangelist," *Pittsburgh Press*, January 1, 1949.

48. "Mrs. Kichline and Son Richard, Cured of Paralysis," *Your Faith and Mine*, c. 1950s, VHS, V496, Collection 212, in KKC.

49. Harrell, *All Things Are Possible*, 99–100.

50. Harrell, *All Things Are Possible*, 100.

51. "Admits He Shot Preacher over 'That Ranting,'" *Chicago Daily Tribune*, January 15, 1946.

52. "Pastor Attacked during Services," *Pittsburgh Post Gazette*, December 30, 1948.

53. "Pastor Attacked during Services," *Pittsburgh Post Gazette*, December 30, 1948.

54. Buckingham, *Daughter of Destiny*, 111.

55. "Press Release c. 1953, Prepared by Howard R. Pearson Representing Kathryn Kuhlman," Collection 212, in KKC.

56. Harrell credits Kuhlman's popularity for Humbard's early success. "Humbard's remarkable success story began in 1952 when, after a successful tent revival by his family, he decided to stay in Akron, Ohio. He asked Kathryn Kuhlman, who had a large following in the area, to help him begin a church. In response, she reportedly attracted 18,000 people in one day." From this beginning Humbard went on to build the eight-thousand-seat Cathedral of Tomorrow for his burgeoning ministry. Harrell, *All Things Are Possible*, 192.

Notes to Chapter 3

1. Jamie Buckingham, *Daughter of Destiny* (Gainesville, FL: Bridge-Logos Press, 1999), 109.

2. I do not want to overlook the importance of print media in Kuhlman's career, but in this chapter the focus will be her role and work in broadcast media.

3. Marshall Fishwick and Ray B. Browne, eds., *The God Pumpers: Religion in the Electronic Age* (Bowling Green, OH: Bowling Green State University Popular Press, 1987), 121.

4. Hal Erickson, *Syndicated Television: The First Forty Years, 1947–1987* (Jefferson, NC: McFarland and Co., 1989), 81–82, does not list *Your Faith and Mine* but does record programs from the 1950s hosted by Oral Roberts and Norman Vincent Peale.

5. "Harry Stephenson, Who Was Healed from Cancer," *Your Faith and Mine*, c. 1950s, VHS, V496, Episode 2, Collection 212, in the Kathryn Kuhlman Collection, Archives of the Billy Graham Center, Wheaton, Illinois; hereafter cited as KKC.

6. *Your Faith and Mine* was syndicated and broadcast in the mid-1950s. Twenty-two

episodes remain. Further information about the television show was very difficult to obtain. The Kuhlman Foundation had no additional data, nor did the Billy Graham Center Archives, where the films are housed. Wayne Warner, Kuhlman's most recent biographer, had no information to add. Rev. David Verzilli, Kuhlman's associate minister who led the weekly Bible studies and assisted with the services at Stambaugh Auditorium from the early 1960s until Kuhlman's death, was also unable to give any details about the show. The episodes are not dated other than "c. 1950s." Rev. David Verzilli, email message to author, July 30, 2007.

7. J. Emmett Winn and Susan L. Brinson, *Transmitting the Past: Historical and Cultural Perspectives on Broadcasting* (Tuscaloosa: University of Alabama Press, 2005), 4.

8. Winn and Brinson, *Transmitting the Past*, 5.

9. Quentin J. Schultze, ed., *American Evangelicals and the Mass Media* (Grand Rapids: Zondervan, 1990), 25.

10. Schultze, *American Evangelicals*, 25

11. Religious television began on Easter Sunday 1940, when separate Roman Catholic and Protestant services were telecast in New York City. Schultze, *American Evangelicals*, 88–89.

12. Lynn Spigel, *Make Room for TV: Television and the Family Ideal in Postwar America* (Chicago: University of Chicago Press, 1992), 32.

13. Tona J. Hangen, *Redeeming the Dial: Radio, Religion, and Popular Culture in America* (Chapel Hill: University of North Carolina Press, 2002), 113.

14. Bernard M. Timberg, *Television Talk: A History of the TV Talk Show* (Austin: University of Texas Press, 2002), 9.

15. Spigel, *Make Room for TV*, 31.

16. John Hinshaw, *Steel and Steelworkers: Race and Class Struggle in Twentieth-Century Pittsburgh* (Albany: State University of New York Press, 2002), 109.

17. Hinshaw, *Steel and Steelworkers*, 66–67.

18. Wayne E. Warner, *Kathryn Kuhlman: The Woman behind the Miracles* (Ann Arbor, MI: Servant, 1993), 150.

19. Samuel P. Hays, ed., *City at the Point: Essays on the Social History of Pittsburgh* (Pittsburgh: University of Pittsburgh Press, 1989), 181.

20. Hinshaw, *Steel and Steelworkers*, 159.

21. The major radio networks had been running limited television service since 1941. Erickson, *Syndicated Television*, 6.

22. R. Laurence Moore, *Selling God: American Religion in the Marketplace of Culture* (New York: Oxford University Press, 1994), 247.

23. Stewart M. Hoover and Lynn Schofield Clark, eds., *Practicing Religion in the Age of the Media* (New York: Columbia University Press, 2002), 142–43.

24. Hoover and Clark, *Practicing Religion*, 151.

25. David Edwin Harrell Jr., *All Things Are Possible: The Healing and Charismatic Revivals in Modern America* (Bloomington: Indiana University Press, 1975), 235.

26. Harrell, *All Things Are Possible*, 235.

27. David Edwin Harrell Jr., *Oral Roberts: An American Life* (Bloomington: Indiana University Press, 1985), 130.

28. Pat Robertson's later shows included an ongoing telethon for prayer and pledges, run by the highly effective fund-raiser Jim Bakker. John Wigger, *PTL: The*

Rise and Fall of Jim and Tammy Faye Bakker's Evangelical Empire (New York: Oxford University Press, 2017), 27. Robertson and his wife at the time, DeDe, appeared in several episodes of *Miracles*. In one episode Robertson reviewed the process leading up to his purchase and development of Christian Broadcasting Network and credited Kuhlman as a significant influence on his life. Robertson's mother requested prayers from Kuhlman's ministry for her wayward son during his early years as a playboy and socialite. Robertson thanked Kuhlman for her ministry to him. "Pat Roberston," *I Believe in Miracles*, August 24, 1972, V230 and V231, in KKC; "DeDe Robertson," *I Believe in Miracles*, August 24, 1972, V232, in KKC. The Robertsons' son Richard and then-wife Patti also appeared on *Miracles* in December of 1973, V44, in KKC.

29. Harrell, *All Things Are Possible*, 105.

30. Harrell, *Oral Roberts*, 129.

31. Harrell, *All Things Are Possible*, 106.

32. Erickson, *Syndicated Television*, 3.

33. Erickson, *Syndicated Television*, 6.

34. Spigel, *Make Room for TV*, 76.

35. Timberg, *Television Talk*, 11.

36. Erickson, *Syndicated Television*, 9.

37. Erickson, *Syndicated Television*, 9.

38. Erickson, *Syndicated Television*, 82.

39. Wigger, *PTL*, 27.

40. Spigel, *Make Room for TV*, 5.

41. Erickson, *Syndicated Television*, 81–82.

42. Warner, *Kathryn Kuhlman*, 14.

43. Moore, *Selling God*, 247.

44. Erickson, *Syndicated Television*, 81.

45. Erickson, *Syndicated Television*, 81.

46. Erickson, *Syndicated Television*, 81–82.

47. Schultze, *American Evangelicals*, 89.

48. When Kuhlman finally allowed the filming of one of her miracle services in Las Vegas, the opening worship sequence was in many ways an exact copy of the introduction to *Your Faith and Mine*. The Kuhlman miracle services likely remained basically true to this early form throughout her career. The films of *Your Faith and Mine* offer a helpful glimpse of what Kuhlman's miracle services were like, despite the very limited visual record of the services and the lack of footage of the actual healings themselves.

49. "Mrs. Fischer, Whose Daughter Had Been a Water Head Baby," *Your Faith and Mine*, c. 1950s, VHS, V490, Episode 2, Collection 212, in KKC.

50. Harrell, *All Things Are Possible*, 87.

51. Grant Wacker notes, "Like countless Christians before them, early Pentecostals assumed that their personal faith stories bore normative implications for others." Grant Wacker, *Heaven Below: Early Pentecostals and American Culture* (Cambridge, MA: Harvard University Press, 2001), 58.

52. Historian Grant Wacker's work on radical evangelical and classic Pentecostal forms of testimony in his book *Heaven Below* sheds helpful light on the basic pattern followed by Kuhlman in her guidance of the guests' stories on *Your Faith and Mine*.

53. As noted, *Your Faith and Mine* was almost certainly a recording of the opening worship and testimonial segment of a Kuhlman miracle service.

54. Kuhlman's careful control over the interpretation of the miracles of her ministry may explain in part why she chose to wait so long to film an "uncontrolled" miracle service. Historian John Wigger states, "Oral Roberts, Billy Graham, Archbishop Fulton Sheen and Kathryn Kuhlman pioneered religious broadcasting in the 1950s and 1960s. But their programs mostly looked like a church service, classroom lecture, or crusade, concepts developed before cameras were a consideration." The inclusion of Kuhlman as a media pioneer is refreshing. A deeper study of Kuhlman's early television show, particularly the testimonial segment, reveals much more than a camera trained on a church service. Kuhlman is already shaping her show to take advantage of the power of television to broadcast an image of charismatic Christianity active in the lives of everyday people. Wigger, *PTL*, 4.

55. Kaufman is quoted in Wacker, *Heaven Below*, 59. Kuhlman at this point was already taking on the role of talk show host, with its responsibility for directing guest interviews toward the narrative demands of the episode. In the twenty-two episodes of *Your Faith and Mine*, Kuhlman succeeded in guiding the guest narratives toward her desired ends. On the almost five hundred episodes of her later television talk show, *I Believe in Miracles*, only a few times was Kuhlman not able to make things "come out right." On scattered episodes, Kuhlman encountered guests unwilling to adhere to her orchestration of their stories. *I Believe in Miracles* will be explored further in subsequent chapters.

56. All quotes are from "Johnny Stake and Family," *Your Faith and Mine*, c. 1950s, VHS, V486, Episode 1, Collection 212, in KKC.

57. Mimi White, *Tele-Advising: Therapeutic Discourse in American Television* (Chapel Hill: University of North Carolina Press, 1992), 129.

58. Wacker, *Heaven Below*, 1.

59. Wacker, *Heaven Below*, 59.

60. "Mr. Reams Who Was Healed of Paralysis," *Your Faith and Mine*, c. 1950s, VHS, V495, Episode 2, Collection 212, in KKC.

61. In an interesting twist, Reams came on screen without being announced by Kuhlman, lending even more drama to the moment.

62. "Mr. Reams Who Was Healed of Paralysis."

63. Wacker, *Heaven Below*, 60–61.

64. Wacker states concerning the role of the healing testimony: "Finally, there was healing, not just the natural mending of the body as acknowledged by all Christian traditions, but Pentecostal healing—the miraculous, inexplicable restoration of bones broken and organs ravaged. From first to last, divine healing remained central to the movement's self-understanding." Wacker, *Heaven Below*, 65.

65. Wacker, *Heaven Below*, 67.

66. Wacker, *Heaven Below*, 64.

67. Harrell, *All Things Are Possible*, 87.

68. "Mr. and Mrs. Turner, Who Was Cured of Cancer," *Your Faith and Mine*, c. 1950s, VHS, V494, Episode 1, Collection 212, in KKC.

69. "A Grandmother and Her Granddaughter, Amelia Who Was Healed from Eczema," *Your Faith and Mine*, c. 1950s, VHS, V491, Episode 2, Collection 212, in KKC.

70. "Harry Stephenson, Who Was Healed from Cancer."

71. "Mr. Suttles Who Was Cured of Cancer of the Tongue," *Your Faith and Mine*, c. 1950s, VHS, V492, Episode 1, Collection 212, in KKC.

72. "It simply never occurred to adherents to interpret their new allegiance as reparation for the loss of something else. They invariably construed the disappointments that preceded conversion as God's way of arousing them from their hell-bent smugness." Wacker, *Heaven Below*, 60.

73. "Maxine Wise Who Tried to Kill Herself," *Your Faith and Mine*, c. 1950s, VHS, V495, Episode 1, Collection 212, in KKC.

74. Wacker, *Heaven Below*, 65.

75. "Mr. Wilson, Mr. Pat 'Paddy' Shovlin, and Mr. Nick Harden, All Former Alcoholics," *Your Faith and Mine*, c. 1950s, VHS, V486, Episode 2, Collection 212, in KKC.

76. Wacker, *Heaven Below*, 63.

77. "Mr. Wilson, Mr. Pat 'Paddy' Shovlin, and Mr. Nick Harden, All Former Alcoholics."

78. "Miss Kilgore and Members of Her Family Who Were Converted," *Your Faith and Mine*, c. 1950s, VHS, V493, Episode 2, Collection 212, in KKC.

Notes to Chapter 4

1. *Healing in the Spirit: A Wide-Ranging Exclusive Interview with Kathryn Kuhlman*, pamphlet published by *Christianity Today*, July 20, 1973, in Box 1, Collection 212, the Kathryn Kuhlman Collection, Archives of the Billy Graham Center, Wheaton, Illinois; hereafter cited as KKC.

2. Grant Wacker observed the same curious behavior in Pentecostal women leaders prior to Kuhlman: "[It is hard to situate on a cultural map] some of the strong women who articulated a conventional or at least a semi conventional position that, if taken seriously, would have prevented them from doing the very things they were doing. . . . All preached. All built and ran institutions. All left legacies of notable accomplishments. Yet to my knowledge none explicitly challenged the assumptions of male clerical and social privilege, let alone received ordination as elders. In words that the feminist theologian Mary McClintock Fulkerson applied to a later generation of Pentecostal women, they simultaneously resisted and reinforced the canonical system." Grant Wacker, *Heaven Below: Early Pentecostals and American Culture* (Cambridge, MA: Harvard University Press, 2001), 172.

3. Marsha F. Cassidy, *What Women Watched* (Austin: University of Texas Press, 2005), 6, 132.

4. Some observers questioned Kuhlman's relationship with her attractive young piano player Dino Kartsonakis. No proof has emerged since Kuhlman's death that Dino was anything more than pleasant "eye candy" for Kuhlman as well as an exceptionally talented piano player for her show.

5. *An Hour with Kathryn Kuhlman*, n.d., T2113 (audiocassette), Collection 212, in KKC; Kathryn Kuhlman, *A Glimpse into Glory* (Gainesville, FL: Bridge-Logos Publishers, 1983), 28.

6. Jamie Buckingham, *Daughter of Destiny* (Gainesville, FL: Bridge-Logos Press, 1999), 117.

7. Wayne E. Warner, *Kathryn Kuhlman: The Woman behind the Miracles* (Ann Arbor, MI: Servant, 1993), 174–75.

8. Letter from Edgar L. Dickson to the *Pittsburgh Post-Gazette*, July 12, 1954, from Kathryn Kuhlman file, *Pittsburgh Post-Gazette*, courtesy of *Pittsburgh Post-Gazette* reporter Ann Rodgers.

9. "Tommy and Ann Levitt for the Dedication of Their Second Child," *Your Faith and Mine*, c. 1950s, VHS, V490, Episode 1, Collection 212, in KKC.

10. Edith Blumhofer, *Aimee Semple McPherson: Everybody's Sister* (Grand Rapids: Eerdmans, 1996), 204–5.

11. Kuhlman never explained her decision not to have children. Her marriage to Waltrip was brief and chaotic, and the two seemed much more interested in joint ministry than in starting a family. She does not make any reference to any medical difficulties. A Pittsburgh reporter asked in a 1974 article, "Ever regret not having a family?" Kuhlman replied, "No. I feel I have a worldful of children." Ann Butler, "She Believes in Miracles," *Pittsburgh Press Roto*, February 3, 1974.

12. Kuhlman discussed corporal punishment with David Wilkerson in an earlier episode; both were firmly in support of the practice. "David Wilkerson, Parenting," *I Believe in Miracles*, August 14, 1968, VHS, V300, Collection 212, in KKC.

13. "Shirley Boone," *I Believe in Miracles*, December 8, 1971, VHS, V209, Collection 212, in KKC.

14. Kuhlman, *A Glimpse into Glory*, 28.

15. "Question and Answer—Youth," *I Believe in Miracles*, September 9, 1971, VHS, V422, Collection 212, in KKC.

16. "Kathryn Kuhlman Answers Questions—Youth, Part II," *I Believe in Miracles*, July 30, 1971, VHS, V426, Collection 212, in KKC.

17. "Kathryn Kuhlman Answers Questions—Youth, Part II."

18. "Duane Pederson, Charles 'Chuck' Smith, Youth Audience," *I Believe in Miracles*, July 22, 1971, VHS, V416, Collection 212, in KKC.

19. "Ad Lib Statements from Group, Charles 'Chuck' Smith, Youth Audience," *I Believe in Miracles*, July 22, 1971, VHS, V202, Collection 212, in KKC.

20. "Duane Pederson, Charles 'Chuck' Smith, Youth Audience." Kuhlman was not one for the designations of "Momma" or "Sister," preferring instead to be called Miss Kuhlman. Biographer Wayne Warner notes, "One former employee told me that if anyone called Kathryn 'Sister Kuhlman' she would let them know she was not their sister." Warner, *Kathryn Kuhlman*, 276n2.

21. "Kecia Fluevog," *I Believe in Miracles*, March 12, 1975, VHS, V94, Collection 212, in KKC.

22. Kuhlman biographers recorded disparate accounts of Kuhlman's wedding day and night. In Buckingham's record, Kuhlman claimed she fainted during the wedding ceremony due to her realization of the mistake she was making, but recovered and went on with the marriage. Warner interviewed a Kuhlman friend who stated that Kuhlman returned to her friends immediately after the service, but then was rejected by her Denver congregation and "driven into Waltrip's arms." Kuhlman lived with Waltrip as man and wife for a short time before separating from him. Buckingham, *Daughter of Destiny*, 77; Warner, *Kathryn Kuhlman*, 93–94.

23. Kuhlman and Dino Kartsonakis parted ways late in her life over professional

and personal differences. During this conflict, Dino was not above implying that Kuhlman's interest in him was sexual, although he also made clear nothing inappropriate ever occurred between the two. More is said about this part of Kuhlman's life in chapter 6.

24. "Mr. Kilgore, Julia Barcage, Red Dolan," *I Believe in Miracles*, 1967, VHS, V497, Collection 212, in KKC.

25. Wacker, *Heaven Below*, 161–62.

26. *I Believe in Miracles*, 1967, VHS, V497, Episodes 1 and 2, and V498, Episodes 1 and 2, Collection 212, in KKC.

27. Patricia Bradley, *Mass Media and the Shaping of American Feminism, 1963–1975* (Jackson: University Press of Mississippi, 2003), 10–11.

28. Celia Lury, in Sue Thornham, *Women, Feminism, and Media* (Edinburgh: Edinburgh University Press, 2007), 12–13.

29. "Book content, whether in hardback or not, was, to some publishers, simply another product, aimed at particular market niches . . . just about any subject matter that might have an audience [was] sought out, sometimes invented, and thence mounted and marketed like any other consumer product." Bradley, *Mass Media*, 6.

30. The fact that Betty Friedan's book was even published at all revealed a newly emerging female market for books, namely, "the women who had settled in the suburbs following the postwar building boom. This market remained largely untapped by major book publishers, except in the area of cookbooks." Thornham, *Women, Feminism, and Media*, 10–11.

31. Bradley, *Mass Media*, 11.

32. Bradley, *Mass Media*, 4.

33. Bradley, *Mass Media*, 11–12.

34. Charles L. Cohen and Paul S. Boyer, eds., *Religion and the Culture of Print in Modern America* (Madison: University of Wisconsin Press, 2008), 273. Neal followed her *Redbook* article with several books of her own on the topic of divine healing. She was known for a healing ministry in the Episcopal Church. She died in 1989.

35. Ruth Milkman, "Before the *Mystique*," *Women's Review of Books* 16, no. 9 (June 1999): 2–3.

36. "*The Fountain of Age*," interview of Betty Friedan by Brian Lamb, *Booknotes*, November 28, 1993, http://www.booknotes.org/Watch/52571-1/Betty-Friedan.

37. Was Kuhlman freed by this manipulation of her persona, or somewhat trapped by it? Her life in some ways seemed to be a lonely one. One of her few close acquaintances was Paul Ferrin, who recalled that Kuhlman "didn't seem to have a lot of personal friends." He continued, "I don't know if she did anything for fun. She was very serious, very intent on the ministry." Perhaps her work was enough; Kuhlman offered little self-reflection to help us know. Paul Ferrin, phone interview with author, March 19, 2013, Harrison, Arkansas.

38. Ann Braude, *Sisters and Saints: Women and American Religion* (Oxford: Oxford University Press, 2008), 99.

39. Significant dates for women in ministry: women ordained in Methodist church and northern Presbyterian church, 1956; women ordained in Lutheran Church in America, 1970; Reform Jews voted to ordain women as rabbis in 1972; Episcopal Church approved the consecration of women as deacons, usually the office that pre-

ceded becoming a priest, then a close vote denied ordination in 1973; voted to ordain women in 1976. Within Catholicism there was also a new openness to women's leadership, within bounds. Vatican II, convened under Pope John XXIII, and running from 1962 to 1965, contained language of equality for women, and in 1974, superiors of Catholic women's orders unanimously endorsed the opening of all forms of ministry to women. See Braude, *Sisters and Saints*, 95–104.

40. Buckingham, *Daughter of Destiny*, 36.

41. The published interview with Kuhlman was an edited version of an oral interview she provided the magazine. The editors of *Christianity Today* gave Kuhlman a list of several questions, and she taped her responses on a series of audiocassettes. The final print form of the interview was significantly shorter than the more extensive answers Kuhlman gave on tape. "Interview with Kathryn Kuhlman for *Christianity Today*," T99-T109 (audiocassette), Collection 192, Papers of Harold Lindsell, Archives of the Billy Graham Center, Wheaton, Illinois.

42. Shirley Boone, *One Woman's Liberation* (Carol Stream, IL: Creation House, 1972), 187, 223–24.

43. Kuhlman, *A Glimpse into Glory*, 28–29.

44. *An Hour with Kathryn Kuhlman.*

45. *An Hour with Kathryn Kuhlman.*

46. "Tongues #1," 1976 (earliest known broadcast date), T327 (audiocassette), Collection 212, in KKC.

47. "Mrs. Matilda Powers, Spinal Healing," *I Believe in Miracles*, September 20, 1967, VHS, V274, Collection 212, in KKC.

48. This passage is quoted in full in chap. 1 above.

49. *An Hour with Kathryn Kuhlman.*

50. Kuhlman, *A Glimpse into Glory*, 29–30.

51. "Interview with Kathryn Kuhlman for *Christianity Today*."

52. *An Hour with Kathryn Kuhlman.*

53. "From Milkpail to Pulpit," VHS, V1, Collection 103: Ephemera of Aimee Semple McPherson, Archives of the Billy Graham Center, Wheaton, Illinois.

54. Kuhlman, *A Glimpse into Glory*, 27.

55. Wacker saw the assertion of the right for females to preach as part of what he termed the primitivist impulse within Pentecostalism. Kuhlman fits nicely within this framework due to her contention that the charismatic renewal and the outpouring of spiritual gifts were a sign of a great "restoration" of God's church. She argued throughout her career that what was happening was not a revival, but a restoration. She believed that in the charismatic renewal movement, God's church was being restored in the latter days, and the prophecy of Joel was being fulfilled. She was certainly affected by the primitivist impulse that "pulled men and women away from inherited assumptions and thrust them outward. Like a kettledrum echoing up from the deep, God's call beckoned women to herald the Word wherever the Holy Spirit directed." Wacker, *Heaven Below*, 164.

56. Wacker, *Heaven Below*, 149.

57. Kuhlman, *A Glimpse into Glory*, 27–28.

58. *An Hour with Kathryn Kuhlman.*

59. Information about Adele and Ralph Carmichael is from an article by Tom

Kisken, Scripps Howard News Service, printed in the online newsletter *New Standard*. Kisken called Ralph Carmichael a "trailblazer in contemporary religious music." In 1997, when the article was written, Adele Carmichael was acknowledged by the Assemblies of God district office as serving the Assemblies of God for seventy-nine years, the longest service of any minister in the denomination's history. Tom Kisken, "Minister, 95, Is an Ageless Pastor," Scripps Howard News Service, accessed December 11, 2006, http://archive.southcoasttoday.com/daily/03-97/03-30-97/e02li181.htm.

60. "Interview with Ralph and Adele Carmichael," *I Believe in Miracles*, 1975?, VHS, V78, Collection 212, in KKC.

61. Carmichael passed away in 2003. She collapsed and died on her way to teach a Bible class. Myrna Oliver, "Adele Carmichael, 101; Longtime Minister Taught Bible Study Classes Till the End," *Los Angeles Times*, October 19, 2003, http://articles.latimes.com/2003/oct/19/local/me-carmichael19.

Notes to Chapter 5

1. "Arlene Strackbein," *I Believe in Miracles*, September 12, 1973, VHS, V31, Collection 212, in the Kathryn Kuhlman Collection, Archives of the Billy Graham Center, Wheaton, Illinois; hereafter cited as KKC.

2. *Miracles* was not produced by CBS, but rather was a production of the Kathryn Kuhlman Foundation. Ray Faiola, director, CBS Audience Services, explains, "While *I Believe in Miracles* was taped at CBS in Hollywood, it was done so merely on the basis of rented space. The program was neither broadcast by CBS nor syndicated by CBS or its subsidiaries." Ray Faiola, email message to author, June 22, 2006.

3. Historian John Wigger gives pride of place to Pat Robertson and Jim Bakker for *The 700 Club*, stating, "Bakker pioneered the Christian talk show format in the 1960s and early 1970s." The debuts of the two shows are only months apart, *Miracles* appearing on the air as early as April 21, 1966, and *The 700 Club* in November 1966. What is more important than the relative start dates are the differences between the presentation of charismatic Christianity on the two shows. As I detail above, Kuhlman worked from the beginning to offer a gentrified vision of charismatic Christianity in line with the shows led by Arlene Francis and Dinah Shore. Jim Bakker was inspired by the late-night talk show format of Johnny Carson, and was inspired to combine the talk show with the telethon fund-raiser. Bakker's emotional appeals, where he broke down and cried on the air, garnered success on the telethons for the new Christian Broadcasting Network in 1965. The emphasis on emotional appeal and "the phones ringing to report healings and miracles" set *The 700 Club* apart from the more restrained *I Believe in Miracles*. Kuhlman, Robertson, and Bakker were all innovators, Bakker primarily in his early adoption of satellite broadcasting. But the goal of transforming the image of charismatic Christianity to one more palatable to the general public was Kuhlman's alone. These early differences signal the coming shift in Bakker's ministry to even more outrageous televangelism and prosperity gospel emphases, patterns Kuhlman did not follow. John Wigger, *PTL: The Rise and Fall of Jim and Tammy Faye Bakker's Evangelical Empire* (New York: Oxford University Press, 2017), 4, 28–29.

4. Bernard M. Timberg, *Television Talk: A History of the TV Talk Show* (Austin: University of Texas Press, 2002), 3.

5. Timberg, *Television Talk*, 1.

6. Timberg, *Television Talk*, 56.

7. "With all its limitations, dangers, potentials, and pitfalls, the TV talk show is now a part of the fabric of modern society. Talk shows represent skewed but instantly recognizable constructions of American experience. Their political and cultural importance can no longer be discounted. An understanding of the TV talk show is now crucial to an understanding of American public life itself." Timberg, *Television Talk*, 1, 18.

8. Hal Erickson, *Syndicated Television: The First Forty Years, 1947–1987* (Jefferson, NC: McFarland and Co., 1989), 158.

9. Erickson, *Syndicated Television*, 162–64.

10. Timberg, *Television Talk*, 66.

11. Mimi White, *Tele-Advising: Therapeutic Discourse in American Television* (Chapel Hill: University of North Carolina Press, 1992), 177.

12. "Elaine St. Germaine, Actress, Drug Addiction," *I Believe in Miracles*, May 17, 1973, VHS, V22, Collection 212, in KKC.

13. Timberg, *Television Talk*, 3.

14. Timberg, *Television Talk*, 3.

15. Timberg, *Television Talk*, 3–4.

16. Wayne Munson, *All Talk: The Talk Show in Media Culture* (Philadelphia: Temple University Press, 1993), 15.

17. Timberg, *Television Talk*, 15.

18. The study was Donald Horton and R. Richard Wohl's 1956 *Mass Communication and Para-Social Interaction: Observations on Intimacy at a Distance*. Munson, *All Talk*, 16.

19. Jeffrey Sconce, *Haunted Media: Electronic Presence from Telegraphy to Television* (Durham, NC: Duke University Press, 2000), 126.

20. Sconce, *Haunted Media*, 126.

21. Munson, *All Talk*, 9.

22. "The big three networks were initiating hardly any shows by the end of the 1960s, but national syndicators outside the networks quadrupled the output of TV talk at the end of the decade." Timberg, *Television Talk*, 72.

23. Munson defines the "fourth wall" as "the defining either-or aesthetic boundaries between performer and text and spectator . . . the clear distinction between public and private." *All Talk*, 117.

24. Munson, *All Talk*, 115.

25. Lynn Spigel, *Make Room for TV: Television and the Family Ideal in Postwar America* (Chicago: University of Chicago Press, 1992), 77.

26. Marsha F. Cassidy, *What Women Watched* (Austin: University of Texas Press, 2005), 33.

27. Radio networks had already achieved great success with the daytime audience through programming "soap operas." "What most Americans have known as soap opera for more than half a century began as one of the hundreds of new programming forms tried out by commercial radio broadcasters in the late 1920s and early 1930s, as both local stations and the newly-formed networks attempted to marry the needs of advertisers with the listening interests of consumers. Specifically, broadcasters hoped to

interest manufacturers of household cleaners, food products, and toiletries in the possibility of using daytime radio to reach their prime consumer market: women between the ages of eighteen and forty-nine." Televised soap operas began in 1950 with Procter and Gamble's *The First Hundred Years*, a fifteen-minute serialized drama broadcast live each weekday. The producers of soap operas shared the same concerns about audience viability as those of talk shows. "It was unclear in 1950 if the primary target audience for soap operas—women working in the home—could integrate the viewing of soaps into their daily routines. One could listen to a radio soap while doing other things, even in another room; television soaps required some degree of visual attention." Robert C. Allen, "Soap Opera," The Museum of Broadcast Communications, accessed May 21, 2018, www.museum.tv/archives/etv/S/htmlS/soapopera/soapopera.htm.

28. "Between 1948 and 1960, viewers were drawn to the television screen in staggering numbers. Television ownership skyrocketed to 87.1 percent of households by the end of the 1950s—a remarkable 45,750,000 homes—and the number of commercial stations grew tenfold, from 50 to 515. Daytime viewership also leaped from virtually zero in 1948 to 7.61 million homes tuned in every minute, on average, between 10:00 AM and 5:00 PM in 1958." Cassidy, *What Women Watched*, 2.

29. Timberg, *Television Talk*, 57.

30. Spigel, *Make Room for TV*, 136.

31. Cassidy, *What Women Watched*, 21.

32. Cassidy notes the practice of using female personalities in local programming during the early fifties before the networks began to dominate the channels. "Dozens of women performers around the country established a daily rapport with viewers in their local markets. Building upon a sense of community cohesiveness, these attractive and personable women helped ease television into the everyday routine of local homemakers." *What Women Watched*, 30.

33. Cassidy, *What Women Watched*, 21; Timberg, *Television Talk*, 39.

34. Cassidy, *What Women Watched*, 146.

35. Arlene Francis's show *Home* "was the first major effort by a national network to capture the daytime audience of women with a woman host and a serious informational format." Timberg, *Television Talk*, 39–40.

36. Cassidy, *What Women Watched*, 132.

37. Timberg, *Television Talk*, 64.

38. Timberg, *Television Talk*, 63, 65.

39. Timberg, *Television Talk*, 65.

40. "David Wilkerson: College," *I Believe in Miracles,* August 14, 1968, VHS, V301, Collection 212, in KKC.

41. "Barbara Walters' rise was associated to some extent with the feminist movement in the United States in the 1960s. She was a transitional figure in this regard, as her own comments and comments of friends and colleagues indicate." Timberg, *Television Talk*, 64, 91.

42. Producer Dick Ross stated, "The garden setting which we gradually evolved was geared to her personality and love for flowers." Helen Kooiman Hosier, *Kathryn Kuhlman: The Life She Led, the Legacy She Left* (Old Tappan, NJ: Revell, 1976), 148.

43. The bird was uncooperative, bobbing and flapping its wings in Kuhlman's face. She became very amused as she tried to handle the animal with some sort of panache.

"I believe in miracles," she said wryly as she finally deposited the bird in its cage. "It's a miracle I ever got that bird off my arm!" Offstage laughter from the crew was audible as Kuhlman turned from the bird to the introduction of her guest. The cockatoo never returned to the show. "David King," *I Believe in Miracles*, February 15, 1974, VHS, V49, Collection 212, in KKC.

44. Hosier, *Kathryn Kuhlman*, 148.

45. Timberg, *Television Talk*, 201.

46. "Heart-To-Heart: Filling of the Holy Spirit," *I Believe in Miracles*, February 14, 1973, VHS, V9, Collection 212, in KKC.

47. Timberg explains, "Shore herself was a hard-driving perfectionist who knew what she wanted . . . and clearly directed her own career. America's girl-next-door had engineered her own success." Timberg, *Television Talk*, 105.

48. "Marko Cockovis," *I Believe in Miracles*, March 30, 1967, VHS, V249, Collection 212, in KKC.

49. "Rodney Allen Rippy," *I Believe in Miracles*, June 10, 1974, VHS, V75, Collection 212, in KKC. This is only one of many examples of this statement.

50. "Charles Bokach and Mrs. David Parr," *I Believe in Miracles*, November 5, 1968, VHS, V314, Collection 212, in KKC.

51. Hosier, *Kathryn Kuhlman*, 148-49.

52. Art Silverblatt, Jane Ferry, and Barbara Finan, *Approaches to Media Literacy: A Handbook* (New York: M. E. Sharpe, 1999), 209.

53. White, *Tele-Advising*, 130–31.

54. Daniel A. Stout and Judith M. Buddenbaum, eds., *Religion and Mass Media: Audiences and Adaptations* (Thousand Oaks, CA: Sage, 1996), 80.

55. Stout and Buddenbaum, *Religion and Mass Media*, 80.

56. Stout and Buddenbaum, *Religion and Mass Media*, 81.

57. Stout and Buddenbaum, *Religion and Mass Media*, 80.

58. Ross also produced seven quarterly specials for Oral Roberts during the late 1960s and was the producer of the feature film *The Cross and the Switchblade* in 1970. "Interview with Mr. Dick Ross by Dr. Lois Ferm," May 1976, Billy Graham Oral History Program, Collection 151, 29-11, Archives of the Billy Graham Center, Wheaton, Illinois.

59. It was surprising that Ross stated Kuhlman was considering televising her miracle services. As outlined in earlier chapters, she began her television career with a program based out of her healing services, but in a move that differentiated her from her contemporaries such as Oral Roberts and A. A. Allen, she chose not to televise the healing miracles themselves. Hosier, *Kathryn Kuhlman*, 146.

60. Hosier, *Kathryn Kuhlman*, 146, 151.

61. Erickson, *Syndicated Television*, 11.

62. Hosier, *Kathryn Kuhlman*, 146.

63. Printed guide to "Videotapes from the Kathryn Kuhlman Collection" and "Office Calendars of the Kathryn Kuhlman Foundation, 1967-1976," Collection 212, Box 1, Folders 1-3 to 1-5, Archives of the Billy Graham Center, Wheaton, Illinois.

64. Erickson, *Syndicated Television*, 10.

65. "Mrs. Edna Wilder," *I Believe in Miracles*, November 27, 1973, VHS, V51, Collection 212, in KKC.

66. Timberg, *Television Talk*, 15.

67. Timberg, *Television Talk*, 15.

68. The phrase "word of knowledge" refers to the second gift of the Holy Spirit listed in 1 Cor. 12:7–10. Within the Pentecostal and charismatic communities, a word of knowledge is "a very special gift, that of knowing what God is doing at this moment in another's soul or body, or of knowing the secrets of another's heart." Stanley Burgess and Eduard M. Van Der Maas, eds., *The New International Dictionary of Pentecostal and Charismatic Movements* (Grand Rapids: Zondervan, 2002), s.v. "knowledge, word of."

69. Kuhlman touched Wolf and prayed for him, but the touch was not a "point of contact" for healing. Wolf was already healed when he came to the service, and Kuhlman's invitation was for those who desired prayer for "spiritual healing." Kuhlman was clear that her touch was not necessary for healing. Her touch during prayer was instead commonly associated with the phenomenon of being "slain in the Spirit." "Richard Wolf, Stroke," *I Believe in Miracles*, January 16, 1973, VHS, V460, Collection 212, in KKC.

70. "Eyona Pargman, Osteoporosis," *I Believe in Miracles*, October 2, 1974, VHS, V67, Collection 212, in KKC.

71. "Father J. Bertolucci," *I Believe in Miracles*, April 17, 1975, VHS, V480, Collection 212, in KKC.

72. "Ruby Haff, Arthritis," *I Believe in Miracles*, May 13, 1970, VHS, V192, Collection 212, in KKC.

73. "Lisa and Isabell Larios," *I Believe in Miracles*, February 14, 1973, VHS, V235, Collection 212, in KKC.

74. "Mr. and Mrs. Robles; Gloria," May 14, 1970, VHS, V193; "Charles Bokach and Daughter, Mrs, David Parr," November 5, 1968, VHS, V314, both on *I Believe in Miracles*, Collection 212, in KKC.

75. "Lorna Gall," *I Believe in Miracles*, July 11, 1975, VHS, V483, Collection 212, in KKC.

76. "Harry Stephenson, Cancer," *I Believe in Miracles*, April 22, 1966, VHS, V138, Collection 212, in KKC.

77. "Colonel Tom Lewis," *I Believe in Miracles*, June 14, 1972, VHS, V1, Collection 212, in KKC.

78. "Mrs. Penny Rohrer and John," *I Believe in Miracles*, 1975?, VHS, V109, Collection 212, in KKC.

79. "Dr. Kahn Uyeyama," *I Believe in Miracles*, April 10, 1969, VHS, V327, Collection 212, in KKC.

80. Dr. Josephine Ford, professor of New Testament at Notre Dame, became a figure of some controversy in charismatic Catholicism in the years following her appearance on *Miracles*. She began at Notre Dame in 1965, and during her time there published several works complimentary of the Catholic charismatic renewal. In 1970 she published *The Pentecostal Experience*, followed by *Baptism in the Spirit* in 1971. Ford was an early critic of sexism within Catholic Pentecostalism, centered primarily in disputes over authority in Catholic "covenanted communities." Ford was associated with the Ann Arbor Word of God Community until she challenged the groups' increasingly sexist hierarchy. She was expelled from the community, and in response wrote a challenging and critical publication, *Which Way for Catholic Pentecostals?*, published in 1976. Ford became full professor of biblical studies at Notre Dame in 1980. Her

most comprehensive article concerning Catholic Pentecostalism was published in 1986, "Toward a Theology of Speaking in Tongues," in *Speaking in Tongues: A Guide to Research on Glossolalia*, ed. W. E. Mills (Grand Rapids: Eerdmans, 1986). Burgess and Van Der Maas, *New International Dictionary*, s.v. "Ford, Josephine Massyngbaerde"; Richard Quebedeaux, *The New Charismatics II: How a Christian Renewal Movement Became Part of the American Religious Mainstream* (San Francisco: Harper and Row, 1983), 131, 137–38.

81. "Dr. J. M. Ford," *I Believe in Miracles*, September 30, 1971, VHS, V423, Collection 212, in KKC.

82. Kuhlman welcomed Catholic guests on at least thirty episodes, nine of which featured priests or nuns. Several episodes also contained references to the prominent place of Catholic religious on the platform at her miracle services. She also interviewed Father Francis McNutt and Father Ralph Martin, two of the most prominent leaders in the Catholic charismatic renewal, both of whom published influential books about the phenomenon.

83. "Father J. Bertolucci."

84. "How could born-again people possibly remain in churches that the fundamentalists, evangelicals, and Pentecostals viewed as the end-time lukewarm church that the Lord said he would spit out of his mouth? This wider view of the kingdom frustrated the Pentecostals and evangelicals but became the means for Kuhlman to influence mainline and Catholic churches to rely more on the ministry of the Holy Spirit and to begin conducting their own healing services." Wayne Warner, "At the Grass-Roots: Kathryn Kuhlman's Pentecostal-Charismatic Influence on Historical Mainstream Churches," *Pneuma* 17, no. 1 (Spring 1995): 51–65.

85. "Jennings and Opal Oertle, Cancer," *I Believe in Miracles*, January 17, 1975, VHS, V85, Collection 212, in KKC.

86. "That the Spirit is, in fact, the center of Christian unity is affirmed in the Vatican Council's decree *On Ecumenism*: 'It is the Holy Spirit, dwelling in those who believe, pervading and ruling over the entire Church, who brings about that marvelous communion of the faithful and joins them together so intimately in Christ that He is the principle of the Church's unity.'" Quebedeaux, *The New Charismatics II*, 214.

87. "Father Robert Arrowsmith," *I Believe in Miracles*, October 28, 1970, VHS, V372, Collection 212, in KKC.

88. Quebedeaux, *The New Charismatics II*, 103–4.

89. Kuhlman asked Shaw earlier in the show, "Tell me your education. You were strong on intellect." Shaw answered, "I guess so," and told of an undergraduate degree from Moody Bible Institute and master's level work from two schools that was never completed. "If a man is going to be heard, he needs educational training," Shaw concluded. Previous to his experience at the miracle service, Shaw would not have considered charismatic Christianity an option for an educated, intelligent person.

90. "Rev. Donald Shaw," *I Believe in Miracles*, April 23, 1968, VHS, V286, Collection 212, in KKC.

91. Dennis Bennett, *Nine O'clock in the Morning* (Plainfield, NJ: Logos International, 1970), ix. John Sherrill likely helped write Bennett's two best-selling books. Sherrill was well known for his own best-selling semiautobiographical book on the charismatic renewal movement entitled *They Speak in Other Tongues* (1964). Sherrill was also

Episcopalian. In 1961, Sherrill approached Bredesen about writing articles about the new movement, but decided to pursue an entire book after he experienced baptism in the Holy Spirit. Sherrill also assisted David Wilkerson in writing *The Cross and the Switchblade* (1963), another highly influential book in the spread of the charismatic movement. Burgess and Van Der Maas, *New International Dictionary*, s.v. "Sherrill, John Lewis."

92. Bennett, *Nine O'clock in the Morning*, 61.

93. David du Plessis, born in South Africa, was known as "Mr. Pentecost" by the 1960s for his work as a spokesperson for Pentecostalism and ecumenism. "No one in the 20th century so effectively linked three of the major movements of the time—the pentecostal movement, the ecumenical movement, and the charismatic movement." Du Plessis was listed in the September 1974 issue of *Time* magazine as "one of the leading 'shapers and shakers' of Christianity." He was particularly known for his efforts to increase dialogue between Pentecostals and Roman Catholics. He was the first non-Catholic ever to have received (in 1983) the pontifical decoration of the Benemerenti award (*Benemerenti* means "to a well-deserving person"). Burgess and Van Der Maas, *New International Dictionary*, s.v. "Du Plessis, David Johannes."

94. Burgess and Van Der Maas, *New International Dictionary*, s.v. "Bredesen, Harald."

95. "Reverend Harald Bredesen and Father Dennis Bennett," *I Believe in Miracles*, December 13, 1969, VHS, V183 and V350, Collection 212, in KKC.

96. "Rachel Phillips and Mr. Mackintosh," *I Believe in Miracles*, April 10, 1969, VHS, V328, Collection 212, in KKC.

97. Janet Thumim, *Small Screens, Big Ideas: Television in the 1950s* (London: I. B. Tauris, 2002), 1.

98. Thumim, *Small Screens, Big Ideas*, 2.

99. Timberg, *Television Talk*, 193.

100. "The second wave [of feminism] emerged at a time when attention from the mass media was commonly held to be imperative for the setting of a political agenda and for influencing national values. . . . Such beliefs were grounded in the successes of the civil rights movement as it unfolded on the nation's television screens and in the lush, large pages of the picture magazines. . . . By mass media's perceived abilities both to pressure and persuade, mass media were to be agents of change." Patricia Bradley, *Mass Media and the Shaping of American Feminism, 1963–1975* (Jackson: University Press of Mississippi, 2003), xiii.

101. Bradley, *Mass Media*, xiii–xiv.

102. Not to paint too rosy a picture here, but television was equally able to silence voices and ignore stories not deemed potentially profitable. Timberg notes this power to define what is important and what is not. "Modern media critics recognize the public space of television is subject to enormous corporate influence and that powerful filters are operating all the time. Alternative ideas . . . are marginalized or not discussed at all." Timberg, *Television Talk*, 193.

103. Timberg, *Television Talk*, 3, 17. While Timberg's assessment of talk shows is astute, it does overlook the powerful role of the host in guiding and controlling the narrative of the show. The hosts were the exact "experts and professionals" Timberg claimed were not at work in the more egalitarian world of television talk shows.

104. Thumim, *Small Screens, Big Ideas*, 3.

105. Munson, *All Talk*, 6.

106. Munson, *All Talk*, 18.

107. "As the exemplary mode of contemporary cultural expression, television significantly rewrites and transforms the cultural and social practices that it references and recombines." White, *Tele-Advising*, 180. Timberg agrees: "The talk show is a porous genre in a porous medium, absorbing everything that comes its way: the economic climate, commercial trends and fashions, political and social movements. The talk show establishes new social rituals." Timberg, *Television Talk*, 194.

108. Marjoe Gortner, *Marjoe: World's Youngest Evangelist*, directed by Sarah Kernochen and Howard Smith (New Video Group, 2006), DVD.

109. *Healing in the Spirit: A Wide-Ranging Exclusive Interview with Kathryn Kuhlman*, pamphlet published by *Christianity Today*, July 20, 1973, in Box 1, Collection 212, in KKC.

110. Eleanor Blau, "Faith Healer Draws the Sick and Anguished," *New York Times*, October 20, 1972.

111. Earl Hansen, "Kathryn Kuhlman Holy Spirit's 'Man'?" *Seattle Post-Intelligencer*, July 22, 1972.

112. William A. Nolen, *Healing: A Doctor in Search of a Miracle* (Greenwich, CT: Fawcett, 1974), back cover. Hereafter, page references from this work will be given in parentheses in the text.

113. Nolen's ethics were questionable. Kuhlman welcomed him as a friend of a friend, not as an author of an exposé on divine healing. Responsible scholarship required him to be more forthcoming to the Ryans and Kuhlman about his intentions.

114. Nolen distinguished between the healing of organic and psychogenic illnesses. Psychogenic illnesses are those in which the psyche often plays a major and dominant role. He included multiple sclerosis, rheumatoid arthritis, undiagnosed paralysis, loss of sight, and allergies under this heading (*Healing*, 92). He acknowledged that some patients with psychogenic illnesses did respond to Kuhlman's healing services.

115. Ann Butler, "Kathryn Kuhlman Calls Her Critic a 'Deceiver,'" *Pittsburgh Press*, November 24, 1974.

116. Kuhlman's interview with Johnny Carson can be found in the introduction.

117. Joyce Haber, "Ruth Buzzi and the Characters She Keeps," *Los Angeles Times*, August 19, 1973.

118. Nolen's book became a best seller in 1974. The next year, Kuhlman allowed cameras into her entire service for the first time. It is possible that Kuhlman decided to film the Las Vegas miracle service in part as a response to Nolen's witheringly critical evaluation.

119. Bradley, *Mass Media*, 5.

Notes to Chapter 6

1. All quotes from *Dry Land, Living Water* are from Kathryn Kuhlman, *Dry Land . . . Living Water* (Pittsburgh: Kathryn Kuhlman Foundation, 1975), VHS. *Dry Land . . .*

Living Water is the title on the VHS tape cover. We will refer to it with the more widely used title.

2. Biographer Wayne Warner suggests Kuhlman also held miracle services as a part of her Denver ministry. Wayne E. Warner, *Kathryn Kuhlman: The Woman behind the Miracles* (Ann Arbor, MI: Servant, 1993), 136.

3. Helen Kooiman Hosier, *Kathryn Kuhlman: The Life She Led, the Legacy She Left* (Old Tappan, NJ: Revell, 1976), 146, 149.

4. Jamie Buckingham, *Daughter of Destiny* (Gainesville, FL: Bridge-Logos Press, 1999), 191.

5. Hosier, *Kathryn Kuhlman*, 146, 149.

6. Buckingham, *Daughter of Destiny*, 191.

7. "Las Vegas Service," *I Believe in Miracles*, 1975, VHS, V100, Collection 212, in the Kathryn Kuhlman Collection, Archives of the Billy Graham Center, Wheaton, Illinois; hereafter cited as KKC. The "we" in this statement is the Kuhlman Foundation. The film of the Melodyland conference was not made by the foundation. Kuhlman also never spoke of *Your Faith and Mine* on *I Believe in Miracles*.

8. "David du Plessis," *I Believe in Miracles*, 1975?, VHS, V105, Collection 212, in KKC.

9. "Heart-to-Heart: Joel 1:2," *I Believe in Miracles*, June 17, 1971, VHS, V411, Collection 212, in KKC.

10. "Heart-to-Heart: Three Questions," *I Believe in Miracles*, December 9, 1971, VHS, V215, Collection 212, in KKC.

11. "Ralph Martin," *I Believe in Miracles*, March 12, 1975, VHS, V93, Collection 212, in KKC.

12. "Heart-to-Heart: Joel 1:2."

13. "Heart-to-Heart: Prophecy," *I Believe in Miracles*, November 5, 1968, VHS, V312, Collection 212, in KKC.

14. "Heart-to-Heart: Joel 1:2."

15. "Hal Lindsey," *I Believe in Miracles*, October 25, 1972, VHS, V234, Collection 212, in KKC.

16. "David du Plessis."

17. Hosier, *Kathryn Kuhlman*, 149.

18. "Hal Lindsey," *I Believe in Miracles*, November 28, 1973, VHS V54, Collection 212, in KKC.

19. Buckingham, *Daughter of Destiny*, 192.

20. Hosier, *Kathryn Kuhlman*, 19. This interpretation of Kuhlman as controlling rather than professional and exacting reflected the sexism she encountered throughout her career as a female religious leader in the essentially conservative and male-dominated charismatic movement.

21. Warner, *Kathryn Kuhlman*, 209.

22. Warner, *Kathryn Kuhlman*, 209–10.

23. Katherine Jane Leisering, "An Historical and Critical Study of the Pittsburgh Preaching Career of Kathryn Kuhlman" (PhD diss., Ohio University, 1981), 107.

24. Paul Ferrin, phone interview with author, March 19, 2013, Harrison, Arkansas.

25. Ferrin, phone interview with author.

26. Lois Armstrong, "Kathryn Kuhlman Is Accused of Not Keeping the Faith," *Peo-*

ple, August 11, 1975, http://www.people.com/people/archive/article/0,,20065526,00
.html.

27. Buckingham, *Daughter of Destiny*, 241–52; Warner, *Kathryn Kuhlman*, 186–89.

28. Helen Kooiman Hosier's account of the Vegas miracle service mentions a testimony given by healed and converted Vegas dancer Sunny Simons, who also appeared on the Kuhlman talk show. This testimony must have been edited out of the final product. The film *Dry Land, Living Water* does not contain any footage of testimonies of people healed at previous services. Hosier, *Kathryn Kuhlman*, 133.

29. Grant Wacker, *Heaven Below: Early Pentecostals and American Culture* (Cambridge, MA: Harvard University Press, 2001), 114.

30. Hosier, *Kathryn Kuhlman*, 46. Kuhlman did know what homiletics meant, of course. As discussed earlier, she failed a course in the subject at Simpson Bible College in her youth. See chapter 1.

31. "Heart-to-Heart: Filling of the Holy Spirit," *I Believe in Miracles*, February 14, 1973, VHS, V349, Collection 212, in KKC.

32. David Edwin Harrell Jr., *All Things Are Possible: The Healing and Charismatic Revivals in Modern America* (Bloomington: Indiana University Press, 1975), 5–6.

33. Leisering, "Historical and Critical Study," 100.

34. Charles Loesch, employee of Kathryn Kuhlman from 1946 until her death in 1976. Ann Butler, "Heirs Suspect Kuhlman Will, Do Nothing," *Pittsburgh Press*, April 1976.

35. Buckingham, *Daughter of Destiny*, 204–5. In subsequent decades, the Vineyard Christian Fellowship emerged as a vital force in charismatic Christianity by encouraging exactly the "dozen little healing services going on in the congregation" that Kuhlman discouraged.

36. Based primarily upon the Vegas message, some studies of Kuhlman's speaking style have included descriptions of her sermons as simplistic and unorganized as well as rambling and lacking coherent structure (see Leisering, "Historical and Critical Study," 177; Todd Vernon Lewis, "Charismatic Communication and Faith Healers: A Critical Study of Rhetorical Behavior" [PhD diss., Louisiana State University and Agricultural and Mechanical College, 1980], 219). This is an unfair evaluation of Kuhlman's preaching ability and a misunderstanding of the role of the message in miracle services. The message captured on the Vegas film was typical in form for Kuhlman's miracle services, but it cannot be used as an example of Kuhlman's overall teaching skills. Other messages recorded for Kuhlman's radio program reveal careful and deliberate construction. She was well known and respected among her colleagues in ministry for her solid doctrinal teaching and her aptitude as a Bible instructor.

37. Wacker, *Heaven Below*, 114.

38. Kuhlman rarely blinked as she preached, which added to the dramatic tension for the viewer of the film. An observer would have trouble "breaking free" from her intense gaze, captured in extreme close-up by Ross's cameras.

39. Hosier, *Kathryn Kuhlman*, 124.

40. Buckingham, *Daughter of Destiny*, 203–4.

41. Leisering, "Historical and Critical Study," 110–11; Buckingham, *Daughter of Destiny*, 203–4.

42. Earl Hansen, "Kathryn Kuhlman Holy Spirit's 'Man'?" *Seattle Post-Intelligencer*, July 22, 1972.

43. Buckingham, *Daughter of Destiny*, 229.

44. Harrell, *All Things Are Possible*, 59.

45. Wacker, *Heaven Below*, 119.

46. Buckingham, *Daughter of Destiny*, 229.

47. Ron Yates, "She Believes in Miracles," *Christian Life Magazine*, November 1972, Collection 212, Box 1, in KKC.

48. Hansen, "Kathryn Kuhlman Holy Spirit's 'Man'?"

49. Evan Pattak, "The Last Miracle Show," *Pittsburgh Magazine*, April 1976, quoted in Leisering, "Historical and Critical Study," 119.

50. *Las Vegas Sun*, May 3, 1975, quoted in Hosier, *Kathryn Kuhlman*, 135.

51. Harrell, *All Things Are Possible*, 99.

Notes to the Epilogue

1. Paul Ferrin, phone interview with author, March 19, 2013, Harrison, Arkansas.

2. Details of Kuhlman's sickness and death are contained in Jamie Buckingham, *Daughter of Destiny* (Gainesville, FL: Bridge-Logos Press, 1999), chapter entitled "The Last Travail," and Wayne E. Warner, *Kathryn Kuhlman: The Woman behind the Miracles* (Ann Arbor, MI: Servant, 1993), chapter entitled "Going Home."

3. "Mrs. Catherine Wright," *I Believe in Miracles*, November 20, 1975, VHS, V242, Collection 212, in the Kathryn Kuhlman Collection, Archives of the Billy Graham Center, Wheaton, Illinois; hereafter cited as KKC.

4. Helen Kooiman Hosier, *Kathryn Kuhlman: The Life She Led, the Legacy She Left* (Old Tappan, NJ: Revell, 1976), 150.

5. Ferrin, phone interview with author.

6. Wilkerson purchased the plane and held its ownership in his automobile leasing company. He argued that the jet would save the foundation money in commercial flight costs. Jamie Buckingham, who did not seem to hold much affection for Wilkerson, notes, "in the end Wilkerson got stuck with not only the plane, but with the two pilots he hired to fly it." *Daughter of Destiny*, 267.

7. "Biography of Kathryn Kuhlman," Collection 212, in KKC.

8. Ann Butler, "'Tink'—the Man Evangelist Kathryn Kuhlman Trusted," *Pittsburgh Press*, April 11, 1976.

9. "Bruno Moss, Back Injury," *I Believe in Miracles*, November 18, 1970, VHS, V380, Collection 212, in KKC.

10. Warner, *Kathryn Kuhlman*, 157.

11. Buckingham, *Daughter of Destiny*, 278.

12. Buckingham, *Daughter of Destiny*, 278.

13. "Wilkerson said he was unaware he and his wife had been named beneficiaries in Miss Kuhlman's will. He did say, however, that his personal lawyer in Tulsa was instrumental in drawing up her will last December 17 which superseded an earlier will signed in January of 1974." Thomas M. Hritz, "Fox Chapel Home, Art

to Tulsa Man: Kuhlman Will Surprises Dealer," *Pittsburgh Post-Gazette*, March 27, 1976.

14. Warner, *Kathryn Kuhlman*, 227.

15. Buckingham, *Daughter of Destiny*, 281–82.

16. "Kathryn Kuhlman OK after Surgery," *Los Angeles Times*, December 29, 1975.

17. Buckingham, *Daughter of Destiny*, 283.

18. "Miss Kuhlman Recuperating," *Pittsburgh Press*, December 30, 1975.

19. Buckingham, *Daughter of Destiny*, 283.

20. Warner, *Kathryn Kuhlman*, 240.

21. Warner, *Kathryn Kuhlman*, 228.

22. Assorted desk calendars, Collection 212, in KKC.

23. *Pittsburgh Press*, February 21, 1976.

24. "Memorial Rites for Kathryn Kuhlman Listed," *Pittsburgh Press*, February 22, 1976.

25. "Kathryn Kuhlman Rites Here Tonight," *Pittsburgh Post-Gazette*, February 23, 1976; "Goodbye to Preacher Lady: 3,000 at Memorial for Kathryn Kuhlman," *Pittsburgh Post-Gazette*, February 24, 1976.

26. "Kuhlman Memorial Service," February 23, 1976, T2116 (audiocassette), Collection 212, in KKC.

27. Warner, *Kathryn Kuhlman*, 281–82n34.

28. Warner, *Kathryn Kuhlman*, 240.

29. *Abundant Life*, May 1976. This magazine is published by the Oral Roberts Evangelistic Association.

30. Hosier, *Kathryn Kuhlman*, 154.

31. In October of 1944, Aimee Semple McPherson was also buried at Forest Lawn, which Edith Blumhofer described as "the beautifully manicured 'supercemetery' favored by the area's rich and famous." Even in death, Kuhlman followed in the footsteps of Sister Aimee. Edith Blumhofer, *Aimee Semple McPherson: Everybody's Sister* (Grand Rapids: Eerdmans, 1996), 379.

32. "Church Gets Nothing from Kuhlman Estate," *Pittsburgh Press*, March 26, 1976. Kuhlman's cash estate alone equaled over $1.2 million in 2018 dollars. According to records produced by Wayne Warner, attorney Irvine Ungerman billed the Kuhlman estate $94,184.50. Warner, *Kathryn Kuhlman*, 281n23.

33. Ann Butler, "Heirs Suspect Kuhlman Will, Do Nothing," *Pittsburgh Press*, April 1976.

34. Butler, "Heirs Suspect Kuhlman Will, Do Nothing."

35. Butler, "'Tink'—the Man Evangelist Kathryn Kuhlman Trusted." The Kuhlman estate was finally valued at $732,543. The Wilkersons cleared $314,500. "Evangelist Kuhlman Leaves Estate Valued at $732,543," *Pittsburgh Post-Gazette*, February 4, 1977.

36. Tink Wilkerson's dubious character was further confirmed with his arrest and conviction in 1991 on federal fraud charges. After serving his eighteen-month prison sentence, he was released in 1993. Sue Wilkerson died in 1997. Tink Wilkerson died in 2003 at the age of seventy-two. "'Tink' Wilkerson, Noted Car Dealer, Dies; Memorial Set," *Tulsa World*, July 26, 2003, https://www.tulsaworld.com/archives/tink-wilkerson-noted-car-dealer-dies-memorial-set/article_0c0b2368-aac8-509a-9052-9be742b915c0.html.

37. Bohdan Hodiak, "Kuhlman's Radio Voice Falls Silent," *Pittsburgh Post-Gazette*, April 24, 1982.

38. Hal Botham, "The Last Broadcast," 1982, T1922 (audiocassette), Collection 212, in KKC.

39. Stanley Burgess and Eduard M. Van Der Maas, eds., *The New International Dictionary of Pentecostal and Charismatic Movements* (Grand Rapids: Zondervan, 2002), s.v. "Kuhlman, Kathryn."

40. Kuhlman's death was featured on the cover of the second issue of *Charisma* magazine in 1976. Reinhard Bonnke, "Why Americans Take the Holy Spirit for Granted," *Charisma*, October 29, 2014, http://www.charismamag.com/spirit/supernatural/1646-dont-lose-the-power.

41. "The Secret to the Power of the Holy Spirit," YouTube, July 7, 2018, https://www.youtube.com/watch?v=yAQlDaEsuY4&vl=en. Not all the comments are positive, and it is interesting to see Kuhlman criticized after death for the same issues that plagued her life: female leadership in ministry, her dramatic presentation style, and the authenticity of her healings, among others.

42. Scott Billingsley, *It's a New Day: Race and Gender in the Modern Charismatic Movement* (Tuscaloosa: University of Alabama Press, 2008), 34, 74.

43. David Edwin Harrell Jr., *All Things Are Possible: The Healing and Charismatic Revivals in Modern America* (Bloomington: Indiana University Press, 1975), 151–56.

44. *Abundant Life*, May 1976.

45. Kate Bowler, *Blessed: A History of the American Prosperity Gospel* (New York: Oxford University Press, 2013), 7. In her notes regarding Kuhlman's part in the emergence of the prosperity gospel, Bowler argues, "Kathryn Kuhlman, the nation's most famous healing evangelist, assumed a prominent place in the charismatic movement but not the faith [prosperity gospel] movement."

46. "Heart-to-Heart: God's Presence Is Fact, Not Theory," *I Believe in Miracles*, December 6, 1967, VHS, V173, Collection 212, in KKC.

47. "Fred Burdick," *I Believe in Miracles*, April 23, 1968, VHS, V287, Collection 212, in KKC.

48. As I argue in earlier chapters, in this and many ways her legacy among female religious leaders is not straightforward; she was not an advocate of women's ordination or women's rights. It was her successful ministry that served as an inspiration to the women who succeeded her, not any vigorous support of a woman's call to ministry.

49. Benny Hinn, *Kathryn Kuhlman: Her Spiritual Legacy and Its Impact on My Life* (Nashville: Nelson, 1999), 16–17, 145.

50. Hinn, *Kathryn Kuhlman*, 146.

51. Hinn, *Kathryn Kuhlman*, 148.

52. Hinn's website claims "tens of millions" attend the Miracle Crusades each year; www.bennyhinn.org.

53. Bowler, *Blessed*, 237.

54. As referenced several times in this work, John Wigger covers this period thoroughly in his book *PTL: The Rise and Fall of Jim and Tammy Faye Bakker's Evangelical Empire* (New York: Oxford University Press, 2017).

55. John Wimber and Kevin Springer, *Power Healing* (San Francisco: HarperCollins, 1991), 20–21.

56. Wimber and Springer, *Power Healing*, 20–21.

57. Billingsley, *It's a New Day*, 31.

58. The majority of the approximately fifty "megachurches" in the world, defined as congregations with fifty thousand or more members, identify themselves as charismatic. Burgess and Van Der Maas, *New International Dictionary*, 300. In addition, according to the Barna report, 49 percent of evangelical individuals self-designated as charismatic. "Is American Christianity Turning Charismatic?" Barna, January 7, 2008, https://www.barna.com/research/is-american-christianity-turning-charismatic/.

59. "Is American Christianity Turning Charismatic?"

60. "Kathryn Kuhlman: A Legacy," July 24, 1976, VHS, V128, Collection 212, in KKC.

Index

Allen, A. A., 69, 70, 160

Bartholomew, Paul, 166–67, 188
Bennett, Dennis, 7, 142, 143, 149,
  229n91
Bertolucci, J., 134, 140
Billington, Dallas, 91, 151
Boone, Shirley, 94, 95, 107
Branham, William, 47, 51, 66
Bredesen, Harald, 6, 7, 142–43
broadcast media
  American Christianity and, 63–64,
    65–66, 114, 128–29, 131
  radio, 120, 225n27
  and social change, 146–49,
    230n102, 231n107
  talk show format (television),
    115–19, 121–22, 123–24, 125
  television, 64–65, 67–68, 119–21,
    226n28

Carmichael, Adele, 112–13
Carmichael, Ralph, 112
charismatic Christianity
  evangelicalism and, 6–7, 19, 81,
    203, 237n58
  popular opinion of, 2–3, 4, 5–6, 14,
    17–18, 59–60, 73, 77, 150, 155–56
  women leaders in, 10–11, 89–90,
    106–7, 109–10, 113
  See also divine healing; faith heal-

ing, faith healers; gentrification
of charismatic Christianity
charismatic renewal movement, 134,
  202
  emergence of, 4–5, 7–8, 61
  female religious leaders in, 89–90,
    109–10, 198, 199–200
  mainline Protestant churches and,
    141–43
  Roman Catholicism and, 139–41,
    229n84
  as sign of end times, 162, 175
  and youth culture, 95–98

Denver Revival Tabernacle, 34–35, 40
Dickson, Edgar L., 91–92
dispensationalism, 7, 18, 23, 25, 59,
  162
divine healing
  radio and, 36, 37, 212n99
  television and, 66, 69–70, 116–17,
    148
  testimonies of, 47, 62–63, 74, 79,
    81, 82, 132–33, 134–36
  twentieth-century development
    of, 15, 18–20, 22–23, 24–25, 48,
    50–52, 58–59, 61, 208n8, 209n33
  See also faith healing, faith healers;
    Kuhlman, Kathryn: divine heal-
    ing ministry of
du Plessis, David, 6, 142, 161–62, 163,
  230n93

Titles published in the

LIBRARY OF RELIGIOUS BIOGRAPHY SERIES

Thomas Merton and the Monastic Vision
by Lawrence S. Cunningham

God's Strange Work: William Miller and the End of the World
by David L. Rowe

Blaise Pascal: Reasons of the Heart
by Marvin R. O'Connell

Occupy Until I Come: A. T. Pierson and the Evangelization of the World
by Dana L. Robert

The Kingdom Is Always but Coming: A Life of Walter Rauschenbusch
by Christopher H. Evans

Francis Schaeffer and the Shaping of Evangelical America
by Barry Hankins

Harriet Beecher Stowe: A Spiritual Life
by Nancy Koester

Billy Sunday and the Redemption of Urban America
by Lyle W. Dorsett

Assist Me to Proclaim: The Life and Hymns of Charles Wesley
by John R. Tyson

Prophetess of Health: A Study of Ellen G. White
by Ronald L. Numbers

George Whitefield: Evangelist for God and Empire
by Peter Y. Choi

*The Divine Dramatist: George Whitefield and
the Rise of Modern Evangelicalism* by Harry S. Stout

Liberty of Conscience: Roger Williams in America
by Edwin S. Gaustad